UNLOCKING LEARNING

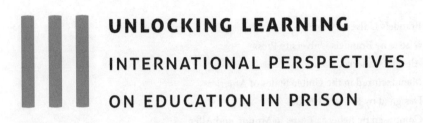

UNLOCKING LEARNING

INTERNATIONAL PERSPECTIVES

ON EDUCATION IN PRISON

EDITED BY

JUSTIN McDEVITT AND

MNEESHA GELLMAN

BRANDEIS UNIVERSITY PRESS Waltham, Massachusetts

Brandeis University Press
© 2024 by Brandeis University Press
All rights reserved
Manufactured in the United States of America
Designed by Richard Hendel
Composed by Rebecca Evans in Minion and Aller

For permission to reproduce any of the material in this book, contact
Brandeis University Press, 415 South Street, Waltham MA 02453, or visit
brandeisuniversitypress.com

Library of Congress Cataloging-in-Publication Data
Names: McDevitt, Justin, editor. | Gellman, Mneesha, editor.
Title: Unlocking learning : international perspectives on education in prison /
    edited by Justin McDevitt and Mneesha Gellman.
Description: Waltham, Massachusetts : Brandeis University Press, [2024] |
Series: Brandeis series in law and society | Includes index. | Summary: "How
    can people involved in carceral interventions learn from work in carceral
    settings outside the United States? This volume addresses this question
    by gathering international perspectives to the field of education in prison
    that could inform carceral interventions elsewhere, including in the
    United States" — Provided by publisher.
Identifiers: LCCN 2023036793 (print) | LCCN 2023036794 (ebook) |
    ISBN 9781684581917 (cloth) | ISBN 9781684581924 (paperback) |
    ISBN 9781684581931 (ebook)
Subjects: LCSH: Prisoners—Education.
Classification: LCC HV8875 .U57 2024 (print) | LCC HV8875 (ebook) |
    DDC 365/.666—dc23/eng/20231012
LC record available at https://lccn.loc.gov/2023036793
LC ebook record available at https://lccn.loc.gov/2023036794

5 4 3 2 1

*For students who are incarcerated
and have taught us more than
we could ever hope to teach*

CONTENTS

ILLUSTRATIONS

Figures

Tables

FOREWORD

"The truth," asserts the alcoholic character Kjær in the classic Danish novel *Havoc* (1930), "is not housebroken." This work of fiction by Tom Kristensen depicts the all-too-real world of keeping reality at arm's length through drink. Truth, however, is ultimately neither tractable nor pliant. As Shakespeare reminds us, the "truth will out."

In the United States, the truth for education in prison is that it was one of many casualties from the "tough on crime" rhetoric of the 1980s and '90s. For electoral gain, politicians outbid one another on doing away with any emphasis on the tradition of what was then termed rehabilitation, and instead valorizing punishment: retribution; (supposed) deterrence through ever-longer prison sentences; and incapacitation by removing the incarcerated from any opportunities to contribute to their communities and nation. The cancellation of Pell funding in 1994 was moral grandstanding by a civil society with little concern for seeking truthful answers to fundamental questions: What actually are the most effective ways to reduce recidivism? How can incarcerated people develop their talents to contribute to their communities and nation—with the "their" really being the communal "our"—both inside prison and when they are reintegrated into their communities? What are the obligations to provide meaningful educational opportunities to incarcerated people as human beings with inalienable rights? As demonstrated in this volume, there exist both ongoing global scholarship and dialogue to lead the way in exploring these questions.

In the United States, the pursuit of truth about education in prison is increasingly back on the table. In my previous role as a college provost, I led the academics on a residential liberal arts campus with traditional undergraduates, overwhelmingly eighteen to twenty-two in age. I also concurrently served as provost for our second site location within a correctional facility, the Moreau College Initiative (MCI). One college, two locations, and two realities that were starkly different and yet similar at the same time. What I would often share with students in both locations is this: Yes, there are differences between students on the traditional campus and the students at MCI, but those differences can often work to the educational advantage of the latter. Those students on average are older with a wide range of lived experiences, including significant challenges and mistakes, which serve as sources of hard-earned insight and wisdom. And although students on our main campus are diverse socioeconomically, culturally, and ethnically, our incarcerated students are *remarkably* diverse, providing a range of perspectives that otherwise would be missing from our college's mix.

While there are differences between the students at the two locations, the similarities are far greater, and in my experience this outlook reassures incarcerated students. From the perspective of higher education, students who are incarcerated are, first and foremost, college students, cherished and respected citizens in good standing of a single college community of both the traditional home campus and a site within a correctional facility. This conception doesn't dismiss or ignore the realities of education in prison, but it foregrounds for these students that they have a shared identity as equals with traditional students, just as they will (or at least should) have a shared equal identity within society as they are reintegrated. An emphasis at our college for all our students, both the traditional and incarcerated, is "to live in the business and problems of the world." Students face uncertainty about the future in job and career challenges in an increasingly competitive global economy. But they are also contemplating many other big questions, such as: What difference—what contribution—will I be able make to my family, community, and country? Many express a desire to set an example for their children, siblings, cousins, nieces, and nephews. It is higher education's responsibility to equip them to deal with the business and challenges of the world.

What I appreciate most about this volume is the holistic approach to the intended outcomes for education in prison. This book identifies and explores the many impediments, both apparent and subtle, that weigh on the success of students while in educational programs and upon their reintegration into society. As noted by Justin McDevitt and Mneesha Gellman in their conclusion, "The work of education in prison does not exist in a universe of its own; it must operate in communication with partners and with an eye toward opportunities for employment after release. More broadly, education in prison will be most effective when it is seen as part of a new approach to public safety, one that . . . is part of centering the holistic well-being of people who are incarcerated" as a goal, rather than only allowing education to happen for the sake of recidivism reduction.

While reducing recidivism is a legitimate goal, people do not typically prioritize their own children's graduation from college so they will statistically be less likely to be incarcerated. What is desired, as many of our parents desired for us, is that college graduates become self-confident, able to stand on their own two feet, to not be fools subject to the manipulation of others, to live the values they claim, and to put their education to use for the common good as best they understand it. That is the road map that this volume provides for education in prison.

ACKNOWLEDGMENTS

It is perhaps an irony that a book about international perspectives on education in prison was conceived and written at a time when, thanks to the Covid-19 pandemic, most of us could neither leave the countries in which we live nor enter the prisons in which we work. Yet bringing this book to life was for us a daily reminder that we are still connected to each other, and that education remains crucial for social transformation. And so, when we could not teach our students, we taught each other.

In accordance with the scope of this book, there are more people to thank than we can fit into a few pages, but first among them are the students, faculty, staff, and supporters of our respective college-in-prison families.

For Justin, the Moreau College Initiative (MCI) was my home for the best part of a decade and helped shape the best parts of me as well. Its longtime director (and my friend), Alesha Seroczynski, took a fledgling Second Chance Pell program and built it into a national model for what is possible in this space, especially as Pell is fully restored nationwide. Likewise, the late Jay Caponigro, Steve Fallon, and the entire MCI Steering Committee are responsible for the program's continued success. In the process of editing the final manuscript of this volume, I was named the new director of the Women's College Partnership (WCP), a college-in-prison program based at Indiana Women's Prison, founded by the Bard Prison Initiative (BPI), administered by the University of Notre Dame, and powered by Marian University. The new Notre Dame Programs for Education in Prison (NDPEP) at the Center for Social Concerns will only add to that work by bringing additional resources and partnerships to bear.

For Mneesha, the Emerson Prison Initiative (EPI) constitutes a hope made real. The EPI students, faculty, and leadership team are the lifeblood of the program. Cara Moyer-Duncan and Stephen Shane, in particular, have given tremendous amounts of time and energy to keep the program on course, along with additional past and present members of the Advisory Council (2022–23 names are included here): Sally Moran Davidson, Lizzy

Cooper Davis, Dana Edell, Natalie Hill, Eileen McBride, Kim McLarin, Yasser Munif, Josh Polster, Joshua Wachs, and Wendy Walters.

Needless to say, these programs themselves would not exist without the generous support and thoughtful nurturing of our larger educational institutions, Holy Cross College and the University of Notre Dame for MCI, Marian University and Notre Dame for WCP, and Emerson College for EPI. The administrations at each institution have created the conditions for these efforts to thrive and grow and do very real good in the world beyond their walls. For Justin Watson, Marco Clark, Tom Burish, Marie Lynn Miranda, Hugh Page, Liz Osika, Amy Ansell, and past Emerson College president Lee Pelton, we are so grateful.

In addition, each of these institutions entered this field only because BPI provided the vision, the expertise, the spark, and the resources to help see MCI, WCP, and EPI established in the first place. For that, thanks must go to Max Kenner, Daniel Karpowitz, Jessica Neptune, Djuan Tatro, and numerous other BPI staff who have supported us along the way. Their guidance through the Consortium for the Liberal Arts in Prison has allowed our respective programs to become leaders in our field, our states, and our corrections departments.

To that end, John Nally and his decades shepherding educational programming in the Indiana Department of Correction have ensured that Indiana has once again regained its status as a national leader in higher education in prison. Special thanks to the staffs at Westville Correctional Facility and Indiana Women's Prison for supporting the mission of MCI on a daily basis. Likewise, we thank Mary Haynes, Dennis O'Neil, and Brian Terhaar for their labor in Massachusetts on behalf of EPI.

We also thank the funders who have allowed our work to flourish. For Justin's work at MCI, WCP, and NDPEP, many thanks are due to the generous support of the Community Foundation of St. Joseph County, the Community Foundation of Elkhart County, BPI, and several anonymous donors. For EPI, the Cummings Foundation, the Boston Foundation, the Gardiner Howland Shaw Foundation, and the Institute of International Education Centennial Grant, along with other foundations and dedicated individual donors, have made it possible to fund instructors teaching college in prison, as well as the development of a reentry program.

We thank Sue Berger Ramin and the editorial team at Brandeis University Press, as well as Rosalind Kabrhel and Daniel Breen at Brandeis University, for including this book in their Law and Society series. Annika

Falconer was an editor extraordinaire on multiple drafts, Abigail Lange assisted in copyediting, and Natalie Jones applied the final polish. We are grateful to you all for helping bring these stories to a wider audience.

On a personal note, Justin would like to thank Zack Imfeld, Andrea Cramer, Emily Ransom, Heather Erwin, Antonella Piconi, Carly Hudson, Sarah Raison, Maya Jain, Justus Ghormley, Caylor Gongwer, the late Barbara Szweda, and many other dear friends for their support through this mammoth project. Thanks to my family for loving and cheering me on. Thanks to the folks at the Shoe, Catch, Bob's, and (of course) the Marine Corps League for hosting the daily grind. And special thanks to Maria McKenna for taking a chance on me teaching in prison and helping me find the rest of my life.

Mneesha would like to thank her family for withstanding her absurd work ethic and reminding her that life is more than sitting at the computer: Joshua, Matolah, and Chayton, you keep me grounded. Also, thanks to family and friends from Boston to California to Mexico and beyond who have affirmed the significance of trying to make the world more humane.

Finally, we extend thanks beyond thanks to all the incredible authors in these pages: for their friendship, their wisdom, their time and expertise, and their offers of a warm welcome when we visit. We (Justin and Mneesha) also thank each other for embarking on the journey of this project together. We are grateful for each other's considerate communication and dedicated work ethic. Coediting is not always easy, and this process has been a microcosm in which we practiced the ethics of care that we both aspire to impart in the larger world.

MNEESHA GELLMAN AND JUSTIN MCDEVITT

INTRODUCTION

WHAT WE CAN LEARN FROM EDUCATION IN PRISON IN COMPARATIVE CONTEXT

Education as Intervention

Incarceration, in its many iterations, is a global strategy to address transgression by putting people behind bars. Such measures are justified as being part of public safety strategies designed to decrease crime and increase security. In fact, public safety policies are, like other policies set out by states in fields such as education and health care, expressions of norms and values. Public safety policies transmit culturally held beliefs about how the world is and should be to people who come in contact with its systems. Such policies are tremendously powerful in creating the daily experiences of incarcerated people around the world.

Incarcerated people everywhere come from many segments of society but are more likely to be poorer than country general populations and of a minority racial or ethnic group. Across the world today, there are an estimated 10.77 million people confined in prisons and jails, a population greater than that of North Carolina, the ninth largest state in the United States, or roughly the population of Greece, the eighty-ninth most populous country in the world (Fair and Walmsley 2021, 2). Though a full quarter of these people are incarcerated in the United States, a country that boasts only 5 percent of the world's total population, the rest are in prisons and jails across the globe (Fair and Walmsley 2021, 2). Breaking down this total by region, while Asia (population 4,184,126) edges out the Americas as a whole (population 3,859,690) for the highest incarcerated population by total number, the Americas (376 per 100,000) far outpace the rest of the world in terms of prison population rate, while Asia's incarcerated population (93 per 100,000) nearly ties Africa (92 per 100,000) for the lowest rate,

1

which is much lower than the incarceration rate for the world population as a whole (140 per 100,000) (Fair and Walmsley 2021, 1).

While some things about incarceration are universal—at its most basic, a restriction on freedom of choice over aspects of daily life—being confined and under supervision necessarily looks different depending on where a person is incarcerated. From punishment to rehabilitation and reintegration, the experience of incarceration can vary widely from country to country, region to region, and state to state. Not only are carceral experiences variable, but critical factors such as justice sector policies, inclusionary or exclusionary state climates, vulnerability to gang and cartel control, and private versus public management all operate as variables that influence the way prisons and other centers of detention operate. The extent and quality of educational access provided within prisons both shape and are shaped by these and many other factors.

Within these significant differences, there is a shared truth across carceral systems in a wide range of places. Access to education for people who are incarcerated continuously proves to be an impactful intervention at both the individual and institutional levels (Hernandez, Murillo, and Britton 2022; Katzenstein, Ajinkya, and Corbett 2019; McMay and Kimble 2020; Novick 2019). Higher education—meaning college- or university-level coursework—has a particularly outstanding track record in this regard. Completing higher educational benchmarks while incarcerated—such as achieving an associate or bachelor's degree in the United States system—reduces recidivism, a long-standing, if imperfect, benchmark of success for many prison systems (Davis et al. 2014; Denney and Tynes 2021; Gellman 2022). Moreover, this level of academic achievement also leads to greater opportunities for people to lead more prosperous lives when they transition back to society, a process that is fraught with hardship and obstacles (Behan 2014; Western 2018). When credentials are gained, upward mobility becomes increasingly plausible, albeit not guaranteed.

Although recidivism rates are a significant factor, they should be only one of many interventionist benchmarks used to evaluate the utility of expanding educational access to people in prison. In addition, providing people who are incarcerated with access to self-actualization tools is part and parcel of this mission. For people serving long-term or life sentences, educational access provides a sense of meaning within prison that allows for a degree of dignity and autonomy in an otherwise bleak landscape. Such a reality is not meant to justify the use of extended sentences commonly issued in the United States, but rather points to the fact that educational access brings a range of positive outcomes for incarcerated people regardless of sentence length or specific circumstances (Gellman 2020). In truth, even correctional administrators acknowledge the power of participation in academic programming as another way to measure reintegration for incarcerated people (Messemer 2011).

Despite the acknowledged benefits to educational access in prison, expanding such access requires navigating a host of bureaucratic and political barriers. Following a confluence of factors—including the global spread of Covid-19, renewed scrutiny of criminal justice systems stemming from racial justice protests, and the restoration of access to Pell Grants for incarcerated individuals in the United States—carceral systems have increasingly been part of public conversations about equality in its many forms. Prisons and jails, as well as the programs providing educational access for the people incarcerated in them, have received more public attention in the past several years as both individuals and institutions struggle to reconcile structural justice with public safety.

By January 2022, two years into the Covid-19 pandemic, nearly 3,000 incarcerated individuals in the United States had died as a result of the disease, with approximately 543,089 infected, numbers that are both woefully undercounted and inadequate to capture the horrors of suffering through a pandemic behind bars (United Nations 2021). The United States has the highest incarceration rate in the world and has also had some of the highest Covid-19 infection and death rates of any country. Globally, as of August 2023 more than 6,882,212 total Covid-19 deaths had been reported worldwide, with the number of total reported cases reaching 678,791,846 (*New York Times* 2023). This is certainly an undercount, as many Covid cases and deaths remain unidentified, underreported, or unreported, with some estimates suggesting the number might be as much as three times as high (Wang et al. 2022, 1534).

The pandemic has been punctuated with events that weave issues of racism and discrimination together with societal values of punitive and restorative justice. Within weeks of the murder of George Floyd on May 25, 2020, outside a corner store in Minneapolis, Minnesota, protests erupted in more than fifty countries as citizens demanded racial justice and police accountability in the United States and beyond. This social movement evinced an amalgam of domestic frustration and international solidarity (Haddad 2020). Amid this upheaval came the announcement in December 2020 that the United States Congress had voted to restore access to federal education grants for college students who were currently incarcerated. This move undid a 1994 provision that had taken Pell funding out of prisons, gutting the financial viability of most programs to extend higher education to people who were incarcerated (Martinez-Hill 2021). The revocation of Pell took place as part of a federal crime bill signed into law by then-president Bill Clinton and happened despite the fact that Pell funding for incarcerated students was seen as "the single most important influence of the growth of prison higher education throughout the 1970s and 1980s" (Wright 2001, 13–14).

Fortunately, with Pell funding slowly being restored, higher education in prisons in the United States has begun to reproliferate and now includes a wide variety of programs, from public to private, liberal arts to vocational, in-person to virtual (Eisenberg 2020). These programs "serve as an important crossroad for civic engagement and cultural exchange" (Utheim 2016, 92), "affect the stigmatization of a criminal conviction" (Evans, Pelletier, and Szkola 2018, 257), and "transform the internal human condition" (Reese 2019, 705). Still, in the same breath, these researchers and practitioners point out obstacles that confound this good work, from "very controlled circumstances" (Utheim 2016, 95) to "social exclusion" (Evans, Pelletier, and Szkola 2018) to lack of "internal desire" on the part of prison administrations themselves as hosts (Reese 2019, 694). The barriers to educational provision in prison are, in short, enormous. To overcome such challenges, Reese suggests an important source of inspiration: "There is a lot the US could learn from other prison systems in the world" (2019, 690). Such a claim is our basic premise in crafting this edited volume.

To be sure, outside the United States, penal practices have led to successful reintegration and have become models for other countries. In Norway, for example, the focus on rehabilitation over punishment has led to some of the lowest rates of incarceration and recidivism in the world (Sterbenz 2014). Similarly, prisons in the Netherlands sit nearly empty thanks to years of pragmatic solutions aimed at implementing what works to reduce recidivism—or crime in the first place—instead of what is politically expedient (Bilefsky 2017). Such approaches to public safety illustrate more holistic visions of how to maintain and restore social harmony.

The United States has at times sought to learn from such successes. For example, in 2018, a delegation of criminal justice administrators from Massachusetts traveled to Germany to tour facilities there in hopes of implementing some of the positive outcomes associated with German corrections policies (Schiraldi 2018). While international exchange can promote positive innovation in carceral intervention, there remains space to grow in both practice and in the literature. Limited views on what public safety should include continue to hamper progress. Punitive, rather than preventive or restorative, justice mechanisms retain favor in many state systems in the United States.

Challenges to carceral interventions abound. On the international horizon, ongoing immigration from areas facing increased insecurity, such as Syria, Central America, and elsewhere in the Global South, continues to bring up questions about the criminalization of immigration. The immigration crisis for Ukrainians fleeing Russian attacks has also shed light on the racial factors at play in the crimmigration—criminalization of immigration—of Black, Indigenous, and People of Color (BIPOC) refugees, asylum seekers, and migrants. More broadly, incarceration as a supposed public safety tool is pushing many states to consider what the purpose of prison truly is. As a result of these and many other factors, a focus on the human rights and dignity of people who are incarcerated around the world has become more salient than ever. There is a growing need for vital and expanding dialogues on the role of education in public safety and justice systems worldwide.

A steady flow of new and insightful empirical research, as well as works on the practice of higher education in prison, have contributed to the increasing prominence of education in prison—especially higher education, or college—in discussions of justice and prison reform. For example, the *Journal of Prison Education and Reentry*, established in 2014, has emerged as an important voice in comparative education in prison, while the Alliance for Higher Education in Prison launched the *Journal of Higher Education in Prison* in 2021. Globally, scholarly research articles on education in prison written in the last decade have appeared in publications ranging from the *International Journal of Educational Development* to *Crime and Delinquency* to the *European Journal of Public Health*, signifying both the interest in and reach of empirical studies in this field. In terms of practice, Daniel Karpowitz's book *College in Prison: Reading in an Age of Mass Incarceration* (2017); Rebecca Ginsburg's edited volume *Critical Perspectives on Teaching in Prison: Students and Instructors on Pedagogy behind the Wall* (2019); Mary Fainsod Katzenstein, Julie Ajinkya, and Erin Corbett's edited symposium in *PS: Political Science and Politics* (2019); and the documentary *College Behind Bars* (2019) by Lynn Novick, Sarah Botstein, and Ken Burns, alongside many others, all show the impact of providing quality education in US prisons and jails. Efforts like these serve to advocate for greater access to education for incarcerated people by illustrating how profound the effects can be.

As administrators in college-in-prison (CIP) programs in our respective home institutions where we are also faculty, we, this book's editors, came together through our shared institutional membership in the Consortium for the Liberal Arts in Prison, hosted by the Bard Prison Initiative (BPI). Both of our CIP programs—the Emerson Prison Initiative at Emerson College (Mneesha) and the Women's College Partnership at the University of Notre Dame and Marian University (Justin)—strive to follow best practices established within the Bard Consortium. Such principles include prioritizing full-time, intensive, credit-bearing curricula that adhere to the same standards as traditional college academics, and not using a deficit approach—an approach centered on what students are lacking—in shaping programming for incarcerated students (Bard Prison Initiative n.d.).

In addition, we are both scholars trained in comparative political traditions and use these lenses in a range of ways in our work. Across political science (both of us) and law (Justin), we have spent years considering how multiple layers of difference and similarity—for example, systemic, individual, state, local—play a role in promoting justice. Comparisons across units in our fields of training allow us to parse the structural from the contextual and the local from the universal, and in doing so, we aim to winnow out the challenges and potential solutions for a variety of situations. In a book of this scope, such comparative framing means we keep our eyes on the larger goal of identifying patterns in education behind bars that can be useful beyond the micro or local context. This volume is reading material for many kinds of scholars and practitioners in any country where prison interventions are of interest.

Contextualizing Incarceration Globally

To be sure, many readers may already have a working knowledge of education in prison, if not on a global scale, then in their own particular contexts. For those less familiar with this terrain, however, to get the most out of the chapters that follow, we provide orientation for the global context of incarceration. As penology scholar David Skarbek writes, "All prisons are similar in fundamental ways" (2020, 149). Freedom is limited, movement is restricted, privacy is disregarded, and full citizenship is denied. And yet there is incredible diversity in almost every aspect of incarceration, from commitment procedure to administration structure, from architecture to social order (Skarbek 2020). Length and severity of imprisonment vary as well, with the United States and several authoritarian regimes leading the way in this notoriety (Dreisinger 2016). Size, location, and proximity to an incarcerated person's home vary, too, and are likewise important in determining efficacy of treatment (Skarbek 2020, 152).

In most of the country-specific chapters that follow, authors have provided an overview of the penal system in their country before centering on specific interventions of note. How many people are currently being held in prisons and jails? What is known about the makeup of this population compared to the general population? How long is the average sentence, and in what conditions is it served? Here, we aim to answer some of the questions at the global level that the individual chapters answer about their respective countries. In doing so, we offer a snapshot of the reality of global incarceration to help make sense of the role of education in prisons and jails around the world.

The first important piece of context in framing the chapters that follow is the size of the prison population worldwide. Though the present chapter, like the volume as a whole, takes a comparative outlook, there is no way to discuss the sheer number of people incarcerated without singling out the United States. The United States consistently leads the world when it comes to the number of its own people it locks up. In terms of raw numbers, in 2021 the United States was the highest of all countries with approximately 2 million people held in its prisons and jails, followed by China (1.69 million), Brazil (811,000), India (478,000), and Russia (471,000) (Fair and Walmsley 2021, 2). In global terms, this means that just under 20 percent of the world's incarcerated people are located in the United States, despite the fact that they contain only about 5 percent of the world's population. To that end, in terms of the proportion of its population currently held in prisons and jails (prison population rate), the United States again leads with 629 per 100,000 people, followed by Rwanda (580), Turkmenistan (576), El Salvador (564), and Cuba (510) (Fair and Walmsley 2021, 2).

In terms of global demographics, recent data shows that 93.1 percent of incarcerated people are male, though the percentage of women has been rising steadily in every continent since 2000 (Walmsley 2017, 2). Likewise, the vast majority (roughly 95 percent) of people incarcerated are citizens of the country in which they are in prison, but the share of incarcerated people who are foreign-born rises to about 7.6 percent in the Americas and more than 22.1 percent in Europe (World Prison Brief 2021). Unfortunately, there are not a lot of reliable aggregate data on the age of incarcerated people around the world, but, for some context, the average age of people incarcerated in the United States is roughly thirty-eight years old (Federal Bureau of Prisons 2022), and the same holds true for Europe (Aebi and Tiago 2020, 42).

The variations in incarceration data also draw attention to the reasons these numbers change across cases. When it comes to philosophies of punishment and how they are translated into penal policy, the literature is vast and impossible to distill in a single section or chapter (see, for example, Tonry 2011). Nevertheless, to understand the context of education in prisons, especially through a global lens, it is necessary to understand the motivations and attendant limitations of the carceral systems in which educators in this field must operate. Doing so will benefit practitioners of education in prison regardless of their specific national or local context. Foremost, it will help educators engage more effectively with systems that are unfamiliar or even antithetical to their own values, but that they must still somehow navigate if they wish to educate this particularly marginalized population. The reality is, even if we wish that "society did not use prisons to solve its problems" (Scott 2013), it does. Educators must "recognize the beast [they are] up against, and then march on" (Peterson 2019, 184). A grasp of the motivations behind incarceration facilitates solutions to address the problems that exist in educational contexts in carceral spaces.

For many reasons, it is important to query why societies use prisons and what they want from them. As Michel Foucault points out in his landmark book *Discipline and Punish* (1995), justice was once paid for with pain, not isolation. Still, before answering the question of "Why prison?" it is worth pointing out that in the majority of democratic regimes, the assumption is that people are in prison because "society," as Robert Scott notes, wants them there. Indeed, in the United States, fluctuations in incarceration levels can best be understood as the result of elite politicians responding to increases and decreases in the level of punitiveness in society at large (Enns 2016). As Rachel Elise Barkow writes, "We do not rely on experts or . . . studies [but] on emotions and the gut reactions of lay people" (2019, 1).

Sometimes this punitiveness can be informed by outright racial animus (Alexander 2020) and a desire for social control (Hinton 2017). At a subtler level, however, it might also be stoked by fears, even among liberals, that "average citizens" (whoever they are) are not safe, an impression that saw increased currency with the widespread ownership of televisions in the 1950s and '60s (Murakawa 2014).

It is true that crime rates did rise in the mid-twentieth century as more and newer drugs poured into the country. This, of course, raises questions about what is criminalized, and how. Even as presidents like Richard Nixon and Ronald Reagan leveraged racist sentiments in the public to shepherd the passage of stricter drug laws and sentencing guidelines, members of the communities hit hardest by the effects of these tougher penalties often supported them because they were also hit hardest by the effects of the crimes themselves (Forman 2018). Viewed in this way, prisons in the United States do not always serve the function of punishment, but instead are used as tools to deliver policy responses to other social forces, such as racial resentment, poverty, mental health crises, addiction, and more. In other words, prisons are "a universal panacea for all forms of delinquency, including the most harmless" (Othmani, Bessis, and Garling 2008, 49).

Before this era of mass incarceration began in the mid-twentieth century, the state played a less active role in the execution of criminal justice, often deferring to notions of "popular justice," even at the expense of the rule of law (Dale 2011, 2). Yet, with the advent of mass incarceration in the United States, there was still a discernible commitment toward rehabilitation, at least in the early days of expansion. In retrospect, it could simply be that the sheer scale of incarceration in the United States had yet to reach the point where even the proponents of rehabilitation realized what it would eventually become: the large-scale warehousing of millions of humans. The closing decades of the twentieth century, however, saw a well-documented pivot away from the rehabilitative ideal to a more punitive posture, "and its tenacity continues even though crime rates have dropped in recent decades" (Ferguson 2014, 172). Evidence of this is clearly discernible in the public response to the availability of education in prison as well. As Erin Kelly reminds us, "A just society would not prosecute criminal wrongdoing for the sake of retribution" (2018, 122).

In other democracies, especially those of Europe, the rehabilitative ideal continues to thrive and remains the linchpin of penal philosophy in dozens of societies in their attempt to maintain social order (Rentzmann 1996, 60). At the same time, it is acknowledged that while incarceration is undoubtedly a form of punishment, it is the maximum amount of punishment appropriate and should be applied in the least damaging way (Rentzmann 1996, 62). Nevertheless, correctional institutions often "reflect a theoretical paradox of mixed intentions," functioning at once to both rehabilitate and dehumanize (Middlemass 2020, 278).

In more autocratic regimes, of course, while prisons still function as maintainers of public order, there is no underlying assumption that they do so to serve the public good. In authoritarian regimes of all sorts, as well as in procedurally democratic ones, prisons have long been used to silence political dissidents, oppress minority populations, and threaten the general public into submission. As Ernest M. Drucker points out, "Hitler, Stalin, and Pol Pot all employed mass imprisonment—each presided over a process that arrested and incarcerated millions" (2011, 41). We cannot assume that incarceration represents valid policy to address transgressions that would hold up to scrutiny under democratic principles or international law.

Finally, whatever their purported aims, it must be noted that there is a robust literature on the criminogenic nature of prisons themselves. In this literature, there is strong evidence that prisons actually *cause* more crime than they solve. Conclusions such as these are based on research that shows that locking up those who have committed crimes for extended periods of time with thousands of others who have committed crimes may lead to the proliferation of both the culture of and the skills involved in crime (Cid 2009; Gaes and Camp 2009). Such conclusions add to the evidence that prisons are either disingenuous or ineffective in their purported attempts to reduce crime. In other words, prisons exist to do something else entirely rather than rehabilitate. Indeed, though incarceration levels in the United States do not shrink when crime rates decrease, they do when budgets shrink, signaling that states only prioritize incarceration as a strategy when it is cost-effective to do so (Drucker 2011, 46).

Again, the question is not whether education should be offered in prison. Education is *always* offered in prison. Simply being in prison instructs people who are incarcerated "that they are incompetent, irresponsible, and without moral or social worth" (Jones and d'Errico 1994, 3). As noted, there is ample evidence that, in the absence of other educational programming, incarceration actually creates opportunities for people who are incarcerated to learn crime-enabling techniques and tips from each other (Cid 2009). In formal terms, the education level of those entering prison is much lower than the typical citizen on the outside, reinforcing the connection between class, education, and involvement with the justice system (Nally et al. 2012).

Our Contribution

This volume is a crucial addition to a literature that allows educators and governments alike to provide the "right" kind of education. But what does education in prison that is connected to intentions of self-transformation rather than punishment look like? We bring together a range of leading global voices—many of whom have firsthand experience as faculty or administrators in education programs in prison in their respective home countries—as well as scholars who study these themes with rigor across a range of social science disciplines.

In creating this book, we provide a detailed and diverse look at educational programs in a global context in the hope that educators and researchers around the world can learn from each other in offering the best possible educational access to people who are incarcerated. One central achievement of the book is that it puts different systems in synthesis with each other in ways that illuminate shared or distinct obstacles and victories. The contexts and program specifics necessarily differ, but we are united in seeking to further understand how we can make the most impactful education available to people serving time behind the wall.

It is important to note that our commitment to facilitating education in prison does not mean that we agree with prison writ large. Many of us who do this kind of interventionist work come from abolitionist orientations, but have chosen to focus our energy on supporting the educational goals of those who are currently incarcerated. We believe that public safety needs to be redesigned, and that making a better system of bringing education into prison is part of it. This is a pragmatic approach, and one that requires a high degree of cooperation with carceral systems themselves. These goals alongside abolitionist thinking that re-envisions what systems of public safety look like. There are as many reasons for doing education in prison as there are people doing it, but as editors, we embark on this book in the spirit of encouraging readers to see education as a fundamental part of a public safety vision that challenges structural injustice in its many forms.

Before we introduce the outline of the book, we offer an important note on terminology. "Prison education" is not necessarily the same thing as "education in prison" (Gellman 2023). The former may refer to what the prison wants to teach, or what one learns from being in prison, while the latter assumes that standard benchmarks of what constitutes education— education that would be recognizable outside prison as well—are used to define the educative process. While it might appear a semantic issue, it is worth being explicit as to why we use some terms over others, given the highly politicized nature of the field. As educators and program administrators adamant about the educational quality of programs in prison being as equal as possible to those outside prison, we use the term "education in prison" to clearly signal that educational standards and practices from outside come behind the wall, and not that educational programs are formed by prison systems.

Similarly, in this volume we refer to people who are incarcerated in person-first language whenever possible—"people who are incarcerated"— and only use terms such as "prisoners" or "inmates" when invoking legal contexts that use those terms. We also use the identity-first phrasing of "incarcerated people." In addition, we follow the practice of capitalizing all racial and ethnic terms, including White (Ewing 2020; Mack and Palfrey 2020). In doing so, we attempt to make visible and interrupt assumptions about cultural baselines that further marginalize BIPOC people. While such capitalization practices are not necessarily the norm in all the countries from which authors in this volume come, conversations about such details took place in tandem with the core content of each chapter. Doing so led to productive learning across editors and authors and is part of the growth mindset we attempt to model in our work.

We invite readers to consider where such language practices might be relevant in their own fields. Through language as well as substance, we hope this volume continues to remind us all of the humanity of those seeking an education while in prison. By intervening in the status quo, we make space for improvement by using language that is both of and for social change.

Outline of the Book

We have collected essays from scholars and practitioners in ten different countries across North America, Central America, and Europe. The case studies, from leaders in the landscape of higher education in carceral settings, articulate a range of successes and challenges in the field of education in prison in general, and of higher education when available. Selected case studies represent an attempt at diversity—of region, topic, and approach—while offering insights that may be of use to scholars and practitioners across the United States and internationally. Though this volume is admittedly geographically limited, it is an important first step. We look forward to future volumes bringing more case studies to light from countries and regions we do not cover here.

The book unfolds in three stages. Part I, titled "Contextualizing Education in Prison," historically places and engages with what has transpired over time—and what is at stake for the future—to bring us to the education-in-prison landscape that exists today. Max Kenner, a luminary in the field and the founder and director of the Bard Prison Initiative—a leading college-in-prison program in the United States with numerous campuses across New York State—opens the volume with a laser-like focus on college in prison in the United States. Kenner's chapter, "The Long History of College-in-Prison," provides a formidable history of college access for incarcerated people in the United States with an emphasis on the impact of Pell Grant availability and restrictions over time. His chapter details how government officials and other policymakers have shaped the educational landscape in US prisons from the second half of the twentieth century to the present day. As a leader in the movement for Pell restoration, Kenner shows what happens when a basic element of college funding is taken away from people in prison, as well as the benefits of bringing it back.

Following this, Maria K. McKenna's chapter, "The Work of Restoration: How to Educate When Education Fails," zooms out to look at the US education system writ large, embedding it in a national history that has great need of restoration. Among its other goals, the chapter serves the important role of grounding our own education-in-prison context within the unique US context, one that can learn from the experience and expertise of scholars from around the globe, but that cannot overcome with scholarship what it has spent centuries seeding with injustice.

In McKenna's construction, education in prison in the United States must be understood—and thus improved—by confronting the injustice in our education system. To McKenna, the important motivation is not the justice system's desire to reform its perceived offenders, but the motivation of each student to "buy in" and take control of their education for their own purposes and goals.

In part II, "Innovations in Teaching and Learning in Prison," the volume moves from general content on education in prison to specific country-based chapters. Six case studies are explored here, detailing how particular countries have innovated to facilitate educational access for incarcerated people. In sharing their successes, authors identify both universally applicable as well as region-specific characteristics of their own programs. Authors are also transparent about hardships encountered along the way, offering what they struggle with and have learned from as helpful insight for others in the field.

Longtime carceral system interventionist Natasha Bidault Mniszek presents an inspiring case study of college access for people incarcerated in Mexico in her chapter, "College Now! A Public University Goes behind the Wall in Mexico City." As the director of a robust college-in-prison program in the heart of Mexico's capital, Bidault Mniszek documents the partnership between government officials and the university, which allows unprecedented access to higher education for highly marginalized populations.

Next, Austrian researcher Walter Hammerschick's "Education and Training in Austrian Prisons: Essential Pieces in the Reintegration Puzzle" approaches education as part of a holistic rehabilitative effort that remains firmly person-centered. Based on data and observations from Austria, Hammerschick makes a strong case for education that is delivered in conjunction with intensive skills training and attention to personal circumstances, offering incarcerated people the best possible chance of success after release. The chapter focuses on creating a set of best practices, rooted in evaluative data, that can be applied in almost any context.

In "Learning behind Bars: Education and Reintegration in Dutch Prisons," communications scholar Chester Lee guides readers into what is often heralded as a paradigmatic success in comparative carceral studies, the case of the Netherlands. Indeed, there is much to be learned from a country that boasts low incarceration, low recidivism, and high positive outcomes for those released from prisons. How can other countries learn from the Netherlands? Which effective intervention strategies are uniquely dependent on other elements of Dutch systems, and which are more or less reproducible in other countries? Lee answers these questions and raises many others in this valuable contribution.

In their data-driven chapter, "Evaluating Education in Norwegian Prisons: Research-Based Approaches," Norwegian researchers Lise Øen Jones, Torfinn Langelid, Terje Manger, Paal Breivik, and Arve Asbjørnsen keep true to the theme of part II by offering innovations for other countries to learn from. Direct partnerships between governments and researchers allow for empirically sound assessment of data on educational access in Norwegian prisons. The authors describe the data collaboration, as well as the national landscape where educational access is prioritized in Norway, and, in doing so, show how much can be accomplished when researchers and government administrators, where possible, work as allies rather than adversaries.

In a cautionary contrast, Slovakian researchers Silvia Lukáčová, Dominika Temiaková, and Marek Lukáč confront the challenges of data collection behind the wall in their vital chapter, "Who Benefits Most from Correctional Education? A View from Slovakia." Rather than taking claims made about educational access in Slovakian prisons at face value, Lukáčová, Temiaková, and Lukáč work through numerous data-gathering challenges to provide their own assessment of who benefits, and how, from education in prison. The Norway and Slovakia chapters taken together offer important lessons about the role of data collection and analysis in tracking the impact of educational access in carceral settings.

In the final chapter of part II, Polish courts expert Grzegorz A. Skrobotowicz examines the dual roles of labor and educational access in "Preparing for Release: Academic and Vocational Education for Incarcerated Persons in Polish Executive Criminal Law." Using his legal training, Skrobotowicz assesses different types of interventions in Polish prisons and concludes that the biggest inhibitor to carceral and educational improvements may be the carceral system itself, with negative subcultures of violence compounded by persistent overcrowding. Understanding the strengths and weaknesses of each potential improvement, as well as the obstacles, is part of identifying the path forward for education in prison.

Part III, "Challenging the Silencing of Marginalized Voices," consists of three chapters that look specifically at whose voices are heard—and whose are not—within education in prison. In the first chapter of this final section, Jennifer Coreas, program coordinator and Authors' Circle founder for the nongovernmental organization ConTextos, addresses the topic head-on in her chapter, "Authorship in Prison: Stories of Identity, Resilience, and Renewal from El Salvador." Coreas documents how incarcerated people are given opportunities to author their own lives through book publishing while incarcerated. In creating these memoirs, students explore their identity, revisit their stories of resilience and struggle by reaching back to before they became victimizers, and reimagine new narratives for themselves. In a place as continually marginalized as El Salvador, Coreas delivers a moving story of hope that reminds readers never to give up on the human capacity to grow and change.

In their case study on the treatment of immigrants in Italian prisons, a team of Italian academics and practitioners—Maria Garro, Massimiliano Schirinzi, Gioacchino Lavanco, and Michelangelo Capitano—identify another type of silencing, that of voices in transit who become targets of the carceral system in Italy. Their chapter, "Rethinking Education and Mediation for Incarcerated Immigrants in Italy," addresses the particular challenges faced by incarcerated people who do not hold citizenship rights within their country of incarceration. The themes explored in their chapter are ones that stretch across many borders and should remind us all that, within incarcerated populations, the experiences of migrant voices continue to be some of the most marginalized of an already marginalized population.

Dorien Brosens, Silke Marynissen, and Liesbeth De Donder, researchers on Belgian prisons, bring the voices of incarcerated peer educators to the page in their chapter, "Effectiveness of Peer Learning and Peer Support in Prison: A Realist-Inspired Review of Outcomes, Mechanisms, and Contextual Factors." Looking across Europe and beyond, Brosens, Marynissen, and De Donder distill numerous studies on peer-based initiatives in prison and show how the voices and actions of incarcerated people play a key role in innovative educational experiences behind the wall.

Finally, in the conclusion to the volume, we take the editors' prerogative to weave together reflections on comparative best practices for education in prison while bringing the lessons of the numerous case studies together, with both US and international audiences in mind. Overall, the volume acknowledges foundational principles of education in prison: expanding access, insisting on parity of quality with education available outside prison, and working cautiously with government and other institutional partners to build systemic support and educational continuity for incarcerated and formerly incarcerated people. Taken together, contributors convey these principles by outlining both notable successes and challenges to be overcome, as well as exploring innovations in the field. By posing persistent questions about who has the right to speak and how they might be heard, we hope to push the education-in-prison conversation forward. In doing so, we work toward a more equitable world, where the promise of education does not remain only in the purview of elites or those who have won the identity lottery, but is instead accessible to all who seek it, no matter their circumstances.

This volume encourages practitioners, educators, administrators, and other interventionists to learn from the experiences of others who openly share their successes, struggles, and lessons learned in expanding educational access in prison. The pages that follow emphasize how countries should invest in educational programs for incarcerated people and argue that transparency about the impact of educational access is vital to better understanding how to support positive societal change. Reviewing various interventions across multiple countries provides a glimpse into both the universality and local specificity of educational access during incarceration. Ultimately, these lessons can help us better understand how to promote remedies in public safety that serve the larger purpose of learning to live together well.

Works Cited

Aebi, Marcelo F., and Mélanie M. Tiago. 2020. "Prison Populations 2020." https:// wp.unil.ch/space/files/2021/04/210330_FinalReport_SPACE_I_2020.pdf.

Alexander, Michelle. 2020. *The New Jim Crow: Mass Incarceration in the Age of Colorblindness.* 10th Anniversary. La Vergne: The New Press.

Bard Prison Initiative. n.d. "National Engagement: Creating Educational Opportunities in Prison Nationwide." https://bpi.bard.edu/our-work/national -engagement/.

Barkow, Rachel Elise. 2019. *Prisoners of Politics: Breaking the Cycle of Mass Incarceration.* Cambridge, MA: The Belknap Press of Harvard University Press.

Behan, Cormac. 2014. "Learning to Escape: Prison Education, Rehabilitation and the Potential for Transformation." *Journal of Prison Education and Reentry* 1 (1): 20–31.

Bilefsky, Dan. 2017. "Dutch Get Creative to Solve a Prison Problem: Too Many Empty Cells." *New York Times,* February 9, 2017. https://nytimes.com/2017/02/09/world /europe/netherlands-prisons-shortage.html.

Cid, José. 2009. "Is Imprisonment Criminogenic?: A Comparative Study of Recidivism Rates between Prison and Suspended Prison Sanctions." *European Journal of Criminology* 6 (6): 459–80.

Dale, Elizabeth. 2011. *Criminal Justice in the United States, 1789–1939.* New Histories of American Law. Cambridge; New York: Cambridge University Press.

Davis, Lois M., Jennifer L. Steele, Robert Bozick, Malcolm V. Williams, Susan Turner, Jeremy N. V. Miles, Jessica Saunders, and Paul S. Steinberg. 2014. "The Case for Correctional Education in US Prisons." *RAND Corporation.* https://rand.org/blog /rand-review/2016/01/course-correction-the-case-for-correctional-education.html.

Denney, Matthew G. T., and Robert Tynes. 2021. "The Effects of College in Prison and Policy Implications." *Justice Quarterly* (November 2021): 1–25.

Dreisinger, Baz. 2016. *Incarceration Nations: A Journey to Justice in Prisons around the World.* New York: Other Press.

Drucker, Ernest M. 2011. *A Plague of Prisons: The Epidemiology of Mass Incarceration in America.* New York: New Press: Distributed by Perseus Distribution.

Eisenberg, Avlana K. 2020. "The Prisoner and the Polity." *New York University Law Review* 95 (1): 1–74.

Enns, Peter K. 2016. *Incarceration Nation: How the United States Became the Most Punitive Democracy in the World.* New York: Cambridge University Press.

Evans, Douglas N., Emily Pelletier, and Jason Szkola. 2018. "Education in Prison and the Self-Stigma: Empowerment Continuum." *Crime & Delinquency* 64 (2): 255–80.

Ewing, Eve. 2020. "I'm a Black Scholar Who Studies Race. Here's Why I Capitalize 'White.'" July 2, 2020. https://zora.medium.com/im-a-black-scholar-who-studies -race-here-s-why-i-capitalize-white-f94883aa2dd3.

Fair, Helen, and Roy Walmsley. 2021. "World Prison Population List, Thirteenth Edition." *World Prison Brief.* London: ICPR. https://prisonstudies.org/sites /default/files/resources/downloads/world_prison_population_list_13th_edition .pdf/.

Federal Bureau of Prisons. 2022. "Inmate Age." Last updated November 11, 2022. https://bop.gov/about/statistics/statistics_inmate_age.jsp.

Ferguson, Robert A. 2014. *Inferno: An Anatomy of American Punishment.* Cambridge, MA: Harvard University Press.

Forman, James. 2018. *Locking Up Our Own: Crime and Punishment in Black America.* New York: Farrar, Straus and Giroux.

Foucault, Michel. 1995. *Discipline and Punish: The Birth of the Prison.* 2nd ed. New York: Vintage Books.

Gaes, Gerald G., and Scott D. Camp. 2009. "Unintended Consequences: Experimental Evidence for the Criminogenic Effect of Prison Security Level Placement on Post-Release Recidivism." *Journal of Experimental Criminology* 5 (2): 139–62.

Gellman, Mneesha. 2020. "Higher Education Access and Parity: The Emerson Prison Initiative's Bachelor of Arts Program." In *Higher Education Accessibility Behind and Beyond Prison Walls,* edited by Dani V. McMay and Rebekah D. Kimble, 47–66. Hershey, PA: IGI Global.

Gellman, Mneesha. 2022. "Afterword: Reflections on Bringing College to Prison." In *Education Behind the Wall: Why and How We Teach College in Prison*, edited by Mneesha Gellman, 186–98. Waltham, MA: Brandeis University Press.

Gellman, Mneesha. 2023. "As Second Chance Pell Grant Program Grows, More Incarcerated People Can Get Degrees—But There's a Difference between Prison-Run and College-Run Education behind Bars." *The Conversation*, April 17, 2023. https://theconversation.com/as-second-chance-pell-grant-program-grows-more -incarcerated-people-can-get-degrees-but-theres-a-difference-between-prison -run-and-college-run-education-behind-bars-202425.

Haddad, Mohammed. 2020. "Mapping Anti-Racism Solidarity Protests around the World." *Al Jazeera*. June 7, 2020. https://aljazeera.com/news/2020/6/7/mapping -anti-racism-solidarity-protests-around-the-world.

Hernandez, Joe Louis, Danny Murillo, and Tolani Britton. 2022. "Hustle in Higher Education: How Latinx Students with Conviction Histories Move from Surviving to Thriving in Higher Education." *American Behavioral Scientist* 66 (10): 1394–1417.

Hinton, Elizabeth Kai. 2017. *From the War on Poverty to the War on Crime: The Making of Mass Incarceration in America*. Cambridge, MA: Harvard University Press.

Jones, Raymond L., and Peter d'Errico. 1994. "The Paradox of Higher Education in Prison." In *Higher Education in Prison: A Contradiction in Terms*, edited by Miriam Williford, 2–16. Phoenix: American Council on Education and The Oryx Press.

Katzenstein, Mary Fainsod, Julie Ajinkya, and Erin Corbett. 2019. "Introduction: Teaching Politics in Jails and Prisons." *PS: Political Science & Politics* 52 (1): 85–88.

Kelly, Erin. 2018. *The Limits of Blame: Rethinking Punishment and Responsibility*. Cambridge, MA: Harvard University Press.

Mack, Kristen, and John Palfrey. 2020. "Capitalizing Black and White: Grammatical Justice and Equity." MacArthur Foundation, August 6, 2020. https://macfound.org /press/perspectives/capitalizing-black-and-white-grammatical-justice-and -equity.

Martinez-Hill, Juan. 2021. "A Monumental Shift: Restoring Access to Pell Grants for Incarcerated Students." *Vera Institute of Justice*, March 2021. https://vera.org /publications/restoring-access-to-pell-grants-for-incarcerated-students.

McMay, Dani, V., and Rebekah Kimble, D., eds. 2020. *Higher Education Accessibility Behind and Beyond Prison Walls*. Hershey, PA: IGI Global.

Messemer, Jonathan E. 2011. "The Historical Practice of Correctional Education in the United States: A Review of the Literature." *International Journal of Humanities and Social Science* 17 (1): 91–100.

Middlemass, Keesha. 2020. "Education's Failed Promise: How Public Policies 'Educate' a Criminal Underclass." In *Beyond Recidivism: New Approaches to Research on Prisoner Reentry and Reintegration*, edited by Andrea Leverentz, Elsa Chen, and Johnna Christian, 275–92. New York: NYU Press.

Murakawa, Naomi. 2014. *The First Civil Right: How Liberals Built Prison America.* Oxford Studies in Postwar American Political Development. New York: Oxford University Press.

Nally, John, Susan Lockwood, Katie Knutson, and Taiping Ho. 2012. "An Evaluation of the Effect of Correctional Education Programs on Post-Release Recidivism and Employment: An Empirical Study in Indiana." *The Journal of Correctional Education* 63 (1): 69–89.

New York Times. 2023. "Coronavirus World Map: Tracking the Global Outbreak." Accessed August 15, 2023. https://nytimes.com/interactive/2021/world/Covid -cases.html.

Novick, Lynn, director and producer. 2019. *College Behind Bars.* Produced by Sarah Botstein and executive produced by Ken Burns. Skiff Mountain Films in association with Florentine Films and WETA-TV. https://pbs.org/kenburns /college-behind-bars.

Othmani, Ahmed, Sophie Bessis, and Marguerite Garling. 2008. "Prisons—A World Apart." In *Beyond Prison: The Fight to Reform Prison Systems around the World,* 1st ed., 49–62. New York: Berghahn Books.

Peterson, Tessa Hicks. 2019. "Healing Pedagogy from the Inside Out: The Paradox of Liberatory Education in Prison." In *Critical Perspectives on Teaching in Prison: Students and Instructors on Pedagogy behind the Wall,* edited by Rebecca Ginsburg, 175–87. New York: Taylor & Francis Group.

Reese, Renford. 2019. "The Prison Education Project." *International Review of Education* 65: 687–709.

Rentzmann, William. 1996. "Prison Philosophy and Prison Education." *Journal of Correctional Education* 47 (2): 58–63.

Schiraldi, Vincent. 2018. "In Germany, It's Hard to Find a Young Adult in Prison." *The Crime Report,* April 10, 2018. https://thecrimereport.org/2018/04/10/in -germany-its-hard-to-find-a-young-adult-in-prison/.

Scott, Robert. 2013. "Distinguishing Radical Teaching from Merely Having Intense Experiences While Teaching in Prison." *The Radical Teacher* 95 (April): 22–32. https://doi.org/10.5406/radicalteacher.95.0022.

Skarbek, David. 2020. *The Puzzle of Prison Order: Why Life behind Bars Varies around the World.* New York: Oxford University Press.

Sterbenz, Christina. 2014. "Why Norway's Prison System Is So Successful." *Business Insider,* December 11, 2014. https://businessinsider.com/why-norways-prison -system-is-so-successful-2014-12.

Tonry, Michael, ed. 2011. *Why Punish? How Much?: A Reader on Punishment.* Oxford; New York: Oxford University Press.

United Nations. 2021. "Impact of Covid-19 'Heavily Felt' by Prisoners Globally: UN Expert." *UN News.* March 9, 2021. https://news.un.org/en/story/2021/03/1086802.

Utheim, Radnhild. 2016. "The Case for Higher Education in Prison: Working Notes on Pedagogy, Purpose, and Preserving Democracy." *Social Justice* 43 (3): 91–106.

Walmsley, Roy. 2017. "World Female Imprisonment List (Fourth Edition)." https://prisonstudies.org/sites/default/files/resources/downloads/world_female_prison_4th_edn_v4_web.pdf/.

Wang, Haidong, Katherine R. Paulson, Spencer A. Pease, Stefanie Watson, Haley Comfort, Peng Zheng, Aravkin Aleksandr, et al. 2022. "Estimating Excess Mortality due to the Covid-19 Pandemic: A Systematic Analysis of Covid-19-Related Mortality, 2020–21." *The Lancet*.

Western, Bruce. 2018. *Homeward: Life in the Year After Prison*. New York: Russell Sage Foundation.

World Prison Brief. 2021. "Highest to Lowest—Foreign Prisoners (Percentage of Prison Population)." https://prisonstudies.org/highest-to-lowest/foreign-prisoners?field_region_taxonomy_tid=All.

Wright, Mary C. 2001. "Pell Grants, Politics and the Penitentiary: Connections Between the Development of US Higher Education and Prisoner Post-Secondary Programs." *Journal of Correctional Education* 52 (1): 11–16.

PART I

Contextualizing Education in Prison

1 ||| THE LONG HISTORY
OF COLLEGE-IN-PRISON

College-in-prison[1] is at once among the most divisive and overlooked subjects in all of the debates about crime, justice, and punishment in the United States. It cuts directly to the question "What are prisons for?" Do they exist purely to punish? Can they add any positive value to the social fabric? The implications of the answers to these questions extend far beyond prisons. College-in-prison raises questions about the purpose of education in American society and who should be entitled to what kind of knowledge.

In the late 1990s, I was a student at Bard College. At that time, the country was in the throes of the tough-on-crime frenzy. It seemed like the college had resources to offer, that some kind of productive relationship could be forged between our small, private college and the prisons surrounding it in rural New York State.

After making some rounds and speaking to anyone knowledgeable who would meet with me, someone suggested I watch the documentary film *The Last Graduation* (1997). It revealed a long, rich history of partnership between these kinds of institutions that had, only recently, ended abruptly. A beautiful film, it tells a tragic story that seemed to me to be familiar to everyone in the field at the time. It went something like this: following the siege at Attica in 1971, a consensus emerged that American prisons had become too violent, too hopeless, too cruel. The scrutiny following those events, and the advocacy of the men who had survived, led to the establishment of college programs within prisons, first in New York and then across the country. College became a central part of what happened in prisons; it imbued the institutions with a sense of hope and meaning while social scientists found that education did more to reduce recidivism than anything else. Despite all that, the 1994 Violent Crime Control and Law Enforcement Act, commonly known as the Clinton Crime Bill, effectively eliminated college opportunity from prisons nationwide when it made incarcerated people ineligible for federal Pell Grants.

The suggestion that Attica led to a more enlightened or progressive period in American corrections was counterintuitive. The decades since the early 1970s were a time of unchecked radical growth of American prisons, which increased dramatically in number and population. But evidence of the power of a college education in prison was convincing. We were on to something; there was a role the college could play in regional prisons that was timely, of crucial importance, and potentially of national significance.

So, in 1999 a group of undergraduates at Bard College founded the Bard Prison Initiative (BPI). Our focus was on institution building, not history. However, the story told in *The Last Graduation*—that college-in-prison arose during the post–civil rights era and was demolished when the Clinton Crime Bill made incarcerated people ineligible for federal education grants—informed our understanding of the work.[2]

In 2017, nearly twenty years later, a colleague at BPI, Jed Tucker, published a terrific article in the *Journal of African American History*. Rooted in archival detail, it describes the process by which Malcolm X sought out and thrived in college during his incarceration in Massachusetts in the late 1940s and early 1950s. For those of us invested in college-in-prison, Tucker's article represented an astounding example of how unfamiliar we are with its history. Contrary to what we generally assume, college-in-prison is not a recent phenomenon born in the era of mass incarceration and the establishment of federal Pell Grants in 1972. If Malcolm X—perhaps the most celebrated incarcerated American of the twentieth century, whose education has figured in bestselling books and major motion pictures—could have enrolled in college during his incarceration, how much more of this history might be hiding in plain sight?

This chapter offers a brief introduction to college-in-prison's origins in the United States. It is essentially an institutional history of colleges, of prisons, and of the ideas that informed partnerships between them. If successful, it will encourage the study of the achievements, disappointments, and hopes that students in these programs experienced over the long history of college-in-prison. It is the accomplishments of those alumni that, ultimately, will be the measure of this field's success.

Prisons are vexing subjects for historians. On the one hand, they represent an unusual archival opportunity: lives and events within them are documented like almost nowhere else. On the other, there is no "prison system" in the United States. There are dozens of prison systems, countless local jails, and various other carceral administrative regimes. Documents are spread from state to state and prison to prison and are often difficult to access. Every individual prison system has customs and procedures that are local and arcane. Sources are fragmented and dispersed; any serious, archival look at the reality of US prisons tends to zero in on one correctional system or, more often, one prison.

Historically, authority over prisons—the power to define their purpose—was often exercised at the level of the individual facility. Until recently, in many states, prisons were commonly managed as fiefdoms of the warden or superintendent. In other words, the question of "What are prisons for?" was answered, in practice, prison by prison. This led to authority that was essentially unchecked, frequently exercised arbitrarily, and generally extralegal. In exceptional instances, broad executive mandates led to prisons that were more forgiving. For many years, much of the literature on the subject documented the efforts of single institutions—or the people who led them—to become more optimistic or "rehabilitative." Recently, scholarship has focused on larger forces: White supremacy, federal policy, and national trends. By observing the history of mass incarceration and focusing on college programs, we may discover how to understand this history in a way that better honors local actors, the decisions they made, and the aspirations they held.

From Postwar Optimism to Cynical Consensus

The Second World War and the ambitious domestic reforms that followed it transformed the American social landscape, creating the conditions for the development of college-in-prison through the late 1940s, '50s, and '60s. The 1944 GI Bill radically increased the number of Americans with access to higher education, and the presence of veterans on college and university campuses helped democratize those institutions (Serow 2004). The bill reflected a widely held belief that education was the best investment for the future that governments could make.

An increasing number of prison systems began offering some kind of education through high school equivalency. There were more incarcerated Americans eager to use their time and improve their lives by pursuing education beyond the secondary level. Prison administrators seeking to make prisons more humane, less destructive, and more focused on the future began creating opportunities to do so. Before the war and on a greater scale in its aftermath, incarcerated people used correspondence coursework to accumulate credits and complete degrees. After the war, colleges and university systems also began to offer "extension" academic programs: fully accredited in-person classes taught by qualified instructors off campus, typically enrolling students part-time (Adams 1973).

At the Norfolk Penal Colony in Massachusetts, the prison from which Malcolm X enrolled in college, leadership worked to make the prison amenable to learning. Norfolk was designed and built in the spirit of the Progressive Era. Its architects believed that its pioneering physical characteristics would help men change their lives. Over time, it featured a significant academic library, a competitive debate society, and an absence of both prison uniforms and the ubiquitous emblems of American confinement: prison bars. The prison not only worked to facilitate higher learning through correspondence coursework, but also invited academics, artists, and teachers to work on-site (Tucker 2017). Malcolm X knew about Norfolk's programs and petitioned the state for years to be relocated there. Once he arrived in 1948, Malcolm took advantage of what Norfolk had to offer, most of all the camaraderie of other incarcerated men with similar interests and ambitions. In the *Autobiography*, Malcolm calls Norfolk "the most enlightened form of prison that I have ever heard of" (X and Haley 1965, 160–61).

Norfolk was unique in many ways; however, in the postwar period, institutions nationwide were beginning to adopt its inclination toward education: In the 1950s, Southern Illinois University in Carbondale introduced academic degree programs in the state prison system; the federal prison at Leavenworth began sporadic college coursework in one of its units; and the University of Maryland started offering courses at the Maryland State Penitentiary (Silva 1994, 25; Adams 1973, 46). Twenty years after the GI Bill, American investment in the expansion of educational opportunity continued; approximately a dozen college-in-prison programs had emerged across the country (Page 2004; Richardson 1965; Willingham 1965b). Moreover, an increase in government spending and private grant-making was about to make formal higher education, though still rare, a more common and prominent feature of American prison life. In 1965, President Lyndon Johnson signed the Higher Education Act (HEA), the Great Society's effort to make college available to as many Americans as possible—and to help them pay for it. Title IV of the HEA featured the Basic Education Opportunity Grant, which would evolve into Pell Grants.

Around this time, the Texas Department of Corrections (TDC)[3] was being run by an outsized figure named George Beto. Intellectual and formidable, Beto earned two PhDs: one in divinity and another in educational administration (Lucko 1994). He is said to have "walked down the hall with a bat in one hand and a bible in the other" (Donna Zuniga [Lee College], interview by author, February 28, 2018). No executive in the history of American corrections did more to secure funding for education within a state prison system. While most of his efforts concentrated on primary and secondary education, Beto eventually recruited colleges to enroll students from within TDC (Bob Evans [Lee College], interview by author, March 5, 2018). In 1966, the TDC partnered with Lee College in Baytown, Texas, to create and maintain perhaps the most resilient and longest-standing program in the country (Zuniga 2015). Beginning with five academic courses, Lee would over time offer an increasing number of subjects, certifications, and degrees across an array of Texas prisons.

Likewise, in 1965, in California, the dean of the School of Criminology at the University of California, Berkeley, rallied the state and potential funders "to develop a new departure in correctional rehabilitation through the creation of an accredited four-year college program within a correctional system" (Elberg 1965). He was inspired by Milton Kotler, an "oddball" (Edley 1964) based at the Institute for Policy Studies in Washington, DC, who had the idea that prisons were the ideal place to begin reforming American education. Before long, the Ford Foundation invested roughly $100,000 for the planning of a new college at San Quentin State Prison to be run by the School of Criminology. "The significance of this proposed grant," wrote Christopher Edley, the first African American officer at the Ford Foundation, "lies in its impact on correctional systems across the United States" (Edley 1965).

Only after committing to the project did Edley learn of college programs at federal prisons in Leavenworth, Kansas, and in Illinois (Richardson 1965; Willingham 1965a). In fact, as early as 1914, college faculty had established opportunities for advanced learning within the expansive perimeters of San Quentin itself (Gehring 1997). Edley (1965) eventually described the California prison system as "the best and most progressive in the nation . . . well-financed, professionally operated, receptive to research and innovations." The collaboration between California's public university and its prison system was a pathway to national impact. The project was funded on the condition that it be launched immediately. By the following year, 1967, there were as many as forty-six prisons across the country offering some kind of college opportunity (Littlefield and Wolford 1982).

That same year, one of New York's largest and most foreboding maximum security prisons hired a new Methodist chaplain. Serious, committed, and ambitious, Edwin Muller set out to establish an array of reform-oriented interventions within Green Haven Correctional Facility. Within a year, Muller secured an alliance with the former governor of Rhode Island, William Henry Vanderbilt III, who provided access to the highest echelons of philanthropy and the best government contacts.

Vanderbilt appointed Muller to become executive director of South 40, his recently established charitable organization, a position the state permitted Muller to hold in addition to his full-time obligations as a New York State employee. With considerable funding and no certainty that it was possible to successfully enroll men incarcerated at Green Haven in higher education, Muller began to recruit local colleges to participate. Most were initially firmly against the idea, but, in 1968, South 40 aligned with Dutchess County Community College and established perhaps the first college-in-prison program in the history of New York. Over time, and with Vanderbilt's access and partnership, South 40 was able to secure a generous matching agreement with the Law Enforcement Assistance Administration (LEAA), a subdivision of the US Department of Justice. For every dollar Vanderbilt would pledge or raise from the private sector, the LEAA offered four. With this commitment in hand, Muller and Vanderbilt raced to create a wide array of pioneering reforms within the seemingly indomitable Green Haven (Charlton 1972; Edward Muller, interview by author, March 2, 2018).

The story of each of these programs—in Texas, California, and New York—reflects an ongoing tension in the work. Each was established with social and educational aspirations in mind. And, over time, each struggled with the question of how to define success: in narrow correctional terms or in some broader and more ambitious way. For example, in New York, Muller's pursuit was to create a collaborative and engaging process through which people in prison could redefine their time and the institutions themselves. South 40's public documents nevertheless point to reductions in recidivism as a core reason for being (Charlton 1972; *Second Chance* 2012; Zahm 1997).

The Ford Foundation cited recidivism as a central justification of the work. In California, the practitioners worried about "a trap" (Edley 1965). Like South 40, the administration at Lee College, and Director Beto at TDC, Milton Kotler envisioned the benefits of college opportunity to extend far beyond incarceration rates. If recidivism was reduced, that would be, in his words, "a happy coincidence" (Kotler 1966).

The consequences of this tension turned out not to be trivial. The quietly growing field of the late 1960s was caught in the increasingly pernicious crosscurrents of its time. While social scientists and funders demanded to measure and to know what "worked" in addressing "deviance" or improving American prisons, advocates, reformers, and radicals increasingly called for a comprehensive rethinking of a response to crime that eschewed prison altogether. The greatest casualty of this phenomenon was Project NewGate, the largest, most ambitious, and most innovative program of the era. After receiving funding from the federal Office of Economic Opportunity (OEO) in 1967, NewGate set out to institute rigorous learning environments in prisons within multiple states. Perhaps its most unprecedented feature was an ongoing commitment to incarcerated students after they returned home. Upon release, students were encouraged to enroll in community-based colleges and offered ongoing support while doing so (Seashore and Haberfeld 1977). NewGate operationalized what would become fashionable and known as "reentry" forty years later (Herron and Muir 1974).

A post-release commitment to students was not NewGate's only distinction. Its programs sought to create a comprehensive educational experience and transform the punitive nature of prison. Students did not engage in coursework on an ad hoc basis; they enrolled full-time and were not expected to maintain additional work assignments. NewGate campuses not only aspired to offer curricula on par with the standards and rigor of campus analogues; they also had a stated objective of "not adapting content" for these particular students (Duguid 2000, 100). By the end of the decade, the OEO was funding NewGate programs in five states. Despite NewGate's aspiration to provide students with an experience liberated from the criminological vocabulary, in the end it served too many masters to succeed. Historian Stephen Duguid, director of Simon Fraser University's Prison Education Program from 1984 to 1993 (Tung 2016), identifies two primary factors in NewGate's demise (Duguid 2000).

First, NewGate failed to realize the purely educational experience suggested by its emphasis on academic standards and autonomy. According to Duguid (2000), NewGate acquiesced to the dominant "medical" model of the day and became, in effect, a prison treatment program. It expected a "prisoner's desire to change his patterns of behavior" to figure in admission decisions, required "intensive therapy and counseling," and, despite a commitment not to tailor curricula, frequently reiterated its mission to help "prisoners achieve a non-criminal lifestyle." These compromises blurred the distinction between college and prison, aligning higher education with other, often coercive, "treatments."

Second, NewGate bound its fortune to an assessment regime for which it was unprepared (Marshall Kaplan, Gans, and Kahn 1975). Like programs elsewhere, NewGate emphasized to funders that the reduction of recidivism was its raison d'être. Ultimately, however, the measurement of recidivism turned out to be considerably more fraught than social scientists had understood. Foremost, recidivism is a result as much of public policy as it is of individual behavior. Furthermore, NewGate did not have at its disposal the kind of sophisticated longitudinal study that could establish the certainty of *any* kind of outcome. When a 1972 evaluation of Project NewGate was conducted only three to five years after programs launched, it failed to demonstrate an impact lowering recidivism rates, and the OEO allowed funding to expire.[4] However, there is no evidence that NewGate did *not* reduce recidivism or improve public safety. According to its evaluators, despite "methodological problems inherent in the original research design . . . the study demonstrates that prison college programs can have significant impact on their participants, namely, in significantly reducing alcohol and drug use, in raising participant aspirations and occupational goals, and in increasing occupational achievement and academic achievement" (Marshall Kaplan, Gans, and Kahn 1975). Nevertheless, NewGate failed to pass muster in the "what works" spirit of its day.

In the end, the OEO expected concrete, criminological measures of impact to justify its support. While NewGate was the outstanding program of the time, it failed to meet funders' criteria for success. The promise of impacting recidivism—and recidivism alone—haunted the NewGate evaluations in precisely the ways that Milton Kotler had predicted from Berkeley five years before. By 1973, NewGate faded as the next era of prison education began. Some of its franchises adapted to survive, and others disappeared. All of its reentry programs closed with the end of OEO support (Duguid 2000, 105). The demise of NewGate was emblematic of an increasingly contentious moment in the history of American criminal justice. As the radical political movements of the 1960s escalated toward their own conclusions, life within American prisons became more explicitly politicized than ever.

Within the academy, particularly among those intellectualizing about crime, a sense that the state could accomplish nothing good through confinement, or nothing good at all, spread rapidly. For example, the medical historian David Rothman wrote in 1971 that the United States was "gradually escaping from institutional responses and one can foresee a period when incarceration will be used still more rarely than it is today" (295). This was not controversial: virtually every leading scholar in the field issued a similar prediction.

A book-length report from the American Friends Service Committee that same year called for the large-scale abandonment of confinement. The report, A Struggle for Justice, argued that the American system of criminal justice magnified inequality "not only because of bias on the part of police or prosecutors but because the substantive content of the law affects those who are not social equals in quite different ways" (AFSC 1971). The following year, the Lutheran Church's Board of Social Ministry issued a damning report of its own, and the Washington Post published a multipart special report, "The Shame of Prisons" (Bagdikian 1972).

The totality of the disruption was captured in a catchphrase promulgated by Robert Martinson, a sociologist based at the City College of New York. Before moving to the East Coast, Martinson had been a long-term graduate student at Berkeley, had run for mayor as a Socialist, and in 1961 had been a Freedom Rider in Mississippi, spending just over a month imprisoned there. In New York, he joined a team of researchers commissioned by the state to perform an enormous literature review of scholarly articles measuring the impact of prison programs designed to curb recidivism. The work was dry; Martinson was flamboyant and prone to getting carried away. He could turn a phrase and blossomed over the early 1970s into a minor celebrity. Intoxicated by the idea that if he could prove prisons and programs serve no positive good, he could upend the system. His pitch—"Nothing works"—influenced readers and government officials of an extraordinary variety (Neptune 2012, 396–409). Liberal academics, left-wing radicals, reactionaries, and emerging neoconservative operatives all found utility in the slogan.

Meanwhile, the furious voices of incarcerated people themselves escaped the confines of prison and reached the general public. Formerly incarcerated authors and activists had joined forces with radical movements of the time, providing firsthand critiques of corrections writ large. In November 1970, radicalized men incarcerated at Folsom State Prison issued a series of demands to authorities. The following August, George Jackson, the prominent author and de facto leader of the Black Panther Party's incarcerated cadre, was killed in circumstances that authorities described as an escape attempt. Two weeks later, the siege at Attica Correctional Facility in New York consumed the prison there and the national media along with it. Leadership of the uprising issued a statement echoing the Folsom Manifesto:

> We, the men of Attica Prison, have been committed to the Department of Corrections by the people of society for the purpose of correcting what [have] been deemed social errors in behavior. Errors which have classified us as socially unacceptable until programmed with new values and more thorough understanding as to our value and responsibilities as members of the outside community. . . . The programs which we are submitted to under the façade of rehabilitation, are relative to the ancient stupidity of pouring water on a drowning man, inasmuch as we are treated for our hostilities by our program administrators with their hostility as a medication. (The Attica Liberation Faction 1971)

The testimony of the men in the D Yard, and the massacre that followed when the National Guard stormed the prison, ultimately killing forty-three staff and incarcerated men, prompted a new spirit of prison reform in New York State, leading to new programs, college, and attention to goings-on in state prisons. The momentum for reform also coincided, unpredictably, with a renewed commitment to punishment and unprecedented growth in the prison system.

Back in Manhattan, Martinson commented that the tumult reflected "growing disgust with what inmates regard as the hypocritical fakery of treatment" (Humphreys 2016). In the New Republic the following April, he declared that the "long history of 'prison reform' is over. On the whole, the prisons have played out their allotted role. They cannot be reformed and must be gradually torn down" (Martinson 1972, 23). Martinson split from the research team that hired him and began a media run that put him on 60 *Minutes*, as well as the pages of *People* magazine, the neoconservative *Public Interest*, and the left-wing *The Nation*. The cry "Nothing works" appealed to radicals, neoconservatives, and the public at large. However, the phrase was weaponized in the opposite way from which he first intended: it amplified skepticism about anything good—but not a desire to mitigate the bad—in prison.

Calls for prison abolition collided with a new commitment to punishment. A dark, unforgiving view of human nature, articulated by James Q. Wilson and fellow neoconservatives, captured the public policy debate sometime in the first half of the 1970s. Wilson, the era's intellectual champion of American punishment, belittled the idea that "programs" or "education" could possibly lead to a significant change in people's behavior.[5] He focused on the other side of the ledger, insisting, as my colleague Ellen Lagemann writes, that "incentives should be changed, with punishment becoming ever more strict and immediate" (Lagemann 2016, 130).

The dynamic of overlapping prison abolitionism with neoconservative calls for a renewed commitment to punishment can be explained as a conflict between competing visions of society. It can also be accurately understood as a perverse kind of consensus. Exhausted by the pitched battles of the late 1960s and early '70s, ideological combatants gave up on the hope of making prisons better or more effective at increasing safety. One side felt that prisons could only be cruel and destructive and therefore shouldn't try to do more; the other understood that prisons *should* only be harsh and cruel. As liberal decision-makers developed an increased skepticism about government's capacity to make any kind of positive social intervention, to conservatives, punishment became a rare facet of American life where state intervention was the one best answer. This cynical consensus left a vacuum leading to radical and unforeseen growth of American prison systems.

The United States was racked by unusually prominent and consequential debates about crime and punishment. Crosscurrents of liberal optimism, radical abolitionism, and conservative reaction cut unpredictably. Throughout the postwar period, discussion of crime, law, and order gradually morphed into an avatar for bitter disagreements and conflict about racial inequality. Prisons themselves, increasingly filled with Hispanic and African American men, became symbols of the shortcomings of—or reaction against—the civil rights revolution, not to mention the New Deal and Great Society. Uprisings in Watts, Newark, and other cities nationwide, along with the presidency of Richard Nixon and, ultimately, the siege at Attica, brought these tensions to the forefront of the public imagination.

Despite all this, the postwar period was, in retrospect, a time of relative stability in American criminal justice. In 1970, roughly 200,000 people were incarcerated in prisons or jails nationwide, with California (25,033), Texas (14,331), and New York (12,059) the most populous systems (Langan et al. 1988). For all their problems, prisons as institutions were not centrally important in American life or government. That was about to change.

The Era of Mass Incarceration

What we now call the era of mass incarceration is the period during which the United States embarked on an experiment of investing in prisons at a scale unprecedented in human history. We began locking up more people for longer periods of time and at younger ages, often for increasingly smaller infractions of the law. And, perversely, the more people were incarcerated in the United States, the more the prisons they were confined in were made to be less livable, less hopeful, and less oriented toward creating a better future for anyone. Mass incarceration as an era can be divided into three stages. The first began with the start of the relentless rise in prison populations and the war on drugs in 1972 and closed with the Clinton Crime Bill in 1994. The second lasted from the implementation of the crime bill until 2008, when, for the first time since 1972, the national prison population did not increase. The third stage runs from 2009 through the present, during which it will be determined whether American prison systems simply stabilize in scale or dramatically downsize to historic or global norms.

First Stage of Mass Incarceration (1972–94)

In 1972, the number of people in prison in the United States began a relentless uptick that continued for a generation. As the incarcerated population began to skyrocket, so too did the number of college programs. By the end of the 1970s, there would reportedly be some three hundred fifty of them (Littlefield and Wolford 1982, 14; Silva 1994, 28). The increase was not the result of central planning. Rather, the spread of community colleges, coinciding with the growth of prison systems and the authorization of Pell Grants, created a demand and a means for funding programs nationwide.

In New York, with pressure mounting following the public hearings about Attica, the state office of education seized the initiative. The new Higher Education Opportunities Program (HEOP), dedicated to increasing college enrollment of academically and economically excluded students, began recruiting colleges to establish programs within a handful of the state's most formidable carceral institutions (Hausrath 2018). HEOP sought first to expand the college at Green Haven, then reached out to colleges that had not previously participated (Hausrath 2018). To the leaders of South 40, who had had a difficult time engaging schools just a few years earlier, it became clear that there was a new calculus driving the decision-making of college administrators. Pell funding had changed the paradigm. In addition, the uprising at Attica made the work more timely, more pressing, and—to the skeptics among us—more in vogue than before (Skidmore College 2011). For Dutchess Community College, there was suddenly competition for students within Green Haven. Marist College entered the same prison with a willingness to enroll considerably more men and the ability to confer a bachelor's degree. North of Albany, along the Vermont border, HEOP was successful in recruiting Skidmore College to enter the prison at Comstock (Skidmore College 2011).

In October 1973, the State University of New York announced its intention to open a "liberal arts prison college" at the prison for women in Bedford Hills (Adams 1973, 49). And, in western New York, HEOP organized a network of three colleges to create what would become the Niagara Consortium. This independent nonprofit partnering with Niagara University, Canisius College, and Daemen College began enrolling students at Attica in 1975. Across New York, funding was in healthy supply. Pell support was supplemented by state-level Tuition Assistance Program (TAP) grants and, often, by additional funds from HEOP (HESC n.d.). By 1980, there would be a college presence in virtually every prison in the state (Ryan and Woodard 1987).

The experience in New York was not uncommon. Pell Grants, often combined with state-level tuition grants, enabled colleges to fund and operate college-in-prison programs nationwide. In Ohio, the growth of the prison system—and of college programs within it—was particularly pronounced. While some programs in Ohio dated as far back as 1964, with Pell funding the programs expanded dramatically. Like in New York,

incarcerated Ohioans were eligible to receive state-level need-based scholarships: the Ohio Instructional Grants. By 1975, every prison in Ohio
hosted a college. In the years that followed, the incarcerated population in
Ohio jumped from fewer than eight thousand to more than fifty thousand.
At its peak, more than five thousand people throughout the Ohio prison
system had enrolled in college through seventeen separate colleges and
universities (GAO 1994; Jerry McGlone [former superintendent of Ohio
Prison Schools], interview by author, December 6, 2017).

By the 1980s, college opportunity had become a central feature of
American criminal punishment and an unusual outlet for optimism in
an otherwise crushing landscape. The number of programs increased from
dozens to hundreds. The dramatic increase in prison populations had left
correctional administrators with an urgent need to "keep people busy."
While people who run prisons are commonly assumed to be hostile to
college, it was often prison staff who sought out colleges to participate. In
other instances, wary administrators became supportive of programs after
seeing the impact they had on morale and safety (Hausrath 2018; Jerry
McGlone [former superintendent of Ohio Prison Schools], interview by
author, December 6, 2017). Over time, many correctional officials came
to view college as a core activity within the prisons. Meanwhile, for many
community colleges, engaging incarcerated people became a central way
to increase enrollment as well as revenue.

Oversight of academic quality was laissez-faire. The dumbing down of
coursework, "no-fail" policies, faculty absenteeism, and missing course-
books all figure in reports of the worst abuses. If anyone should have been
responsible for regulating standards, it was not clear who. In some states,
educators and correctional officials collaborated to provide governance or
to create an oversight regime, most prominently in Ohio and New York.
These organizations were exceptions, however, not the rule (Hausrath
2018; Jerry McGlone [former superintendent of Ohio Prison Schools],
interview by author, December 6, 2017).

In the mid-1980s, after fifteen years of unabated growth, college-in-
prison programs in the United States began to face resistance. At first,
murmurs about the abundance of low-quality academics and abuse of
government funding raised concerns about the future. Prison-based education was hardly unique in this. Reports of abuse of the Pell program grew
in number over the same period and exploded into genuine scandal in 1993
(Opinion 1993). However, concern over quality was not what would lead

to the programs' demise. In the end, an apparently persuasive argument that these programs were morally wrong and their students undeserving carried the day.

In 1982, Congressman William Whitehurst proposed legislation limiting the use of Pell Grants in prison to a cap of $6 million per year. This was the first of what became annual attempts by members of Congress to limit or eliminate—and politicize—Pell funding within prisons (Gehring 1997, 48). At the same time, the cost of college began to rise, while government tuition aid started a fast decline. By 1986, the College Board reported increases over a five-year period of 12–26 percent for annual tuition, while federal financial aid dropped nearly 20 percent (Cross 1986). As the 1990s approached, skepticism about the Pell program and tough-on-crime hysteria began to merge. The Drug Free Workplace Act of 1988 required "anyone who receives a Federal grant" to "pledge that he will not be involved in drug-related activities." Pell Grant recipients on campuses had to take an "anti-drug oath" (*New York Times* 1989).

By the 1990s, college-in-prison was a matter of public debate. Massachusetts governor Bill Weld claimed that, if the Pell program continued in prison, "people who cannot afford to go to college are going to start committing crimes so they can get sent to prison to get a free college education!" (Gilligan 2000). In 1991, Senator Jesse Helms introduced a bill intended to eliminate Pell funding within state and federal prisons (Page 2004). Then, *60 Minutes* ran a feature in which Governor Weld told Morley Safer that Boston University should make its program available "to poor, law-abiding citizens who have committed no crime" and that incarcerated students could become reacquainted with "the joys of making small rocks from big rocks" (Silva 1994, 29). Back in Washington, DC, a limited version of Helms's amendment passed, banning anyone serving a life sentence from receiving Pell Grants (Page 2004).

In 1993, polling indicated a dramatic rise in public anxiety about crime. Midway through his first term, President Bill Clinton viewed a major crime bill as a top legislative priority. Toward the close of the year's congressional session, Texas senator Kay Bailey Hutchison introduced Amendment 1158, which would eliminate Pell Grant eligibility for any person in prison. It passed the Senate with little debate or resistance. By the spring of 1994, the House was debating the extensive legislation—a debate intended to demonstrate the Democratic Party's ability to address the crime issue.

The most frequent, pernicious, and false claim in the increasingly contentious debate about Pell funding in prison was the assertion that a Pell Grant issued to an incarcerated person meant a Pell Grant taken from someone else. In November 1993, Senator Hutchison addressed her colleagues to garner support for her amendment: "What has happened is that because prisoners have zero income, they have been able to step to the front of the line and push law-abiding citizens out of the way to get these grants for college educations. . . . This amendment will . . . free up the $200 million dollars that was going to prisoners to have their educations funded and it will now go to the children of these low-income families for whom the Pell Grants were originally intended" (Senate Session 1993). Hutchison misrepresented the cost of Pell in prison, exaggerating the total by nearly 600 percent, inflating $35 million to $200 million. More importantly, cutting the program did not "free up" monies to help pay for college for students anywhere.

The inaccuracy of the argument was lost in one-sided "debates." On April 19, 1994, NBC's *Dateline* aired a segment presenting the Pell issue as a competition between conventional and incarcerated undergraduates. When asked if he thought "more students could get a Pell Grant if you took them away from prisoners," congressman Bart Gordon of Tennessee replied, "There's no question that they could" (*Dateline* 1994). The morning after the broadcast, along with two other members, Representative Gordon proposed an amendment to make incarcerated people ineligible for Pell. In the House, one representative took the lonely position of defending the programs. Albert Wynn of Maryland suggested modestly that the program be extended two years while the federal government measure its success (Page 2004). He was unsuccessful.

To some, the public's animosity and the revocation of Pell Grants for incarcerated students came as a surprise. Most programs were entirely unprepared. The Niagara Consortium, the collection of New York colleges based at Attica, was a unique exception and had been squirreling away savings for years. At first, the conservative financial approach reflected concern about the possibility of another prolonged shutdown at the prison and the need to pay core staff when financial aid might temporarily disappear. By the early 1990s, the Consortium was putting aside money because of a different fear: due to public hostility, federal grants and state scholarships—or both—could evaporate.

In August 1994, New York's college providers met in the Hudson Valley for their annual retreat, planning for the upcoming academic year. The gathering was scheduled months in advance, before it was clear that this meeting might be the last. Over the summer, New York had been sending delegations to Washington to oppose Pell revocation. Every college working in the state system attended, along with some correctional personnel, totaling roughly one hundred people. In Congress, the provision to eliminate Pell funding had made its way into the final version of the bill, which had already passed the House. On August 25, while the conference of college providers was in session, word came from the Capitol that the Crime Bill had passed the Senate, 61–38. The corrections officials in attendance knew that the scope and purpose of their work was going to change immediately, perhaps forever; the representatives of colleges and universities understood their programs would not last long. Virtually all were shuttered within the academic year (Hausrath 2018).

On September 13, 1994, leaders from Congress and law enforcement officials gathered in the Rose Garden for the signing ceremony of the Clinton Crime Bill. President Clinton assured leaders that "the laws of the land will be brought back into line with the values of our people and begin to restore the line between right and wrong" (*ABC News* 1994). In the twenty years since Folsom, Attica, and Robert Martinson, the problem of prisons had grown radically worse, but it no longer inspired intense intellectual debate. Liberals looked the other way.

The Crime Bill ended an era when prisons were multiplying in size and number across the United States but, perhaps paradoxically, quietly became a site for the establishment of hundreds of new little colleges. Whether one considers these schools to be *correctional* or *rehabilitative* is a matter of semantics: education anywhere is the cultivation and development of a personality. Within American prisons, the establishment of "programming" that was not coercive represented a quiet watershed. College practices did not resemble the *treatment* of the so-called *medical* era that leaders at Folsom and Attica specified in their list of grievances. Rather than being vehemently opposed by them, the colleges were championed by incarcerated people, families, and advocates. Eddie Ellis was in Attica during the uprising and in Green Haven through the golden years of the college programs. He was perhaps the most influential formerly incarcerated advocate of his generation. In his words, "prisoners, very early, recognized that they needed to be better educated—that the more education they had the better they would be able to deal with themselves, their problems, the problems of the prison, the problems of communities from which most of them came" (Zahm 1997).

In the end, every incarcerated person in the United States became ineligible for a Pell Grant. Lawmakers who supported the change often argued that the United States could not financially afford college-in-prison. The legislation they supported, and that decimated in-prison education nationwide, earmarked $7.5 billion for the construction of new prisons (Mauer 2006, 22)—enough to maintain the Pell program for incarcerated Americans for more than two hundred years (GAO 1994).

Second Stage of Mass Incarceration (1995–2008)

The passage of the Clinton Crime Bill marked the end of the first period of mass incarceration. From 1995 to 2008, prison populations continued to rise nationwide even while crime, especially violent crime, dropped precipitously. As Ian Buruma has written, this change in public policy represented a shift in governments' approach from being "tough-on-crime" to "tough-on-criminals" (Buruma 2005). It removed the pretense of rehabilitation or "correction" from American prisons at precisely the moment that prisons had become a more central part of our societal fabric than ever before.

The end of Pell decimated the college programs. In many states, college disappeared from prisons altogether. Nationally, enrollment dropped 40 percent in the first year and more in the years immediately following. A national survey of correctional education directors found that nearly half reported that the elimination of Pell funding "completely changed" their systems (Tewksbury et al. 2000). Meanwhile, other funding also came under attack. Anything that seemed to make the experience of incarceration more tolerable faced severe public scrutiny. So-called "No Frills" legislation was introduced in Congress and passed by state legislatures. "To habitual criminals, prisons are resorts with televisions, weight training facilities and libraries that some colleges would envy," said one New Jersey state senator. "For a lot of them, jail time is just an extended vacation" (Peterson 1995).

In the 1990s, the cynicism of the 1970s turned into outright government hostility toward those ensnared in the criminal justice system and toward young people in general. John DiIulio Jr., a protégé of James Q. Wilson, popularized the phrase "superpredators" to describe a generation of children. In 1995, DiIulio published a highly influential essay in the *Weekly Standard* and was subsequently welcomed at the Clinton White House to expand on it (DiIulio 1995). Meanwhile, prison officials were not uniformly supportive of the new, singular direction in which policy was moving. A spokesman for the American Correctional Association declared that "the pendulum is swinging too far" toward harsh measures and that it "is not the politicians" who have to contend with the fallout from their bad decisions (Johnson 1996).

In 1995, state governments nationwide debated eliminating funding or outright banning college programs within prisons. In New York, George Pataki was inaugurated governor and quickly moved to revoke state-level TAP grants. The change took effect immediately, compounding the loss of Pell funding and eviscerating programs statewide (Bernstein 1995). While Governor Pataki repeated the false claim that college-in-prison made college access more difficult for conventional students, he also moved to cut financial aid for students on campuses across New York. The priorities were clear: punishment was a good investment, education less so.

In 1998, the Center on Juvenile and Criminal Justice reported, "Whereas New York spent more than twice as much on universities than on prisons in 1988, the state now spends $275 million more on prisons than on state and city colleges. The 1997–98 figures represent only the corrections operating cost, and do not include the $300 million approved for the construction of 3,100 new prison spaces approved in the state budget for that year" (CJCJ 1998).

Other state capitals' results were less predictable. In Texas, with its tradition and commitment to education in prison dating back to the directorship of George Beto, legislators did not succeed in eliminating the $7 million line item for college in the state budget. Unlike New York, Texas found a compromise to keep programs running, though it featured a drastic 50 percent budget cut (Erisman and Contardo 2005; Donna Zuniga [Lee College], interview by author, February 28, 2018). In North Carolina, a formalized relationship between the Department of Corrections and the Community College System insulated programs from revocation of Pell funds. In Ohio, where prominent members of the state senate vehemently opposed the programs, the head of the state corrections department told his team to "get ready to fight" (Jerry McGlone [former superintendent of Ohio Prison Schools], interview by author, December 6, 2017). The programs reduced recidivism—his department had documentation to prove it, and it set out to defend the programs from the legislature. Ultimately it succeeded, but only to a point. State funding continued, but under two extraordinary conditions. Study of the liberal arts—history, mathematics, science, and literature—had to be excluded. In addition, college study in Ohio prisons could never, no matter how many credits a student accumulated, culminate in a college degree (Erisman and Contardo 2005; Jerry McGlone [former superintendent of Ohio Prison Schools], interview by author, December 6, 2017). Across the country, in a hostile environment, educators and correctional officials were forced to make difficult decisions and forge uncomfortable compromises to keep any degree of education going.

The elimination of Pell funding was the most dramatic and important moment in the history of higher education in prison. It exemplified the punitive national mood and had a drastically effective impact. However, the decisions of legislatures in these states proved that Pell was not in fact the alpha and omega of college-in-prison, but that state and local funding was essential to its existence (Erisman and Contardo 2005). They also demonstrated that college-in-prison does not operate on a conventional left-right axis and, even through the worst times, continued to have advocates in legislatures, correctional systems, and communities.

While allies in government preserved as much of the programs as they could, in other states different groups worked in new ways to reinvent college-in-prison for the post-Pell era. Incarcerated people, religious communities, undergraduates and graduate students, and other private citizens created new initiatives. Gradually, diversely funded individual efforts marked the landscape. These programs restored the presence of college on a small scale and functioned as a reminder to the country that better things were possible within its enormous systems of punishment.

At Bedford Hills, the maximum security prison for women in New York State, incarcerated women organized, advocated for, and, in 1996, successfully reestablished college there (Worth 2001; Fine et al. 2001). At Sing Sing, incarcerated men and allies followed suit, establishing a program there. This program would come to be called Hudson Link and, after receiving significant media attention, would go on to establish franchises with various academic partners across New York State. In California, after exceptional college faculty and correctional staff attempted to keep some semblance of college programming intact within San Quentin, Jody Lewen, a graduate student at the time, took charge of the floundering remains of the college program and built a lasting institution that became the Prison University Project (PUP) in 2003 and eventually the fully accredited, independent Mount Tamalpais College, in 2020 (Jody Lewen [executive director, Prison University Project], interview by author, March 7, 2018). In 1999, in New York, my fellow undergraduates and I at Bard College petitioned the college administration to enroll incarcerated people and negotiated access into the state prison system, creating the Bard Prison Initiative (BPI).

In time, these initiatives became analogs to the 1960s programs: demonstration projects for the post-Pell era. Hudson Link, PUP, and BPI were built on the expectation that private funding was the immediate-term path to survival. Proximate to Manhattan and San Francisco, fundraising was more viable than elsewhere. Still, each was unlikely to last. They faced long odds but, with time, became nationally recognized for, if nothing else, our ability to survive in a hostile climate. Whatever recognition was deserved, none would have made it if not for the commitment of the administrative leadership of the specific prisons that hosted our programs. However unfriendly the media and politicians had become, there continued to be a belief in education among some people who oversaw or worked in prisons for a living.

Whatever the level of support at the local level, we were very much in the wilderness politically. Until 2005, our understanding at BPI was that we were tolerated by the political leadership so long as we essentially worked in secret. From California, when I asked Jody Lewen (interview by author, March 7, 2018) to describe the field at the time, she replied: "The thing I think of; just that it was incredibly small. It felt like there were five of us, it was like us and Bob Hausrath: very isolated, very committed people digging their own trench." And, without any aspiration or hope of statewide or national initiatives, "it was very focused on quality." Reflecting on his forty-one years directing the Niagara Consortium, Bob Hausrath (2018) describes, "the last 20 years [were] the most difficult. . . . I felt like I was alone in corrections and that I had a target on my back." We worked with the feeling that the field was infinitesimally small and that we were, essentially, alone (Jody Lewen [executive director, PUP], interview by author, March 7, 2018).

In 2005, a white paper issued by the Institute for Higher Education Policy suggested otherwise. It reported that during the 2003–2004 academic year, more incarcerated people had enrolled in college than prior to the end of Pell funding. By 2004, over 20 percent of people in North Carolina prisons were enrolled in some form of postsecondary education (Erisman and Contardo 2005). Federal Incarcerated Youth Offender (IYO) grants, along with state funding and private philanthropy, were being used to cobble together new educational programs and to maintain, in reduced form, older ones. Strikingly, however, courses available to people in prison were now overwhelmingly vocational, not academic. The authors note that "prison inmates are not earning college degrees, even at the associate's level, in any significant numbers" (Erisman and Contardo 2005). As had happened in Ohio and states across the country, breadth, choice, and degree completion in education had been all but eliminated from American prisons.

There were exceptions, however. In Texas, Lee and a number of other colleges soldiered on with some state and occasionally limited federal funding. Indiana, a state that hosted almost no programs during the Pell era, became a hotbed of college-in-prison. And, in western New York, the Niagara Consortium managed to stay afloat, first spending down savings, then enjoying brief success with philanthropy, and finally, relying on the support of a duo of legislators—a liberal city-based assemblyman and a conservative rural state senator—year after improbable year.

Throughout this period, the politics of the issue gradually improved. The existence of outstanding demonstration projects, the dramatic decline in crime, and the emergence of new groups of advocates for prison reform all contributed to the change. By 2008, a generation of formerly incarcerated advocates coalesced into the makings of a genuine social movement. Some of these people were young enough to have been precisely the individuals that John DiIulio was referring to when he popularized the concern about "superpredators." Meanwhile, in Texas, a group of reformers gradually emerged from the conservative movement and the advocacy of Charles Colson, who had spent time in prison for his involvement in the Watergate scandal.

A growing body of research contributed to the change in public opinion and contextualized the historic investment in punishment. One set of researchers found that in some of New York's poorest neighborhoods, governments were spending over $1 million per year to incarcerate residents of single urban blocks. These "million-dollar blocks," which researchers started to identify in various cities, provoked debate about how taxpayer money could be put to better use (Badger 2015; Kurgan et al. n.d.; Orson 2012).

For college-in-prison, the second stage of mass incarceration was defined by retreat and resilience. Programs vanished, reemerged, often in secret, and gradually reentered the national conversation on new terms. State-funded programs stabilized after the shockwaves of 1994, but with limited funding and sometimes with mandated curricular restrictions. Even federal funding returned, quietly and briefly, albeit with other restrictions of its own. Publicly supported programs were almost always vocationally oriented. The small number of privately-funded programs—the boutiques—were almost all liberal arts programs. Mostly, these programs operated in different social and governmental networks and remained remarkably unaware of one another.

During this period, the number of people held in prison systems in the United States soared from the now quaint numbers of 1972. In New York, for example, the population of the state prison system peaked around seventy-two thousand, while Texas surpassed a hundred fifty thousand, and California approached a hundred seventy-five thousand (California Department of Corrections 2007). Nationally, the number of incarcerated people inched toward a previously unthinkable two and a half million. However unpopular the work was thought to be, or how easily legislators made a scandal out of it, college-in-prison was never more imperative than under the new regime and extraordinary scale of American incarceration.

Third Stage of Mass Incarceration (2008–22)

In 2009, after nearly forty years of perpetual growth, the number of incarcerated people in the United States did not show an increase year over year. During this third and current stage of mass incarceration, we have seen modest decreases in prison populations, though rates remain extraordinarily high by any measure. After peaking in 1991, the national crime rate has steadily decreased, and the violent crime rate has fallen nearly 50 percent (Friedman, Grawert, and Cullen 2017). As this is being written, well over six million Americans are without voting rights; in fact, more Black Americans are legally denied the franchise today than prior to the Voting Rights Act (Uggen, Larson, and Shannon 2016). The financial crisis of 2008 was followed by another series of cuts in government spending for college-in-prison (Mitchell, Leachman, and Masterson 2017). In the handful of states that continued to invest after Pell was eliminated, the budget sessions of 2010 and 2011 enacted severe setbacks.

If the second stage of mass incarceration was defined by retreat and resilience, the current one is characterized at once by further defeat, a return to prominence, and considerably more acceptance than in the past. As a national phenomenon, college-in-prison is back, and not as a pariah. However, for the programs that hung on through the darkest years of the 1990s, the recent period has been challenging. The life cycle of some of the oldest programs has ended. Simultaneously, a groundswell of small independent programs has created grassroots communities of providers that are aligned with a growing network of formerly incarcerated advocates and a bipartisan coalition committed to a transformation of criminal justice in the United States.

In Texas, legislative budget cuts in 2011 coincided with the expiration of federal funding. The IYO program, which buoyed many holdouts from the Pell era, was eliminated in 2011. In a single year, Lee College lost 72 percent of its support for prison education. The combination devastated but did not destroy all programs in Texas. Instead, there were the predictable casualties: programs in the liberal arts, the humanities, and coursework designed to be transferable to four-year degree programs post-release. Professional coursework and certifications continue unabated to this day (Bob Evans [Lee College], interview by author, March 5, 2018; Marc Levin, interview by author, March 13, 2018; Donna Zuniga [Lee College], interview by author, February 28, 2018). Similar phenomena also led to the gradual elimination of North Carolina's programs.

In Indiana, the simultaneous end of federal IYO and state funding led to a precipitous decline (John Nally, interview by author, March 18, 2018). Indiana is peculiar in that there was not widespread college-in-prison during the Pell era, but in the late 1990s, with IYO and some state investment, it became one of the richest environments for higher education in prison nationwide. Through the first decade of the twenty-first century, Indiana issued an ever-increasing number of college degrees in prison until funding was pulled in 2011. At its peak, the programs in Indiana led to the conferral of over eight hundred associate degrees and nearly three hundred bachelor's degrees per year (Patrick Callahan, email message to author, March 9, 2018).

Not long before, at BPI, we had entered the business of recruiting other colleges and universities in states across the country to join this line of work. Following a *60 Minutes* feature in 2007, philanthropists approached us with questions about how to do more (Olian 2007). In contrast to the large bureaucracies of corrections, education within prisons is best offered at a human scale. Rather than franchise BPI in different states, we decided that the best thing to do with more resources was to share them and spread them among dedicated colleges and universities.

By 2011, BPI had made significant investments in new programs at Wesleyan University in Connecticut, Grinnell College in Iowa, and Goucher College in Maryland. With this in mind, then-BPI Director of Policy and Academics Daniel Karpowitz set out to see whether anything could be salvaged from the legacy in Indiana. After some initial groundwork, he recruited the University of Notre Dame and Holy Cross College to collaborate in the work of restoring college-in-prison in the state. With the participation of the most influential university in the state, Indiana Department of Correction (IDOC) then agreed to collaborate and provide public funding. The state's contribution was minuscule compared to that of its recent past, but in the new climate it was far from trivial. In 2013, it led to the establishment of the Moreau College Initiative (MCI), which now confers bachelor's and associate degrees every spring. This moment of crisis in higher education generally provided colleges of every variety an opportunity to rethink "mission" and access. Louis Nanni, vice president of University Relations at Notre Dame, said of college-in-prison, "There are few engagements more meaningful to our faculty and speak more deeply to the soul of this University. The void of educational opportunities extended to those in prison is alarming. We need to expand our efforts and invite more partners to join [the effort] to make a lasting difference" (Jay Caponigro, email to author, December 13, 2017).

Of the new era's crop of demonstration projects, the University of Illinois Urbana-Champaign has made a particular contribution; in Washington State, the Freedom Education Project of Puget Sound enrolls women in degree-granting programs; Goucher College's terrific contribution in Maryland offers bachelor's degrees and wields unusual influence due, only in part, to its proximity to Washington, DC; efforts in states including Maine, New Jersey, Arizona, and Massachusetts have taken a variety of forms depending on funding mechanisms. Some elite universities, reluctant to dilute the market value of their transcripts, have established partnerships with local community colleges to offer associate degree programs. Others have been more forthcoming: Washington University in St. Louis and New York University have established small but robust degree-granting programs.

One group of researchers reported in 2017 that as many as 177 colleges

and universities were participating directly in college-in-prison programming at that time (Castro et al. 2017). By comparison, in 1971, another
optimistic researcher estimated 150 schools were involved immediately
preceding the explosive period of growth following access to Pell Grants.
In that year, 200,000 people were incarcerated in the United States; in
2018, there were 2.3 million in American prisons and jails.

Meanwhile, in New York, the sole holdout from the Pell era, the Niagara
Consortium, finally closed without fanfare in 2016. Its director of forty-one
years, Bob Hausrath, who had quietly persevered through the toughest
times, reflected recently on the meaning of his work in Attica and elsewhere: "I think the legacy is that we understand that it is ideas that change
men's lives. Usually through the liberal arts . . . ideas change lives" (Hausrath 2018). Voters and decision-makers are beginning to agree with him.
In 2013, national philanthropy, led by the Ford Foundation, partnered with
Republican governors attempting to reestablish programs in New Jersey,
North Carolina, and Michigan. In 2014, in New York, Governor Andrew
Cuomo announced his intention to restore state funding. While the proposal failed in the face of traditional, visceral opposition, public polling
was conducted on the issue for the first time, and the results surprised
many of us. The data showed that the public favored Cuomo's proposal
by a double-digit margin (Harding 2014).

In 2015, a collective of major philanthropic players set out to restore
college-in-prison programs across California. In January 2016, the District
Attorney of New York announced a major investment in college-in-prison
statewide. This was perhaps the first time since the 1970s that law enforcement acknowledged education as a form of crime prevention worth
investing in. It was the closest thing to a restoration of public funding
for college-in-prison that New York had seen since 1995. Remarkably, in
2016, Jody Lewen, on behalf of the PUP, accepted the National Humanities
Medal from the president of the United States.

At the same time, two different political movements working behind
the scenes or at the grassroots level gained influence and prominence.
First, conservative thought-leaders whose discomfort with mass incarceration was first articulated in private and then in relative obscurity burst into
mainstream conservative debate. What had originated with Chuck Colson's
brief incarceration and the long advocacy of his deputy Pat Nolan now
involved former House Speaker Newt Gingrich, the libertarian-leaning
Koch brothers and their network, and an active Texas-based think tank,

Right on Crime, which served as a nerve center for policy cultivation and implementation. These efforts, parallel to a growing grassroots progressive movement for wholesale change, gradually helped turn criminal justice reform into perhaps the single issue in contemporary American political life with promise for bipartisan action and agreement.

In 2018, Marc Levin, the leader of Right on Crime, described conservative thinking on the specific question of college-in-prison, saying that there are two central policy concerns dominating conservative thought on higher education. The first is that government tuition aid, like Pell Grants or the state-level equivalents, have the counterintuitive effect of driving up the cost of college. The second is that not enough resources are directed toward teaching as opposed to the production of obscure scholarship. The absence of either of these considerations in our context, he suggested, leaves room for support in the new climate of criminal justice reform.

During Barack Obama's second term, the administration turned to address criminal justice in an increasingly serious and focused way. The pivotal moment came in October 2015. The Federal Interagency Reentry Council, an innovation of Attorney General Eric Holder, later continued by the Trump administration, invited a group of formerly incarcerated advocates to lead a discussion. This followed years of grassroots efforts to ensure that people with direct experience of incarceration have a place of influence and prominence in policy debate. Eight leaders, women and men, arrived from Alabama, California, North Carolina, and New York. They addressed a room of roughly forty senior government officials. Each of them described the work they were doing in their home communities: housing advocacy; voting rights; "ban the box"; criminal justice reform in the South; education; and leadership development.

At the conclusion of the presentation, the director of the Federal Bureau of Prisons rose and declared, "I will never do my job in the same way again." Individuals directly impacted by mass incarceration had been released, paid their dues, created organizations, done advocacy, and, now, stunned a room of officials who were tasked with rethinking criminal justice policy in the United States. One fact struck the leadership of the council: nearly every one of the eight leaders present went to college in prison. They each spoke about the role of education in their lives and in solving the most vexing social problems we face as a country (Vivian Nixon, interview by author, March 13, 2018).

Conclusion

The presentation by the eight formerly incarcerated leaders led to an Obama-era "experiment" named Second Chance Pell: a temporary, limited reinstatement of Pell Grant eligibility for incarcerated students. Remarkably, as a part of Donald Trump's final budget in 2020, Congress approved an expansion of Second Chance Pell to gradually restore Pell eligibility nationwide. In 2022, after twenty-six years, New York State lifted the ban on incarcerated people receiving TAP grants. Both of these changes followed a generation of advocacy, and neither elicited much public discussion or caused controversy. Both happened as part of large omnibus bills and during the shroud of Covid-19; their impact and the public's reaction remain uncertain.

As I write, the battles to define, evaluate, and justify this work have returned. We spent twenty-six years arguing what college-in-prison would be; now we will argue about what it *could* or *should* be. New decision-makers will want to define or measure the success of college-in-prison in old ways. For students and practitioners, however, the reality of the work confirms its human importance. Milton Kotler's insistence that recidivism be one benefit among many, not college-in-prison's entire reason for being, is as true today as ever before.

The conflict represented in *The Last Graduation* is, in part, a setup. It is the story of a seemingly hopeless, Manichean battle between large forces and small people: Bill Clinton, Congress, and White supremacy versus incarcerated people, college educators, and correctional officials. The truth is that more of the outcome is determined at the local level—within states and prisons themselves—than we knew. Moreover, the battle is not all or nothing. The greatest and least-recognized conflict in this story pertains to the question of what kind of knowledge people in prison deserve access to. More precisely, to what knowledge of history, mathematics, or science should members of America's most forgotten class be entitled?

For those seeking metrics or context, the literature that exists provides some certainty: college-in-prison does reduce recidivism; it increases the likelihood of meaningful employment for people returning home; even when people are unsuccessful finding work, they are still less likely to return to prison; and education also reduces violence in the prisons and increases public safety outside of them (Karpowitz and Kenner 2003; Johnson 2001; Fine et al. 2001; Davis et al. 2013; Harer 1994). In other words, it accomplishes all the things that the optimistic or genuine practitioners of the "treatment" regimes sought to do. But college is not done coercively *to* people in prison; it is practiced collaboratively *with* or *by* them.

As Vivian Nixon, one of those eight leaders who visited the Reentry Council in 2015 told me, "There is extraordinary support [for college] among incarcerated and formerly incarcerated people. Very little of it has to do with public safety or recidivism. It is about giving people the capacity and the tools to make independent and informed decisions about what they want to do with their lives and lifting the bar, raising the ceiling of what's possible to them. It's not about the 'system'; it's about themselves and their life capacity" (Vivian Nixon, interview by author, March 13, 2018). College-in-prison "works" for precisely the same reasons it is controversial: because it treats people in prison with dignity, because it provides something desirable, and because it looks forward to a promising future rather than backward to a contentious past.

Notes

A previous version of this chapter was published as Max Kenner, "The Long History of College in Prison," in *Education for Liberation: The Politics of Promise and Reform Inside and Beyond America's Prisons*, edited by Gerard Robinson and Elizabeth English Smith, 9–29 (Lanham, MD: Rowman & Littlefield, 2019).

1. While elsewhere in the volume the editors use "college in prison" as the noun form and "college-in-prison" as the adjective form, the policy of the Bard Prison Initiative (BPI) is to use "college-in-prison" for both, so it appears that way in this chapter.

2. While I cannot recall how I initially encountered the film, one of the three women who produced *The Last Graduation* was also instrumental in the very early years of BPI and helping me navigate the field very early on. Benay Rubenstein had been a program director for Marist College, then a director of the college program at Bedford Hills; I am, and all of us at BPI are, exceptionally indebted to her.

3. In 1989, the TDC was absorbed into the new Texas Department of Criminal Justice (TDCJ).

4. It is worth pointing out the near impossibility of measuring recidivism in relation to programs that had only been established three to five years prior. The number of students who could have completed college coursework, been released, and remained out of (or returned to) prison, all in a period of only three years, could not have been substantial enough to draw any reliable conclusions about the efficacy of programs in reducing recidivism.

5. For example, with characteristic verbosity, he writes, "It requires not merely optimistic but heroic assumptions about the nature of man to lead one to suppose that a person, finally sentenced after (in most cases) many brushes with the law, and having devoted a good part of his youth and young adulthood to misbehavior of every sort,

should, by either the solemnity of prison or the skillfulness of a counselor, come to see the error of his ways and to experience a transformation of his character."

Works Cited

ABC News. 1994. "President Bill Clinton Signs the Crime Bill." September 13, 1994. http://abcnews.go.com/Politics/video/archive-video-president-bill-clinton-signs-crime-bill-38309076.

Adams, Stuart. 1973. "Higher Learning behind Bars." *Change* 5 (9): 45–50.

American Friends Service Committee (AFSC). 1971. *Struggle for Justice: A Report on Crime and Punishment in America.* New York: Hill & Wang.

The Attica Liberation Faction. 1971. "Manifesto of Demands." *Race & Class* 53 (2). https://doi.org/10.1177/0306396811414338.

Badger, Emily. 2015. "How Mass Incarceration Creates 'Million Dollar Blocks' in Poor Neighborhoods." *Washington Post,* July 30, 2015. https://washingtonpost.com/news/wonk/wp/2015/07/30/how-mass-incarceration-creates-million-dollar-blocks-in-poor-neighborhoods/?utm_term=.78befa35b52f.

Bagdikian, Ben. 1972. "The Shame of Prisons." *Washington Post,* January 29, 1972— February 6, 1972. https://undercover.hosting.nyu.edu/s/undercover-reporting/item-set/34.

Bernstein, Emily M. 1995. "Pataki's Budget Would Pare College Grants." *New York Times,* December 19, 1995. http://nytimes.com/1995/12/19/nyregion/pataki-s-budget-would-pare-college-grants.html.

Buruma, Ian. 2005. "Uncaptive Minds." *New York Times Magazine,* February 20, 2005. http://nytimes.com/2005/02/20/magazine/uncaptive-minds.html.

California Department of Corrections. 2007. "Fall 2007 Adult Population Projections." https://cdcr.ca.gov/Reports_Research/Offender_Information_Services_Branch/Projections/F07pub.pdf/.

Castro, Erin L., Vanessa Johnson-Ojeda, Tara Hardison, Rebecca Hunter, and Sean Crossland. 2017. "Researching Postsecondary Educational Opportunity in Prison: What Do We Know?" (PowerPoint presentation). *Alliance for Higher Education in Prison.* Dallas. November 4, 2017.

Center on Juvenile and Criminal Justice. 1998. *New York State of Mind? Higher Education vs. Prison Funding in the Empire State, 1988–1998.* http://cjcj.org/uploads/cjcj/documents/new_york.pdf/.

Charlton, Linda. 1972. "'South 40' Tries to Aid Convicts." *New York Times,* April 23, 1972. https://nytimes.com/1972/04/23/archives/south-40-tries-to-aid-convicts-education-program-and-rehabilitation.html.

Cross, Dolores E. 1986. "Letter to the Editor: How Student Financial Aid Has Become a Barrier to Education." *New York Times,* October 18, 1986. https://nytimes.com/1986/10/18/opinion/l-how-student-financial-aid-has-become-a-barrier-to-education-828986.html.

Dateline. 1994. "Society's Debt?" Aired on April 19, 1994, on NBC.

Davis, Lois M., Robert Bozick, Jennifer L. Steele, Jessica Saunders, and Jeremy N. V. Miles. 2013. *Evaluating the Effectiveness of Correctional Education: A Meta-*

Analysis of Programs That Provide Education to Incarcerated Adults. Santa Monica, CA: RAND Corporation.

DiIulio, Jr., John J. "The Coming of the Super Predators." *Weekly Standard*, November 27, 1995. http://weeklystandard.com/the-coming-of-the-super -predators/article/8160.

Duguid, Stephen. 2000. *Can Prisons Work?* Toronto: University of Toronto Press.

Edley, Christopher. 1964. Christopher Edley to Paul Ylvisaker, Ford Foundation Records, Rockefeller Archive Center, May 11, 1964.

Edley, Christopher. 1965. Docket Excerpts: University of California (Berkeley) Planning of a Prison College, Ford Foundation Records, Rockefeller Archive Center, July 12, 1965.

Elberg, Sanford S. 1965. Sanford S. Elberg to Christopher Edley, "Prison College Proposal." Ford Foundation Records, Rockefeller Archive Center, July 20, 1965.

Erisman, Wendy, and Jeanne Bayer Contardo. 2005. *Learning to Reduce Recidivism: A 50-State Analysis of Postsecondary Correctional Education Policy*. Washington, DC: The Institute for Higher Education Policy.

Fine, Michelle, Maria Elena Torre, Kathy Boudin, Iris Bowen, Judith Clark, Donna Hylton, Migdalia Martinez, "Missy," Rosemarie A. Roberts, Pamela Smart, and Debora Upegui. 2001. *Changing Minds: The Impact of College in a Maximum-Security Prison*. New York: Ronald Ridgeway, Inc.

Friedman, Matthew, Ames C. Grawert, and James Cullen. 2017. "Crime Trends 1990–2016." *Brennan Center for Justice*. https://brennancenter.org/publication /crime-trends1990-2016.

Gehring, Thom. 1997. "Post-Secondary Education for Inmates: An Historical Inquiry." *Journal of Correctional Education* 48 (2): 46–55.

General Accounting Office (GAO). 1994. "Pell Grants for Prison Inmates." https:// gao.gov/assets/90/84012.pdf/.

Gilligan, James. 2000. *Violence in California Prisons: A Proposal for Research into Patterns and Cures*. Sacramento, CA: Senate Publications.

Harding, Robert. 2014. "Siena Poll: Majority Supports Cuomo's Plan to Offer College Courses for Inmates in New York Prisons." *The Citizen*, March 24, 2014. http:// auburnpub.com/blogs/eye_on_ny/siena-poll-majority-supports-cuomo-s-plan -to-offer-college/article_02b576c6-b372-11e3-88ae-0019bb2963f4.html.

Harer, Miles D. 1994. "Prison Education Program Participation and Recidivism: A Test of the Normalization Hypothesis." Federal Bureau of Prisons, Washington DC. https://bop.gov/resources/research_projects/published_reports/recidivism /orepredprg.pdf/.

Herron, Rex, and John Muir. 1974. *History and Development of Project NewGate— A Program of Post-secondary Education for Incarcerated Offenders—Final Report*. Washington, DC: Eric Clearinghouse. https://ncjrs.gov/App/Publications/abstract .aspx?ID=74550.

Higher Education Services Corporation (HESC) of New York State. n.d. "Appendix E: New York's Tuition Assistance Program—A History." Accessed November 23, 2022. https://hesc.ny.gov/partner-access/financial-aid-professionals/programs

-policies-and-procedures-guide-to-grants-and-scholarship-programs/appendix
-e-new-york-s-tuition-assistance-program-a-history.html.

Humphreys, Adam. 2016. "Robert Martinson and the Tragedy of the American
Prison." *Ribbon Farm*. Accessed November 23, 2022. https://ribbonfarm.com/2016
/12/15/robert-martinson-and-the-tragedy-of-the-american-prison/.

Johnson, Annette. 2001. "Post-Secondary Education and Reductions in Recidivism:
A Selected Bibliography." *The League of Women Voters of New York State:
Balancing Justice Task Force on Correctional Education.*

Johnson, Dirk. 1996. "Taking Away the Privileges of Prisoners." *New York Times*,
September 8, 1996. https://nytimes.com/1996/09/08/us/taking-away-the
-privileges-of-prisoners.html.

Karpowitz, Daniel, and Max Kenner. 2003. *Education as Crime Prevention: The Case
for Reinstating Pell Grant Eligibility for the Incarcerated.* Annandale-on-Hudson,
NY: Bard Prison Initiative. https://static.prisonpolicy.org/scans/crime_report
.pdf/.

Kotler, Milton. 1966. Prison College Conference, Ford Foundation Records,
Rockefeller Archive Center, November 5, 1966.

Kurgan, Laura, Eric Cadora, Sarah Williams, David Reinfurt, and Leah Meisterlin.
n.d. "Million Dollar Blocks." *Center for Spatial Research*. Accessed on
November 23, 2022. http://c4sr.columbia.edu/projects/million-dollar-blocks.

Lagemann, Ellen Condliffe. 2016. *Liberating Minds*. New York: The New Press.

Langan, Patrick A., John V. Fundis, Lawrence A. Greenfield, and Victoria Schneider.
1988. *Historical Statistics on Prisoners in State and Federal Institutions, Yearend
1925–86*. Washington, DC: US Department of Justice. https://ncjrs.gov/pdffiles1
/digitization/111098ncjrs.pdf/.

Littlefield, John F., and Bruce I. Wolford. 1982. "A Survey of Higher Education in
US Correctional Institutions." *Journal of Correctional Education* 33 (4): 14–18.

Lucko, Paul M. 1994. "Beto, George John." *Handbook of Texas Online*. November 1,
1994. http://tshaonline.org/handbook/online/articles/fbenm.

Marshall Kaplan, Gans, and Kahn. 1975. "Additional Data Analysis and Evaluation
of 'Project NewGate' and Other Prison College Programs." San Francisco, March
1975. https://ncjrs.gov/pdffiles1/Digitization/45655NCJRS.pdf.

Martinson, Robert. 1972. "The Paradox of Prison Reform–IV, Planning for Public
Safety." *New Republic*.

Mauer, Marc. 2006. *Race to Incarcerate*. New York: The New Press.

Mitchell, Michael, Michael Leachman, and Kathleen Masterson. 2017. "A Lost Decade
in Higher Education Funding: State Cuts Have Driven up Tuition and Reduced
Quality." *Center on Budget and Policy Priorities*. https://cbpp.org/research/state
-budget-and-tax/a-lost-decade-in-higher-education-funding.

Neptune, Jessica. 2012. "The Making of the Carceral State: Street Crime, The War
on Drugs, and Punitive Politics in New York, 1951–1973." PhD diss., University of
Chicago.

New York Times. 1989. "Campuses Coping with a Drugs Oath." October 8, 1989.
https://nytimes.com/1989/10/08/us/campuses-coping-with-a-drugs-oath.html.

Olian, Catherine, producer. 2007. *60 Minutes*. "Maximum Security Education." Aired April 15, 2007, on CBS.

Opinion. 1993. "The Pell Grant Mess." *Washington Post*. October 30, 1993. https:// washingtonpost.com/archive/opinions/1993/10/30/the-pell-grant-mess/2b23c0dc -8c57-430b-a984-eae29eb6511a/?utm_term=.43455cc45a9a.

Orson, Diane. 2012. "'Million-Dollar Blocks' Map Incarceration's Costs." *NPR*, October 2, 2012. https://npr.org/2012/10/02/162149431/million-dollar-blocks-map -incarcerations-costs.

Page, Joshua. 2004. "Eliminating the Enemy: The Import of Denying Prisoners Access to Higher Education in Clinton's America." *Punishment & Society* 6 (4): 357–78.

Peterson, Iver. 1995. "Cutting Down on Amenities to Achieve No-Frills Jails." *New York Times*, July 10, 1995. http://nytimes.com/1995/07/10/nyregion/cutting-down -on-amenities-to-achieve-no-frills-jails.html.

Richardson, G. V. 1965. G. V. Richardson to Christopher Edley, Ford Foundation Records, Rockefeller Archive Center, July 29, 1965.

Rothman, David J. 1971. *The Discovery of the Asylum: Social Order and Disorder in the New Republic*. Boston: Little Brown.

Ryan, T. A., and Joseph Clifton Woodard Jr. 1987. *Correctional Education: A State of the Art Analysis*. U.S. Department of Justice.

Seashore, Marjorie J., and Steven Haberfeld. 1977. *Prisoner Education: Project New Gate and Other College Programs*. New York: Praeger.

Second Chance. 2012. "Know the Facts About Prison Education in Texas." November 2012. https://lee.edu/publications/files/2012-11-second-chance.pdf/.

Senate Session. 1993. *C-SPAN*, Washington, DC. November 16, 1993.

Serow, Robert C. 2004. "Policy as Symbol: Title II of the 1944 G.I. Bill." *Review of Higher Education* 28 (1): 481.

Silva, Walter. 1994. "A Brief History of Prison Higher Education in the United States." In *Higher Education in Prison: A Contradiction in Terms?*, edited by Miriam Williford. Phoenix, AZ: Oryx Press.

Skidmore College. 2011. *Commemorative Book of Reflections: University without Walls*. https://skidmore.edu/odsp/documents/UWWReflections.pdf/.

Tewksbury, Richard, David John Erickson, and Jon Marc Taylor. 2000. "Opportunities Lost." *Journal of Offender Rehabilitation* 31 (1–2): 43–56.

Texas Department of Criminal Justice. 2008. "Statistical Report: Fiscal Year 2008." http://tdcj.state.tx.us/documents/Statistical_Report_FY2008.pdf/.

Tucker, Jed B. 2017. "Malcolm X, the Prison Years: The Relentless Pursuit of Formal Education." *Journal of African American History* 102 (2): 184–212.

Tung, Allen. 2016. "Capping off an Illustrious Teaching Career." *Simon Fraser University News*. March 10, 2016. https://sfu.ca/sfunews/stories/2016/meet-the -2015-sfu-excellence-in-teaching-award-winners/stephen-duguid-humanities .html.

Uggen, Christopher, Ryan Larson, and Sarah Shannon. 2016. "6 Million Lost Voters: State-Level Estimates of Felony Disenfranchisement." *The Sentencing Project*.

http://sentencingproject.org/wp-content/uploads/2016/10/6-Million-Lost-Voters
.pdf.

Willingham, J. T. 1965a. J. T. Willingham to Christopher Edley. Ford Foundation
Records, Rockefeller Archive Center, July 20, 1965.

Willingham, J. T. 1965b. J. T. Willingham to Christopher Edley, Ford Foundation
Records, Rockefeller Archive Center, July 29, 1965.

Worth, Robert. 2001. "Bringing College Back to Bedford Hills." *New York Times*,
June 24, 2001. http://nytimes.com/2001/06/24/nyregion/bringing-college-back
-to-bedford-hills.html.

X, Malcolm, and Alex Haley. 1965. *The Autobiography of Malcolm X*. New York:
Grove Press.

Zahm, Barbara, director. 1997. *The Last Graduation*. New York: Deep Dish TV, DVD.

Zuniga, Donna. 2015. Special Regents Briefing, Lee College.

2 ||| THE WORK OF RESTORATION

HOW TO EDUCATE WHEN EDUCATION FAILS

Introduction: Embedding the Current Educational Ecosystem in United States History

The United States of America has a long record of turning a blind eye to those things that do not fit its founding narrative as traditionally told. Familiar tropes about the country—a supposed nation of manifest destiny, free from the tyranny of monarchy, and one of "the American dream," whereby people "pull themselves up by their bootstraps"—abound in US culture. Countless stories about resilience, can-do attitudes, and "we work for what we earn" mentalities are found in stories from Paul Bunyan and Johnny Appleseed to more recent examples like Bill Gates and Steve Jobs. Never mind that these narratives are devoid of women and completely, and most often deliberately, ignore the gruesome history associated with the birth of this nation. It is often forgotten that the United States was built on one of the largest genocides ever to take place in the modern world, with scholars estimating that throughout the early twentieth century, upward of twelve million Indigenous people died on the land of what is the present-day United States (Smith 2017). We must consider all of this history seriously and consistently when discussing education in any form.

The traditional founding narrative of the United States also ignores the fact that wealth generated from its founding to the present day is based on not only stolen land and genocide but also the commodification of Black and Brown bodies, the forced enslaved labor of people of African descent, and the exploitation and indentured servitude of non-European immigrant peoples. Individual people, entire communities, and even governmental bodies of the United States have long been willing to kill, maim, disenfranchise, and marginalize those elements that do not fit the White, Christian, and Eurocentric version of the United States. The educational enterprise of the United States is not immune to this history, especially as it pertains to incarceration and the education of those incarcerated.

Acknowledging the global readership of this volume, one might ask: How can someone write about the United States in broad strokes when it is so diverse in so many ways? And yet, there are political, economic, social, cultural, and even historically Christian religious norms and trends that have marked the nation since its inception. Certainly, there are individuals, groups, and larger events or movements one can point to that defied and fought against the conditions and norms described in this chapter. This does not, however, detract from the central point: namely, that one of the most important threads in the history of the United States is the extensive length to which exclusionary practices, especially economic and political practices, were—and continue to be—embedded in the fabric of the United States.

Examinations of contemporary circumstance in any arena, especially education within a carceral setting, cannot be disentangled from practices of violent, racialized, and systematic disenfranchisement that over time became, and remain, normative aspects of culture in the United States (Bell 1992; Harris 1993). These same practices of disenfranchisement and inequity, particularly around race and ethnicity, not only undergird the system of incarceration in the United States, but are also present in its education system, public and private (Ladson Billings and Tate 1995). It comes as no surprise, therefore, that the United States leads the world in the number of people it incarcerates (Anderson 2017; Hinton 2016). This is in large part due to policies implemented in the latter part of the twentieth century and early 2000s, whereby the response to the increase in the availability and sale of illegal drugs drove incarceration rates and sentences exceptionally high (see, for example, Provine 2007; Taifa 2021; Williams and Coffee 1938). These more recent trends and their subsequent impacts, including those related to education, only make sense in the wider historical and, importantly, racialized context.

A Brief History of Violence and Exclusion in the United States

One need only look at the history of enslavement in the United States to consider why contemporary rates of incarceration are so high. Prior to the Emancipation Proclamation and the ratification of the thirteenth, fourteenth, and fifteenth amendments to the Constitution of the United

States, people of African descent were considered legally and socially inferior, incomplete persons, property to be owned. Their rights as human beings were second to their economic value and to the economic engine of the United States as a whole. The Reconstruction Era that followed the Civil War was, in some ways, a time of great promise. And while significant progress was made for many formerly enslaved African Americans, other White and wealthy stakeholders in our country were hard at work figuring out new ways to continue to disenfranchise Black Americans. This led to a new era of "Black codes" and Jim Crow segregation (Packard 2002; Zinn 1990).

Throughout the country, but particularly in the southern United States, municipalities and states found new ways to segregate, disenfranchise, and diminish the purchasing and political power, social acumen, and educational access of the nation's Black people. Property ownership for Black Americans was a fraction of that of White Americans, which is due to the fact that by the end of the nineteenth century, the White segment of the United States had centuries of property ownership to build upon while most Black Americans were starting with nothing (Williams 2017). Through sharecropping and subpar, abusive employment in agricultural and industrial settings, Black and Brown Americans were consistently relegated to employment where they were underpaid, taken advantage of financially, abused, and subjected to miserable working conditions (Royce 1993). These trends still continue today, with Black American men and women making seventy-three and sixty-five cents, respectively, on the dollar relative to White Americans (Patten 2016). At the same time, educational access was stymied and segregated, despite a deep and abiding understanding by Black America about the value of free public education and literacy for all (Bagley 2018).

Indeed, the same could be said for other non-European immigrant populations of the time. Asian immigrant communities in the West, hired first as agricultural, goldmine, and railway workers and later as textile and factory employees, were often the victims of contract-for-passage employment, and most wages went directly back to employers for basic needs such as room and board (Day 2016). Immigrants from Mexico and elsewhere in Central and South America fared no better, often being relegated to backbreaking agricultural work across the United States (Borjas and Katz 2007). Following the genocide of the Indigenous peoples of the Americas and the westward push of manifest destiny, Native Americans were confined to reservations with little possibility of economic self-sufficiency. Anti-immigration and anti-Indigenous laws of the nineteenth and twentieth centuries—such as the Indian Removal Act of 1830, the prejudicial US Supreme Court ruling of *People v. Hall* in 1854 (prohibiting anyone who was not European from testifying against White people in courts), the Chinese Exclusion Act of 1882, the Immigration Acts of 1917 and 1924, and others—codified exclusion from US society for most immigrants, Native Americans, and Black Americans. Policies and practices stemming from these laws continued well into the latter half of the twentieth century.

Despite the inequity, there were a number of incredibly successful politicians, businesspersons, educators, entrepreneurs, and inventors in the African American, Indigenous, and immigrant communities throughout the history of twentieth-century United States (Bogan and Darity 2008; Hsu 2016; Nembhard 2014). Rather, the previous passages serve to illustrate the ways in which White America did very little to support, buoy, or encourage spaces for non-White Americans to develop or flourish, and instead actively discouraged this from happening. As non-White Americans gained freedom and immigrants continued to see the United States as a land of possibility, there was little willingness on the part of many White Americans to support the livelihoods or well-being of others, particularly Black Americans.

In fact, when non-White American communities thrived, White American politicians, entrepreneurs, and others often stepped in to hinder progress without fear of retribution or political peril. Take, for example, the Federal Housing Authority's redlining practices of the 1930s and '40s, the burning of Black Wall Street, or the ways in which industrial magnates tried to control the types, locations, and content of schools for Black Americans and others in the United States (Rothstein 2018; Watkins 2001). For non-White America, the story of the twentieth century in the United States is one of wealth suppression, housing discrimination, and voter disenfranchisement.

Despite these efforts, non-White Americans found ways to persist. Black Americans did thrive in many locations and first began to mobilize and organize around the Niagara Movement, which later became the NAACP. Publications like *Crisis Magazine* and the *Chicago Defender* provided information and suggestions around political empowerment, wealth accrual, cultural contributions, and general well-being. Similar efforts in immigrant populations emerged as well, with periodicals in various languages and the emergence of several ethnically diverse advocacy organizations, including the nonpartisan Chinese-language newspaper *Chung Sai Yat Po* and the League of United Latin American Citizens (LULAC). The body politic could no longer ignore the diverse and vocal populations of US citizens demanding their rightful place at the tables of industry, politics, and community life.

By the mid-twentieth century, the civil rights movement was in full swing. And yet, once again throughout the United States, local, state, and federal policies; community opposition; judicial decision; individual prejudices; and systemic disenfranchisement in lending, housing, and education gave rise to a new phase of discriminatory practices in the United States. We need only look to the internment of Japanese Americans from 1942 to 1945 for evidence of sustained and irrational violence against US citizens of non-European backgrounds. Only a decade later, the landmark US Supreme Court case *Brown v. Board of Education* decision was handed down with a mandate from the high court to integrate K-12 schools with "all deliberate speed." This was justly hailed as progress with the court's unanimous decision to strike down the separate-but-equal interpretation of the US Constitution.

While the court decisions of *Brown I* (1954) and *II* (1955) were laudable for their unanimous agreement that Black Americans deserved the right to integrated educational access that was equally resourced, the result was complicated. The decision did nothing to prescribe remedies for how that might be actualized in a racially divided nation, nor did the court make any attempt to encourage schools across the country to act with urgency (Ogletree 2004). Some would argue that this was purposeful, forcing the burden of integration to rest squarely on those impacted by segregation. Similar measures regarding the integration of Mexican American children in California were required by the 9th Circuit of the US Court of Appeals earlier in 1946 as a result of *Mendez v. Westminster School District of Orange County*, when then-governor Earl Warren ultimately signed a law ending long-standing school segregation in California, impacting children from all ethnic backgrounds, including Indigenous Americans (Wollenberg 1974). Between *Westminster* and *Brown I* and *II*, the United States saw challenges to segregated educational spaces across the United States. From this point on, the country entered an ongoing fight for educational equality, as well as workplace and housing equity for people of non-European descent. The Civil Rights Act of 1964, the Elementary and

Secondary Education Act of 1965, the Immigration Act of 1965, the Fair Housing Act of 1968, the Indian Education Act of 1972, and the Individuals with Disabilities Education Act in 1975 all ushered in an era of attentiveness to equity in education stemming in part from Lyndon Johnson's War on Poverty, which began in 1964.

One could almost be forgiven for thinking that this was the beginning of a happier, or at least more egalitarian, period in US history. Unfortunately, this is, in many ways, exactly where the current state of affairs began with both the education system and the system of mass incarceration in the United States. With increasingly fewer legal means available to suppress the success of people of color in the United States, the lengths to which everyday people—and often regulatory agencies and governmental policies and programs—would go to protect enclaves of privilege grew rapidly in the latter quarter of the twentieth century and into the twenty-first century.

In fact, in 2021 the FBI noted the highest level of hate crimes in recent history in the United States (Equal Justice Initiative 2021). These actions occurred alongside a rapid acceleration of wealth accrual for White America, a doubling down on suburban life with its de facto segregation, and an ever-increasing surveillance of Black and Brown bodies via increased policing, while the construction of areas of dire poverty brought on by the creation of federal housing projects and the emergent zero-tolerance policies concerning illicit drug use and distribution also played a role (Rothstein 2018). With this admittedly incomplete but necessary history as the backdrop, the discussion now turns specifically to schooling and the ways that domestic educational settings have contributed to the current state of incarceration in the United States.

Education (Not) for All

Within the landscape of education in the United States, it is important to lay bare some larger contexts for consideration. According to the National Center for Education Statistics (NCES), the following figures reflect the most recent school-level data available for consideration as of 2022. The educational system serves just under fifty-five million students each year, almost fifty million of whom use the free public schooling system in their local community (National Center for Education Statistics n.d.). More than half of the public-school community in the United States is composed of children of color, while approximately 80 percent of our teaching force is White and 70 percent is female (National Center for Education Statistics 2021). Almost a full 10 percent of children are multilingual learners. Approximately 30 percent of school-age children attend school in rural settings, while another 30 percent are found in urban settings, with the remaining 40 percent attending suburban schools. Suffice it to say that the landscape of schooling in the United States can accurately be described as diverse, complicated, fluid, diffuse, and mismatched between the adults and students sharing the same space. This complicated array is also reflected in prisons and jails nationwide.

Additionally, over the past twenty years, more attention has been paid to the disparities between discipline policies and outcomes in schooling. For over thirty years, the Civil Rights Project housed at the University of California, Los Angeles (UCLA), has focused on the various facets of segregation, inequities, and disenfranchisement. The project, beginning at Harvard in 1996 and moving to UCLA in 2007, is responsible for some of the most comprehensive and intricate data around schooling and disenfranchisement that exists to date in the United States.

The Civil Rights Project's landmark study "Brown at 60: Great Progress, a Long Retreat and an Uncertain Future" (Orfield et al. 2014) reminded the nation that schools must continue to navigate complicated racial and economic landscapes. Orfield and colleagues note, "Contrary to many claims, the South has not gone back to the level of segregation before Brown. It has lost all the additional progress made after 1967 but is still the least segregated region for Black students. The growth of segregation has been most dramatic for Latino students, particularly in the West, where there was substantial integration in the 1960s, and segregation has soared. A clear pattern is developing of Black and Latino students sharing the same schools" (2014, 2). The authors go on to inform their readers that interactions between race, ethnicity, and poverty are also quite common. "Black and Latino students tend to be in schools with a substantial majority of poor children, but White and Asian students are typically in middle-class schools. Segregation is by far the most serious in the central cities of the largest metropolitan areas, but it is also severe in central cities of all sizes and suburbs of the largest metro areas, which are now half non-White. Latinos are significantly more segregated than Blacks in suburban America" (2).

Troubling patterns emerge when combining this information with reports on lost instructional time due to punitive discipline policies and the vast differences in the application of these policies between White and non-White students. Daniel Losen and Paul Martinez's report "Lost Opportunities: How Disparate School Discipline Continues to Drive Differences in the Opportunity to Learn" (2020) brings to light the ways in which there is not only a persistent "achievement gap" in schools but also a "discipline gap," as they term it (xi). For example, based on the most recent data available from the 2015–16 school year, Black boys lost instructional time at a rate five times higher than White boys, while Native American and Pacific Islander children lost instructional time at rates over twice that of their White peers. The same was true for children with disabilities. Black girls lost instructional time at a rate seven times higher than their White peers (Losen and Martinez 2020, vi).

Perhaps most important for the work at hand is Losen and Martinez's finding that there is "an association between being suspended and a threefold increase in the risk for juvenile justice involvement" (1). The authors point to a recent piece by Janet Rosenbaum, whose work outlines an extensive body of research about harm and the relationship between absenteeism, suspension, expulsion, and general educational attainment and involvement in the criminal justice system.[1] Additionally, Losen and Martinez find that, though these particular data are difficult to come by and reporting is sparse (despite being legally mandated), arrests and referrals to law enforcement impact children of color and immigrant children more frequently than their White counterparts (2020, 77).

Overlay these statistics with the most recent data on incarceration rates and the patterns further crystallize. According to research by the Institute for Crime and Justice Policy, there are over two million people in prisons or jails in the United States. While there is some hope on the horizon, as incarceration rates have declined for the past two years, prisons and jails across the United States remain full (Gramlich 2021). Even with the decline, incarceration rates remain comparatively high, and the vast majority of incarcerated people are from impoverished backgrounds. For example, though Black Americans make up only 12 percent of the US adult population, they make up a full third of the federal and state prison population. Likewise, Hispanic adults make up about 12 percent of the US population but almost 30 percent of incarcerated individuals. Overall, more than two-thirds of the US prison population is non-White (Federal Bureau of Prisons 2022; Nellis 2021; Pew Research Center 2020). These numbers are even higher when factoring in individuals held in local and county jails.

Finally, while reliable data on English language learners is not readily available in the US context, it too plays a factor in the carceral landscape of the United States. Importantly, noncitizens are underrepresented in the prison population (The Sentencing Project 2017). Finally, in a study for the Prison Policy Initiative, authors Bernadette Rabuy and Daniel Kopf (2015) outline the impoverished conditions that most individuals who are incarcerated in state prisons suffer from prior to finding themselves in prison. In their work, they noted that the average annual prior income of male individuals who were in prison in 2014 was slightly higher than $19,000, less than half that of their nonincarcerated peers.

Moving to explore the processes and dispositions required to (re)develop a love of learning and a trust of education as a system and institution, with individuals who are incarcerated we must do so with open eyes concerning the racial, economic, and historical backdrops impacting their lives in the United States. Furthermore, one must add to this the political and racial unrest of the recent past. It is easy to imagine the vulnerability that students in prison might experience as they venture into a space of formal learning that may have once been familiar but is now foreign. And, while no two students are alike in their lived experiences, it is safe to say that the trauma of incarceration alone is enough to make education in prison a complicated endeavor.

Pedagogy of Care and Vulnerability

In a research project completed over a decade ago that studied the lived experiences of educational care in schools with a group of adolescent coresearchers, chewing gum came up more often than one might expect (McKenna 2015). In fact, chewing gum was noted repeatedly, at first as an answer to the question "What is the most important rule in your school?" Without missing a beat, one child said definitively, "Chewing gum. *Absolutely no* chewing gum," to which the rest of the room vigorously agreed. The researcher expected the answer to be something about treating people and things with respect, or children doing their best, or something that had to do with learning, but it was none of those things. It was about chewing gum: how sticky it was, how gross it was under the desks, and how teachers *hated* gum more than anything else. From there, chewing gum became a regular topic of conversation. With time, the researcher realized that while "No chewing gum" was a real rule, it was also representative of the arbitrary and capricious nature of so much of the US (dare I say global?) educational landscape. It was about a foundation in control and rules, not unlike prison itself.

Rules in schools are often made in response to behavior, and in the antiquated system of education enacted around the world, behavior is to be controlled. Controlled means predictable, and predictable means boring. Boredom, more often than not, is a state that veers students off track, causing them to seek the intellectual or social stimulation needed in less-than-ideal ways. This is not the only pattern of trouble, nor is it fair to attribute this iterative description of school to every teacher, classroom, or child. It is representative of a cycle that was repeatedly apparent in conversations with the youth involved in this project, one that is seen daily in classrooms around the country and is reflected in the school stories and experiences of men who are incarcerated and working their way through school once again.

Closing one's eyes long enough, one can picture it—the gum, the child trying to pay attention, and the ones who just cannot quite do it. One can picture the defiant child sneaking a piece of bubble gum *and* the one who simply forgot he was chewing it on the bus. One can also picture the conversation when the teacher got angry about the bubble gum under the desk or the testy exchange about spitting the gum out.

Now substitute sunglasses, a backpack, an open bag of chips, and one can imagine those same exchanges. Add in conversations about respecting authority, respecting property, and respecting rules. There is a lot of unearned respect expected from the child to adult in educational spaces, with little promised in return. Truth be told, it sounds a lot like carceral culture—an expectation of respect toward those in charge without the guarantee of anything in exchange. Add in the silent student (child or adult) who wants to avoid conflict at all costs but is mistaken for defiant, or the child whose safe haven is school but who dreads themselves or other kids getting in trouble. It is likely that one can picture those children (or adults) too.

Somewhere in these examples are the men and women being taught in prison. They, too, were the gum chewers, the teacher's pets, the tattletales, and the challengers. As they progressed in school, they were the young people tracked into the wrong classes, told by their counselors that college was not for them or that "this class might be too difficult." They were the ones who lived for ball practice after school, sticking around for the team that was their community—their brothers or sisters. Quite often, they were also the young people sorting out difficult challenges outside of school hours: a relationship gone bad, the unexpected pregnancy, or finding "the one." They were on student council or had a job at the local grocery or were working to be part of the Quiz Bowl team. They were the caretakers for their younger siblings, and they were the kids who used marijuana or alcohol to self-medicate and protect themselves from difficult experiences. And, once upon a time, no matter which one of these kids they were, they dreamed of something completely different from landing in prison at age seventeen, twenty-three, twenty-eight, thirty-five, or fifty-three. Of everything to know of the students learning while in prison, this last one is an absolute certainty.

Taking a Chance on Learning

When students arrive at a "school in prison" setting to learn, whether they are enrolling in a college-in-prison program, a high school credit recovery program, or a therapeutic learning platform, they have already made a difficult choice to return to a learning environment. This requires them to trust institutional structures that failed them at some earlier point in their lives. For educators in these settings, this is one of the first and most important premises we must consider. These are individuals, once again, giving education a chance when much of their lived experiences tell them to run far away from the structures and programs that failed to serve them well the first time around. And yet, they do show up and they do try again. This is where the work of restoration begins.

Given this context, while content is still important, the pedagogy surrounding that content is even more important. Education in all spaces, but particularly places like prison, must begin with a pedagogy of vulnerability (Brantmeier 2013). This includes a disposition of the instructor and student alike toward restoration, reparation, and community. Some scholars and others associated with carceral culture will talk about rehabilitation; while this is perhaps an outcome to consider, this cannot be the sole focus if one wants to fundamentally restore a student's faith in the power of learning.

In educator preparation, students are often taught about the triad of "knowledge, skills, and dispositions" related to the craft (McKenna 2009). In the case of learning in prison, educator disposition holds a place of primacy, while knowledge and skills follow. Students can immediately tell whether their instructor is nervous, scared, or worried. This is true whether one is teaching in a prison or a traditional classroom, but it is doubly true when teaching behind bars. It is never far from the students' minds that, at the end of a class, session, or program, the instructor gets to leave the confines of the space they must call home. So, as the students take a chance on learning, the educators involved must take a chance on vulnerability and engagement of a different sort. This requires thoughtful relationship-building and patience. Of course, all the rules of the carceral setting still apply in the traditional classroom, so one must be mindful of the boundaries and parameters in the larger context. Nonetheless, it is still the instructor's job to instill a sense of wonder and trust and to encourage a hopeful disposition with the aim of having students become intrinsically motivated.

At the end of any given day, learning ideally continues without daily check-ins, office hours, easy access to electronic communication, or any of the other modern conveniences of formal education. Motivation theory teaches us that intrinsic motivation—the desire for an individual to learn or participate simply for the sake of doing so, independent of external rewards—is important to lifelong learning and well-being (Ryan and Deci 2000). In the space of incarceration, where the instructor gets to leave but the students must stay, this has never been more important. As such, part of the work of restoration means moving beyond the "No chewing gum" mentality, where rules and boundaries force compliance and fear, and into a space of deep discourse, listening, and communal support.

This communal nature of learning is at the heart of a pedagogy of vulnerability (Brantmeier 2013; Brantmeier and McKenna 2020). When a learner struggles to understand a concept, the entire community of the classroom is impacted. If a learner resists a concept within a course, the entire community must be patient while they come to their own understanding of the idea. When learners fundamentally disagree with one another about a theory, construct, application, or view of the world, time must be taken to parse out new ideas, find common ground, and forge a pathway to understanding. This is true whether one is speaking of the sociology of race or the value of linear algebra. Restorative education anywhere, but particularly in prisons, is slow, slow work. Content might be sacrificed for developing the dispositions needed to be lifelong learners. In fact, it may take weeks simply to get students to speak. It may take even longer to get students to believe that what they are learning matters or that they can do it. It takes the longest to get students to trust that they themselves oversee their learning and have the capacity to do so in deep and meaningful ways.

Recent neuroscience suggests that trauma can cause epigenetic alterations in the brain, leading to changes in stress responses and other reactions over time (Lang et al. 2020). Neuroscience is also leading the way in research around resilience and interventions of care and relationality that counterbalance these epigenetic impacts and act as protective factors in the lives of young people and adults (Felitti 2002; NCSCDC 2015). Many, though not all, incarcerated students come back to education while also working to make sense of difficult lived experiences and their residual impacts. In most instances, they have built up a thick, sometimes seemingly impenetrable, armor to protect themselves from hurt and further trauma. This can make teaching difficult, but, for the individuals in these classrooms, finding ways through that armor is part of the work of restoration. It is learning on top of learning, asking them to lay down their metaphorical armor and find the willingness to be vulnerable. The simple task of asking a question or helping them admit when they do not know something is the long-term project. It is then, and only then, that they can become masters of their own understanding and learning, asking questions of themselves and others in and out of the classroom, seeking out expertise, and challenging one another and themselves to think about the world differently and more fully.

This is lifelong and challenging work for all involved, but one must not forget that these students are working especially hard to make this happen. It does not happen overnight, nor is it work that the instructor is exempt from having to consider. Learning is always an act of restoration for all of us, an ongoing project of inventing and reinventing and understanding anew; when done right by anyone, it takes a considerable amount of energy. Finally, consider the energy needed to seek formal education while in prison. This is energy on top of the energy that one needs to survive, to follow all the rules, not to become cross with those who will be in one's orbit for potentially years and years to come. This energy must be mustered after constant nagging or the sometimes-paralyzing thought that one day they will also need to be prepared to go back into the world.

Learning (and even surviving) in prison operates differently than in the outside world, but the opportunity to learn together and in community does not change. As educators of individuals in prison, we want people to do more than survive. Alongside them, we mean to do more than simply "do no harm." We want them to flourish, to find beauty, to develop more nuanced technical skills and acumen, to value relationality, and to live in community. This is a tall order with high expectations for people who have been disappointed by the world. Still, creating a classroom space, literally and figuratively, one course, one day, one book, painting, or discussion at a time, where the possibility of recognizing one's own agency as a learner once again (or perhaps even for the first time) is possible, is a worthy undertaking.

Conclusion

To close, consider the chewing gum study for just another moment. In this study, the youth who were interviewed shared a great deal of wisdom and insight on what the concept of care meant on a day-to-day basis in schools. Ultimately, their lived reality of care centered on five distinct elements: deep relationships, clear and consistent guidelines, opportunities for student voice, quality content and delivery, and awareness of the environment (McKenna 2015). As the youth explained what these ideas meant, it became clear that, first and foremost, their understanding of education was ultimately defined as the ability for students to see that educators had thought about and brought the best versions of themselves, their expertise, and their expectations into the classroom. They cared about their surroundings and their materials: were students cared for, and had someone realized what they needed to complete their work successfully? And finally, the youth understood that caring in education meant that education is a relational undertaking, one with a clear disposition toward inclusion, trust, and always looking for the best in an individual.

In this way, the youth had handed researchers a road map for caring and a pedagogy of restoration that could be applied in classrooms near and far. Even within the walls of prison. Even to a classroom full of men or women for whom school was not a caring place. Even in a nation fraught with challenges and a deep history of neglect and exclusion. To be sure, the model requires diligence, communication, patience, and forgiveness. It also requires bravery, high expectations, and truthfulness about ability, effort, and outcomes. Edward Brantmeier and I (2020) write, "We understand vulnerability to be an essential construct to advance teaching and learning but recognize it as just one of the many lenses that one must embody to fully appreciate a pedagogical stance that honors all types of knowledge and all ways of knowing. . . . In fact, a pedagogy of vulnerability is about bringing the lived curriculum of both teachers and students alike into the classroom as a source of valid knowledge" (4–5).

And yet, there are limits to how one can and should do this in the context of individuals who are incarcerated. A. D. Seroczynski (2020) writes thoughtfully about exactly this in her contribution to *Pedagogy of Vulnerability*, noting, "The walls [of a prison] symbolize a strong physical and emotional dichotomy between being in and being out. The walls also keep the human mind locked up, both literally and epistemologically and emotionally. Indeed, prison is a sea of sameness. Some students have compared it to the military, but even enlisted individuals can touch a tree or look upon the stars at night. Incarcerated individuals are restricted from these basic human endeavors" (208). And so, how one engages students who also happen to be incarcerated becomes a tricky undertaking, one requiring care and awareness, hope with a dose of pragmatism, and the infinite patience to unwind the mistrust that the world in its complicated myriad of ways has bred into each of the students.

So, how does one navigate through the crack, if one opens it with students who are also in prison, to the joys of learning and the value of exploring something new? It requires going back to the beginning, both of this chapter and of the story. Whether that story is the history of the United States, the history of education (the courses I teach), the history of their time in school, or the history of their time in the education program in the here and now, context matters. Context is part of truth telling, bearing witness, and bringing light into the world. But truth telling is hard, hard work. It requires educators to have a sense of humor and to be ready to be deeply relational, overprepared, flexible, and consistently vigilant.

By delving into these varied histories, especially histories for which the students already have a prescribed narrative, when you (or they) are able to interrupt, complicate, and widen their lens on these same histories, new possibilities emerge. New explanations for why things "are the way they are" develop, and students begin to connect the dots between what is, what was, and what might be. When incarcerated students become defined by more than just the fact that they are incarcerated, this too complicates their story in positive and challenging ways. And though we pretend to relish the simplicity, what we really relish is to be seen—in all our complexity.

Note

1. Rosenbaum's "Educational and Criminal Justice Outcomes 12 Years after School Suspension" (2020) in *Youth & Society* is an excellent discussion of the various ways education and criminal justice overlap, with copious source material on the topic.

Works Cited

Anderson, Carol. 2017. *White Rage: The Unspoken Truth of Our Racial Divide.* Paperback edition. New York: Bloomsbury USA.

Bagley, Joseph. 2018. *The Politics of White Rights: Race, Justice, and Integrating Alabama's Schools.* Athens: University of Georgia Press.

Bell, Derrick. 1992. *Faces at the Bottom of the Well.* Paperback edition. New York: Basic Books.

Bogan, Vicki, and William Darity, Jr. 2008. "Culture and Entrepreneurship? African American and Immigrant Self-Employment in the United States." *The Journal of Socio-Economics* 37 (5): 1999–2019.

Borjas, George, and Lawrence Katz. 2007. "The Evolution of the Mexican-Born Workforce in the United States." In *Mexican Immigration to the United States: A National Bureau of Economic Research Conference Report,* edited by George J. Borjas, 13–56. Chicago: University of Chicago Press.

Brantmeier, Edward. 2013. "Pedagogy of Vulnerability: Definitions, Assumptions, and Applications." In *Re-envisioning Higher Education: Embodied Pathways to Wisdom and Transformation,* edited by Jing Lin, Rebecca Oxford, and Edward Brantmeier, 95–106. Charlotte: Information Age Press.

Brantmeier, Edward, and Maria McKenna, eds. 2020. *Pedagogy of Vulnerability.* Charlotte: Information Age Press.

Day, Iyko. 2016. *Alien Capital: Asian Racialization and the Logic of Settler Colonial Capitalism.* Durham, NC: Duke University Press.

Equal Justice Initiative. 2021. "FBI Reports Hate Crimes at Highest Level in 12 Years." https://eji.org/news/fbi-reports-hate-crimes-at-highest-level-in-12-years/.

Federal Bureau of Prisons. 2022. "Blacks, Hispanics Make Up Larger Shares of Prisoners Than of US Population." https://bop.gov/about/statistics/statistics _inmate_ethnicity.jsp.

Felitti, Vincent. 2002. "The Relation between Adverse Childhood Experiences and Adult Health: Turning Gold into Lead." *The Permanente Journal* 6 (1): 44–47.

Gramlich, John. 2021. "America's Incarceration Rate Falls to Lowest Level since 1995." *Pew Research Center.* https://pewresearch.org/fact-tank/2021/08/16/americas -incarceration-rate-lowest-since-1995/.

Harris, Cheryl I. 1993. "Whiteness as Property." *Harvard Law Review* 106 (8): 1707–91.

Hinton, Elizabeth Kai. 2016. *From the War on Poverty to the War on Crime: The Making of Mass Incarceration in America.* Cambridge, MA: Harvard University Press.

Hsu, Madeline Yuan-yin. 2016. *Asian American History: A Very Short Introduction.* New York: Oxford University Press.

Ladson Billings, Gloria, and William Tate. 1995. "Toward a Critical Race Theory of Education." *Teachers College Record* 97 (1): 47–68.

Lang, Jason, Judith McKie, Helene Smith, Angela McLaughlin, Christopher Gillberg, Christopher, Paul Shiels, and Helen Minnis. 2020. "Adverse Childhood Experiences, Epigenetics and Telomere Length Variation in Childhood and beyond: A Systematic Review of the Literature." *European Child & Adolescent Psychiatry* 29 (10): 1329–38.

Losen, Daniel, and Paul Martinez. 2020. "Lost Opportunities: How Disparate School Discipline Continues to Drive Differences in the Opportunity to Learn." Palo Alto/Los Angeles: *Learning Policy Institute; Center for Civil Rights Remedies at the Civil Rights Project*, Stanford/UCLA.

McKenna, Maria. 2009. "Dispositions: Responsibilities of Teacher Educators and Teacher Candidates." In *Affective Teacher Education*, edited by Patrice LeBlanc and Nancy Gallavan, 29–38. Massachusetts: Rowman & Littlefield Education.

McKenna, Maria. 2015. "When I Explain It You'll Understand: Children's Voices on Educational Care." In *Pedagogies of Kindness and Respect: On the Lives of Education and Children*, edited by P. Thomas, Paul Carr, Julie Gorlewski, and Brad Porfilio, 83–98. New York: Peter Lang.

National Center for Education Statistics. n.d. "Back-to-School Statistics." Accessed April 7, 2022. https://nces.ed.gov/fastfacts/display.asp?id=372#K12-enrollment.

National Center for Education Statistics. 2021. "Characteristics of Public School Teachers." https://nces.ed.gov/programs/coe/indicator/clr.

National Scientific Council on the Developing Child. 2015. *Supportive Relationships and Active Skill-Building Strengthen the Foundations of Resilience: Working Paper No. 13.* http://developingchild.harvard.edu.

Nellis, Ashley. 2021. "The Color of Justice: Racial and Ethnic Disparity in State Prisons." *The Sentencing Project.* https://sentencingproject.org/publications/color -of-justice-racial-and-ethnic-disparity-in-state-prisons/.

Nembhard, Jessica Gordon. 2014. *Collective Courage.* State College: Penn State University Press.

Ogletree, Charles. 2004. *All Deliberate Speed: Reflections on the First Half Century of Brown V. Board of Education*, 1st ed. New York: W. W. Norton & Co.

Orfield, Gary, Erica Frankenberg, Jongyeon Ee, and John Kuscera. 2014. "Brown at 60 Great Progress: A Long Retreat and an Uncertain Future." *The Civil Rights Project.* https://civilrightsproject.ucla.edu/research/k-12-education/integration-and -diversity/brown-at-60-great-progress-a-long-retreat-and-an-uncertain-future /Brown-at-60-051814.pdf/.

Packard, Jerrold M. 2002. *American Nightmare: The History of Jim Crow*, 1st ed. New York: St. Martin's Press.

Patten, Eileen. 2016. "Racial, Gender Wage Gaps Persist in US Despite Some Progress." *Pew Research Center.* https://pewresearch.org/fact-tank/2016/07/01 /racial-gender-wage-gaps-persist-in-u-s-despite-some-progress/.

Pew Research Center. 2020. "Blacks, Hispanics Make Up Larger Shares of Prisoners Than of US Population." https://pewresearch.org/fact-tank/2020/05/06/share

-of-Black-White-hispanic-americans-in-prison-2018-vs-2006/ft_20-05-05
_imprisonmentrates_2a/.

Provine, Doris Marie. 2007. *Unequal under Law: Race in the War on Drugs*. Chicago:
University of Chicago Press.

Rabuy, Bernadette, and Daniel Kopf. 2015. "Prisons of Poverty: Uncovering the Pre-
incarceration Incomes of the Imprisoned." *Prison Policy Initiative*. July 9, 2015.
https://prisonpolicy.org/reports/income.html.

Rosenbaum, Janet. 2020. "Educational and Criminal Justice Outcomes 12 Years After
School Suspension." *Youth & Society* 52 (4): 515–47.

Rothstein, Richard. 2018. *The Color of Law: A Forgotten History of How Our
Government Segregated America*. New York; London: Liveright Publishing
Corporation, a division of W. W. Norton & Company.

Royce, Edward Cary. 1993. *The Origins of Southern Sharecropping*. Philadelphia:
Temple University Press.

Ryan, Richard, and Edward Deci. 2000. "Self-Determination Theory and the
Facilitation of Intrinsic Motivation, Social Development, and Well-Being."
American Psychologist 55 (1): 68–78.

The Sentencing Project. 2017. "Immigration and Public Safety Fact Sheet." https://
sentencingproject.org/wp-content/uploads/2017/04/Immigration-and-Public
-Safety-Fact-Sheet.pdf/.

Seroczynski, A. D. 2020. "Becoming Vulnerable with the Vulnerable: A Pedagogy of
Hope for Incarcerated Students of the Liberal Arts." In *Pedagogy of Vulnerability*,
edited by Edward Brantmeier and Maria McKenna, 203–22. Charlotte:
Information Age Press.

Smith, David Michael. 2017. "Counting the Dead: Estimating the Loss of Life in
the Indigenous Holocaust, 1492–Present." *Native American Symposium 2017:
Representations and Realities*. Southeast Oklahoma State University. https://
se.edu/native-american/wp-content/uploads/sites/49/2019/09/A-NAS-2017
-Proceedings-Smith.pdf/.

Taifa, Nkechi. 2021. "Race, Mass Incarceration, and the Disastrous War on Drugs."
Brennan Center for Justice. https://brennancenter.org/our-work/analysis-opinion
/race-mass-incarceration-and-disastrous-war-drugs.

Watkins, William. 2001. *The White Architects of Black Education: Ideology and Power
in America, 1865–1954*. New York: Teachers College Press.

Williams, Henry Smith, and John Main Coffee. 1938. *Drug Addicts Are Human
Beings*. Washington, DC: Shaw Publishing Company.

Williams, Robert. 2017. "Wealth Privilege and the Racial Wealth Gap: A Case Study in
Economic Stratification." *The Review of Black Political Economy* 44 (3–4): 303–25.

Wollenberg, Charles. 1974. "*Mendez v. Westminster*: Race, Nationality and Segregation
in California Schools." *California Historical Quarterly* 53 (4): 317–32.

Zinn, Howard. 1990. *A People's History of the United States*. New York: Harper & Row.

PART II

Innovations in Teaching
and Learning in Prison

3 ||| COLLEGE NOW!

A PUBLIC UNIVERSITY GOES BEHIND
THE WALL IN MEXICO CITY

Introduction

The Higher Education Program for Social Reintegration Centers of Mexico City (Programa de Educación Superior para Centros de Readaptación Social, PESCER) is the culmination of my life's work.[1] From the time I was a young girl growing up in Mexico City and watching US television, my idol was Columbo, the 1970s homicide investigator, and I liked to imagine myself with a magnifying glass and a trench coat, solving crimes. But when I was fourteen, I saw the movie *Midnight Express* (1978), about an American imprisoned in Turkey and the terror, injustice, and denigration he faced. In that moment, I decided to dedicate my professional life to people deprived of liberty.

I have worked in carceral institutions for the last twenty years, and I am sometimes asked why it is important to bring higher education to the jails and prisons of Mexico City. I respond with a broader question: Why is it important anywhere? Idleness, as the saying goes, is the root of all mischief.[2] In prison, people deprived of their freedom diminish day by day. They are consumed with life inside prison walls. Educational access, vocational programming, recreation, cultural events, work, friends, and family are all important for maintaining a relationship with the outside world.

In addition, the human capacity for change begins through education, culture, the arts, and other endeavors that push us to explore the self. For incarcerated people, being able to discover for themselves that the door to knowledge is always open is powerful, even if for others, especially powerful elites, it is convenient that knowledge remain in the hands of

79

the privileged few. Nevertheless, empowering everyone brings us all to a better way of being in the world together.

In this chapter, I discuss PESCER, which provides high-quality college education to the penitentiary system of Mexico City. In the first part of this chapter, I outline the purpose, mission, and vision of PESCER's host university to provide context for how PESCER operates. In the second section, I discuss PESCER in detail, including the program's educational model, admissions overview, commitment to students, and material and human resources, as well as some key achievements and obstacles, all of which may help practitioners initiate and grow similar programs around the world.

Higher Education Access Expanded in Mexico City

Mexico City wrestles with high unemployment, pervasive informal employment, chronic underemployment, wages far below a livable standard, and other indicators of economic insecurity. Inequality and social marginalization exacerbate already widespread poverty and impede the exercise of a pluralistic and inclusive democracy, active citizenship, and human rights. For their part, incarcerated people often suffer these realities before, during, and after their detention.

In populations marked by poverty and its many associated issues, education is not always considered among the most basic and pressing needs. Vulnerable populations are consistently exposed to human insecurities in a range of basic categories, such as insufficient food and shelter, and these insecurities can lead to high degrees of violence. In the context of this socioeconomic instability, bringing college programming into prisons in Mexico can be seen as a mechanism for the prevention of violence and for amplifying the potential of true social reintegration. The importance of education is tremendous in a country that still has relatively low levels of high school completion, let alone college. In short, the promise of education is that it can prepare individuals for a better future. Education, both formal and informal, encompasses the endowment of values, principles, skills, aptitudes, and attitudes toward life, and this is especially pertinent to the prison population in aiding with the social reintegration of formerly incarcerated people.

The Autonomous University of Mexico City (Universidad Autónoma de la Ciudad de Mexico, UACM) is committed to the mission of education as a means of liberation. The UACM was founded as an institution of higher education on April 26, 2001, by Andrés Manuel López Obrador, then the head of Mexico City's federal government and, since 2018, Mexico's president. On December 16, 2004, the UACM obtained autonomous status through the Law of the Autonomous University of Mexico City, approved by the Legislative Assembly of Mexico City (Autonomous University of Mexico City n.d.), cementing its role as an educational institution able to determine its own path forward, including carrying out its educational offerings in prison. The statute that founded the UACM outlines its transformative mission and vision, as well as programs and courses of study focused primarily on developing citizens who possess the ability to critically analyze the world around them (Autonomous University of Mexico City n.d.). Philosophically, UACM is committed to training students in a multidimensional understanding of social problems and providing students with sufficient scientific and humanistic knowledge as well as tools to facilitate their ability to propose viable solutions to relevant problems (Autonomous University of Mexico City n.d.). UACM is the university host of PESCER, responsible for its accreditation, funding, staffing, and day-to-day operations as a college-in-prison program.

PESCER, of which I have been the director since 2005, spans socioeconomic borders and has international resonance because, at its base, it is very simple. The program stipulates that the university campuses in prisons across Mexico City should be treated as college campuses just like any others. PESCER adopts the institutionalized model of any university in that the university provides education to all students without constraints due to geography, criminal history, or any other limitations. It is truly a campus of the world and a model of education for the twenty-first century, where universities embrace a commitment to bringing educational access to everyone, not just elites. PESCER's careful attention to teacher qualifications is a special element of the program that has been instrumental to its success and is a feature that can be replicated by college-in-prison programs in other countries. Before outlining the specifics of PESCER, let me provide context for educational access in Mexico, as well as our university partner, the UACM.

Education as Redistributive Policy at UACM

The mission of the UACM is to help meet the pressing needs of Mexico City in the field of higher education.[3] This is especially important considering that a large part of the Mexico City population has not had the privilege of obtaining a university education. The creation of the UACM addresses this need and demonstrates the government's commitment to education, especially for the segments of the population that have lacked them. The UACM's entire raison d'être is to allow access to higher education for more and more people. To this end, the UACM regards both the consolidation of acquired knowledge and progress toward the truth as core values. The communities of educational institutions are constituted by teachers and students, and this requires that students and teachers have a common interest in knowledge and culture (Autonomous University of Mexico City n.d.). To this end, the UACM works to ensure that all students who begin their studies can successfully complete them.

As for its educational mission within prison, PESCER seeks to replicate the mission and vision of the UACM within the Mexico City penitentiary system.[4] The prisons of the Federal District of Mexico, located in Mexico City—the capital of Mexico and one of the world's largest cities—are an important space to develop ways to meet the need for higher education.

PESCER is innovative because it is the first and only program at the national level in Mexico that offers the prison population in-person higher education classes as well as continuing education opportunities as a university extension (PESCER n.d.). Before PESCER began, the education offered in Mexico City's prison schools ran only from literacy to upper secondary, or high school, level. Interestingly, the classes were provided by incarcerated people themselves, who exercised the role of academic advisers as specified by governmental education programs designed by the National Institute for Adult Education (Instituto Nacional para la Educación de los Adultos, INEA) through the Open High School government program.

UACM's work to bring higher education into Mexico City's prison system officially began with its first classes on April 26, 2001. The next step of programmatic consolidation came to fruition in 2004, when the UACM and the Government Secretariat of Mexico City signed an inter-institutional collaboration agreement, creating programmatic autonomy for the UACM within the prison system. The parties agreed to facilitate programs of higher education, research, dissemination of culture, and university extension in the schools of the Penitentiary System of Mexico City (Autonomous University of Mexico City n.d.). For context, Mexico City is home to nearly 25 percent of the country's more than 220,000 incarcerated people—more than 50,000 people (Romero 2021)—housed in thirty-seven separate penitentiaries (Cooper 2020).

On April 18, 2005, academic activities related to one governmental program, termed an integration cycle, began in the form of in-person classes at the school facilities of Santa Martha Acatitla Women's Social Reintegration Center (Centro Femenil de Reinserción Social Santa Martha Acatitla, CEFERESO) and at the Mexico City Penitentiary. At the time, these programs began with two groups of just thirty-five students and nine teachers (Higher Education Program for Social Rehabilitation Centers of Mexico City, PESCER n.d.). As of 2022, PESCER serves 1,160 incarcerated people across seven penitentiaries in Mexico City.

PESCER's Educational Model

As with many premier college-in-prison programs, PESCER seeks to replicate the academic programming of the UACM as fully as possible in prison. Incarcerated students and students at the five outside campuses have the same educational rights and access to the same benefits. The higher education programming offered by the UACM is public and free, requires no entrance exam, and does not take into account the prestige of a student's secondary education. All that is required is a high school diploma (or equivalent) and a birth certificate.

In both the outside UACM campuses and through the PESCER program within the broader system of education in prison, students move through three distinct cycles or stages of college. First, all students take the mandatory integration program to begin their college-level work, then the basic cycle that consists of three semesters, which would be comparable to general education requirements in most university systems. Finally, in the superior cycle, students carry out specific studies for their chosen degree.

First, integration (which in English and within the US college system would be most comparable to orientation or first-year programming) lasts one semester and focuses on preparatory, pre-college skill-building. Prior to beginning a PESCER degree pathway in the detention centers of Mexico City, the UACM requires that all students participate in this one-semester integration program, which includes topics such as mathematics, cultural studies, and language and thinking. These three topics help students gauge their current academic level and what they will need to do to be college-ready.

At PESCER, as with UACM, there is no admissions exam. Instead, the program accepts everyone who has completed high school and has the necessary identification documents. In order to continue to the next stage of academic offerings, the basic cycle, students must successfully complete the orientation semester. Participants also complete a diagnostic evaluation, which tests knowledge of mathematics as well as oral and written language skills. The results of the diagnostic determine whether students enter the basic cycle of PESCER directly or if they need to review any modules before proceeding onward. The purpose of this intervention is to equip students with a more uniform level of mathematical knowledge, communication skills, and reading comprehension to ensure their success once they enter the demanding bachelor of arts (BA) pathway. Once the integration stage is completed, students advance to the three-semester basic cycle.

Next, the basic cycle sees students take a range of entry-level college courses. In this phase of the program, students acquire knowledge in historical, scientific, cultural, and language topics, which allows them to express critical opinions inside and outside of PESCER. Students also work to set clearer goals about their future academic pursuits. The basic cycle includes a common curriculum that all students at UACM take, whether in or out of prison, that is roughly equivalent to the general education requirements in US higher education, and which includes classes on culture, politics, and writing. These courses are more tailored to matriculated students headed for degree-granting programs but are general enough to serve as a common foundation. The courses on their own do not yet culminate in a degree but are part of a pathway to a degree if a student chooses to continue on to the higher cycle.

In the fifth semester of college, students look toward regularizing their status as matriculated students in their majors. To do this, they must have completed the basic cycle and passed into the higher cycle, which includes preparation for the bachelor's thesis, social service work, and specialized courses. There are special scholarships for students who make it to the higher cycle as they move through the remaining semesters of coursework. Upon completion of the higher cycle, at the conclusion of additional semesters of study, students graduate with a bachelor's degree. The higher cycle varies in length depending on the major selected, and students carry out specific studies for each chosen degree. In this period, students either fulfill the standard curricular trajectory established in the study programs or create their own slate of subjects selected from the requisite credit hours and academic interests over six semesters. For example, the higher cycle requires seven total semesters for law, six for creative writing, or five for political science and urban administration (PESCER n.d.).

In 2020, when this chapter was first drafted, students were enrolled in the following degree-granting programs within PESCER: law (232 students), political science and urban administration (2 students), and creative writing (2 students). Of these students, 37 identified as women and 199 as men. By education level, in PESCER in 2020, there were 205 undergraduates and 31 graduate students enrolled. PESCER continues to grow over time.

PESCER uses the same sequences of academic preparation as for students on traditional, noncarceral campuses. Importantly, this means that by the time university students leave the penitentiary centers, PESCER has provided them with the guidance and preparation necessary to adapt to a change of campus. Even if students are transferred to other prisons within Mexico City, their ability to conduct their higher education studies would not be impacted if they are able to join UACM groups at their new detention center and continue their studies.

In order for the educational model proposed by UACM to be adequately implemented, PESCER provides a range of additional academic supports. For example, PESCER utilizes an education model complemented by advising and ongoing tutoring, which is a key part of the responsibility of the teaching faculty. This approach contributes to the comprehensive professional training of students. Just as for outside students, incarcerated students in PESCER have scholarships to help purchase materials they need for classes, and faculty come to the prison to teach the same kind of in-person classes they offer on the traditional campuses. Every prison in which PESCER operates contains a prison school where people who are college-eligible are able to study with classmates and faculty.

PESCER's educational programming is carried out in eight detention centers across Mexico City,[5] and the program has shown robust participation. For example, in 2009, there were 15 courses (1 integration, 5 basic cycle, and 9 higher cycle), comprised of 189 matriculated students and 70 nonmatriculated, as well as a faculty of 44 instructors (PESCER n.d.). By 2021, when the Covid-19 pandemic was ravaging Mexico, 155 courses had to be canceled across two semesters, while only ten courses were able to continue under adverse conditions, serving 59 students with 4 faculty.

As of 2022, PESCER has served a total of 19 cohorts of students taught by a total of 391 instructors.

As for the impact of the Covid-19 pandemic, as of the first semester of 2022, four courses were canceled, but forty-five more were able to go ahead as planned, with 29 professors and 161 students served. While Covid-19 has posed many challenges for Mexico as a whole and for higher education in general, it has pushed the PESCER program to imagine new and innovative possibilities, especially when it comes to the delivery of education through technology. As it became clear that the pandemic was a long-term problem, PESCER worked to provide virtual classroom teaching via Zoom, though technology-based virtual learning is still being built in many of the prisons and is not yet universally available. End-of-semester final assignments and evaluations in 2022 were carried out via multiple distance-learning methods, through packets of hard-copy materials made available to students, as well as through both electronic and in-person meetings with PESCER faculty, administrators, and incarcerated students whenever possible. These innovations allowed approximately 60 percent of PESCER students to stay on their academic pathways during the pandemic.

Student Life in PESCER

The central labor of PESCER resembles in many ways the typical daily work of a college or university. Courses are planned out over time and placed in a weekly schedule, and faculty are recruited and appointed to serve as instructors. This second role is critical to teaching in prison because we not only select faculty; we also orient them and prepare them for what it means to teach in a prison. Then, when classes begin, we accompany them in their classes as well, until teachers have both the confidence to teach alone and the trust of the students to do so effectively. In the sixteen years we have been teaching in the prisons, faculty who have taught for PESCER generally enjoy it, and we have worked with the university in a variety of situations to make teaching in prison accessible for faculty.

Like a typical university, PESCER conducts course scheduling, provides administrative and student support, and connects students with opportunities for service in the community. National social service, for example, is a requirement for all Mexican university students, including for those in PESCER. Upon completion of their degrees, Mexican college graduates from public universities are required to work for one year in some type of service role—many are paid jobs that provide career-specific training, much like a paid internship, and are competitive to acquire. PESCER students who finish their degrees outside of prison will also carry out this year of service outside, but for those who are serving longer sentences and graduate inside, service opportunities are made available inside prison as well. Roughly 80 percent of all social service work for PESCER students is performed while students are still incarcerated within their penitentiary settings. As of 2022, a hundred thirty-one students have completed their social service.

In addition, PESCER implements, in collaboration with the office for Coordination of Cultural Diffusion and Extension, a broad program of artistic and cultural events for the prisons and jails in which PESCER operates. Such activities include cinema club and cinema debate team, independent and university shows, workshops, seminars, meetings, courses, book presentations, conferences, photographic exhibitions, organization of an exposition for the sale of penitentiary-produced crafts, and promotion of calls for poetry contests, among others. PESCER also oversees the publication of the program's newspaper, *La Musa del Estafeta*,[6] available on both the prison campuses and traditional campuses. Because of UACM's commitment to offering a high academic caliber and degree requirements to incarcerated students equal to those at UACM's main campuses, PESCER provides a range of student services in prisons. These include career advising, scholarship application assistance, academic support, referrals for health services, and robust cultural programming. This is all part of PESCER's commitment to educational access as a redistribution mechanism in Mexico City.

Human and Material Resources of PESCER

Like all other aspects of the program, instructors who teach with PESCER are held to the same standards as those teaching on the main campuses of the UACM. Those who are selected to teach in PESCER must have a solid and broad curricular background with verifiable academic degrees at the master's level, teaching experience, and, above all, the proper disposition and comfort level necessary to teach college in a prison setting. Accordingly, most faculty are highly motivated, and recruitment is quite competitive, as teaching with PESCER is seen as a desirable post. This is a shift from the early days of the program's existence, when it was difficult to recruit faculty from within the existing teaching staff at the university. Before PESCER was well known and established as an educational program, faculty participation depended on the goodwill of those who wished to collaborate and required overcoming judgment about the unfavorable reputation of the detention centers. Now PESCER is seen as a clear way for educators to practice social justice and educational redistribution.

Our success with faculty recruitment has relied on recruiting teachers with a high sense of humanity and sensitivity to carceral issues. We do not present teaching in PESCER as being a high-status position. On the contrary, we describe the role as one that necessitates humility and sensitivity. At first, teachers frequently wonder why they should go to teach at the prisons, but as they begin to work with the program, they dispel their doubts through their own education about incarcerated students and the mission of the program.

In terms of preparation, faculty are oriented to their roles at the beginning of each semester. Instructors who participate in PESCER for the first time are generally given an introduction to the prison system and are taken individually to the classroom in which they will teach their course, where they are greeted by administrators and students alike. Following this formalized protocol also allows faculty to gain the confidence of security personnel within the assigned prisons.

PESCER associates include qualified personnel who work in prisons as officials. They, like all faculty and staff, must understand the prison regulations, policies, ideals, mission, and vision for each of the prisons where PESCER operates. Above all, they must know the population that participates in the program. Our teachers also learn these systemic and personal contexts as they get to know the world within prison, and this informs their teaching and overall experience.

All PESCER instructors are supported by a collegial cluster of faculty and staff grouped by research specialty and made up of teachers from the UACM campuses and from PESCER. Key functions of these clusters include teaching, research, dissemination of academic work, and social cooperation, and they also function as intellectual solidarity groups. In short, a characteristic of the academic work of the UACM is a kind of collegiality carried out in groups with shared interests and purposes. Cluster work is common in Mexican universities and is another way that PESCER integrates its model as fluidly as possible into standard academic practices.

The clusters develop from the exchange of knowledge and experiences and are based on respect for plurality of thought, freedom of expression, the right to disagreement, and academic freedom (which is limited only by the rights of students who are incarcerated).

Another priority of PESCER is to meet the requirements for professional growth that teachers and administrative staff need to be successful and thrive. PESCER carries out this mission through courses and conferences that faculty and staff request. In this way, PESCER leadership provides informative and sensitizing talks aimed at newly admitted faculty and staff, with the goal of introducing them to intra-prison teaching work. Moreover, to reinforce the academic project of UACM within PESCER, the libraries of the prison schools have been strengthened by bolstered catalogs according to the educational projects and the careers that are offered in each. Each campus of PESCER has a library with between five hundred and eight hundred books available for students to peruse or check out. In addition, books published by the UACM are also delivered to the prison schools, as are magazines and newscasts. In fact, four basic library science courses in a workshop style have been offered to incarcerated students who volunteered to classify, order, and care for the bibliographic collection, with a total of fifty-eight attendees (PESCER n.d.).

Student Evaluation and Administrative Operation

Any administrative academic procedure that students request—transcript updates, exam review, course selection, degree progress, or making suggestions or complaints—is carried out through PESCER assistants in order to be managed in a timely manner. Student work is evaluated by faculty each semester and receives numeric scores—from five (lowest) to ten (highest)—along with qualitative written and oral evaluations. If a student receives a low grade on an assignment, they are allowed to redo the assignment or exam until they receive a grade that is satisfying to them. This is not a PESCER requirement, but rather it is a program policy. The policy creates space for students to learn from past mistakes and garner an achievement they can feel good about, even if it takes longer than other students. PESCER staff maintain records of student academic progress to assist this process.

Fortunately, PESCER students tend to be very high achieving and hardworking. This may be in part because they are typically adults who know they have a chance to make something worthwhile out of their situation of being incarcerated. PESCER students usually come prepared to work hard and often encourage the faculty to give them more work and additional information on their topics. Faculty at UACM can choose to teach for PESCER as part of their course obligations, and many do so because the quality of work in the classroom is high, and students' enthusiasm for learning is gratifying for professors. Overall, PESCER students get very good grades and write excellent theses.

Successes and Innovations

As other programs look for ways to expand or innovate, PESCER may offer some suggestions about what might be possible in the prison space. For example, the postgraduate course "Masculinity in Confinement" took place in a Mexico City penitentiary. At one point in the postgraduate program, UACM professor Adriana Terán Enriquez delivered a keynote presentation on masculinities in the history of Mexico. This line of inquiry in the postgraduate program served as a space for reflection of how traditional Mexican masculinity, exercised since pre-Hispanic Mexico, affects the relationships of men with women, with other men, and with themselves. The purpose is to create a new masculinity that is more responsible both to individuals and communities, and to create a more harmonious, equitable, and inclusive society. Delivering courses and programming such as this allows PESCER to challenge societal norms and facilitate forward thinking on socially relevant issues, a positive role that many college-in-prison programs could or do play.

Other PESCER initiatives include workshops in puppetry, advanced chess, jazz dance, software applications, and many other topics. As for the arts, the cinema club and cinema debate team have screened films such as *Zelig* (1983), *Viólame* (2000),[7] *Traffic* (2000), *Interiors* (1978), *Músico, poeta, y loco* (1948),[8] as well as a cycle of erotic cinema. Among the shows presented have been the Symphonic Band of the National School of Music of UNAM, a concert with Negro Ojeda, presentation of the groups Son como Son and Arte por Todos, monologues, jarocha rumba, Spanish pop rock, radio blues, and many others. PESCER has also hosted conferences such as "Cooperative Self-Management," "Coffee and Mathematics," "The Rise of the Social Sciences," and "The Mesoamerican Worldview."

It should be mentioned that the rest of the prison population not involved in the program has benefited from the cultural offerings of PESCER as well. Indeed, PESCER has even collaborated in the training of prison staff, offering courses such as "Writing, Spelling, and Reading Texts" and "Psychological Aspects." The participation of the university in this space has fostered the sensitization of prison personnel to the work carried out by the university, fostering a more favorable climate for university life.

Regarding the field of research, the UACM through PESCER has initiated a study entitled "University Training in Total Institutions," which seeks to analyze the meanings, beliefs, perceptions, and expectations of a university education for incarcerated students. It is also an ideal instrument to support the work of PESCER on a scientific basis, representing in turn the historical and theoretical record of the program. So far, the research has yielded positive results, internally reflecting in students a reification of their human condition, not only in their confinement but also in their opportunities for freedom.

Obstacles Faced by PESCER

PESCER has seen many innovations and is on a trajectory for long-term success and stability. Of course, PESCER must confront obstacles similar to those of many other college-in-prison programs. One significant obstacle to the consistent advancement of the program has been higher-than-ideal student turnover, typically due to factors such as students focusing on their legal situation, the trauma of imprisonment, abandonment by family, disciplinary measures imposed by the prison authorities, living conditions, and more.

Another difficulty has been not being able to meet the requests of students who wish to study topics such as engineering, due to the lack of resources and adequate facilities for this purpose inside the prisons. Limitations on technological and laboratory-type resources for incarcerated students is an ongoing challenge that many college-in-prison programs navigate. Sometimes it means students do not get their first choice of major, but they will still get a quality college education in an area that they can apply to future studies outside prison, where they will not have the same resource constraints. To this point, it is worth noting that as of 2022 approximately three hundred fifty students who have been released have elected to continue their studies at five different campuses of the university.

As is common in this field of work, PESCER faces a range of resource obstacles, but our deep relationships within the university as well as with prison officials and other government officials has helped PESCER make a beachhead into Mexico City's carceral system. In this way, we are able to continue to expand and serve more incarcerated students in a range of prisons and jails throughout the city.

Other chapters in this volume speak to difficulties and successes around data access to document the results of educational interventions in prison. PESCER does not necessarily frame that as an obstacle, but we know this work lies ahead of us. We need to develop an investigatory framework to document whose lives have changed, and how, with access to and participation in PESCER. For example, did obtaining a college degree change people's lives through employment opportunities or other ways? Also, has crime in Mexico City been impacted at all by PESCER's intervention? Is the societal value of education worth the investment that PESCER is making in the penitentiaries? These questions will need to be answered in the years ahead.

As the director, I have seen many powerful changes by incarcerated students as well as formerly incarcerated students. But we must have empirical research that can test the credibility of what we have anecdotally seen to be true. With the 1,035 enrolled PESCER students of 2021, we need to see percentages of degree completion, what can be improved, and to what end. Assembling this data may be perceived as an obstacle, but it is truly an opportunity to document the impact of our work. We currently have forty students set to graduate: thirty-nine with a licensure in law and one in political science and urban administration.

Conclusion

The future for PESCER is bright, and there are many exciting areas for growth. PESCER may continue to expand with additional educational programs in detention centers and also increase the number of partners we work with. Similarly, regarding the teaching staff, the aim is to increase consistency, with the goal of having professors within PESCER teach courses for at least two semesters. This would promote more long-term exchange between the prison and university environments, deepening the commitment of faculty to this work within the departments to which they belong. We are interested in making a PESCER publication, including publishing a magazine that contains the poetic and literary works of students of the program, as well as a book that collects the experiences of both students and teachers alike. Such documentation of the program will bring the voices of PESCER students to wider audiences.

There are always obstacles inherent in work that directly interfaces with structural inequality. Nevertheless, PESCER continues to serve as an educational tool of liberation for an otherwise marginalized population. In providing this case study of PESCER, my hope is that it will provide an example to others striving to deliver equal access to high-quality education for incarcerated individuals worldwide.

Notes

1. This chapter was translated from the original Spanish by Mneesha Gellman and Justin McDevitt.

2. In Spanish, "La ociosidad es la madre de todos los vicios." (In English, literally: "Idleness is the mother of all vices.")

3. More on the mission of UACM can be found here: https://uacm.edu.mx/inicio /institucion/mision_vision.

4. Forming the core administrative team of PESCER are Manuel Perez Rocha, engineer and founding rector of the UACM, Jaciel Luis Ortega, subsecretary for the Mexico City prison system, and myself.

5. These include the Penitentiary of Mexico City, the Tepepan Women's Social Reintegration Center, the Santa Martha Acatitla Men's Social Reintegration Center, the Santa Martha Acatitla Women's Social Reintegration Center, Martha Acatitla, East Male Preventive Prison, South Male Preventive Prison, and North Male Preventive Prison. As of 2021, PESCER continues its work in three *reclusorios* (presentencing detention centers) and four *penetenciarias* (postsentencing prisons). In the penetenciarias, there are six groups divided across three facilities, including two groups in the women's prison. In the reclusorios, there are four groups in three facilities: the North, South, and East reclusorios. There are four groups of students in North Reclusoria, two in South, and four in East.

6. In English, *The Courier's Muse.*

7. The original French title is *Baise-moi.*

8. In English, *Music, Poetry, and Madness.*

Works Cited

Cooper, Caitlin. 2020. "Prisons, Covid-19 and Mexico's Permanent War." *OpenDemocracy.* https://opendemocracy.net/en/democraciaabierta/carceles -Covid-19-guerra-permanente-mexico-en/.

Mendes, Jose Manuel, Manuela Guilherme, and Teodoro António. 2014. "Equality, Democratic Citizenship and Solidarity: Is There a Role for Higher Education in the Framing of an Alternative Paradigm?" In *European and Latin American*

Higher Education Between Mirrors: Conceptual Frameworks and Policies of Equity and Social Cohesion, edited by António Teodoro and Manuela Guilherme, 23–39. Rotterdam: Sense Publishers.

PESCER. n.d. "Programa de Educación Superior para Centros de Reinserción Social de la Ciudad de Mexico." PESCER. Universidad Autónoma de la Ciudad de Mexico. Accessed November 25, 2022. https://portalweb.uacm.edu.mx/uacm/pescer/es-es/antecedentes.aspx.

Romero, Teresa. 2021. "Number of Imprisoned Persons in Mexico: 2010–2021." *Statistica*. https://statista.com/statistics/1280844/prison-population-mexico/.

Universidad Autónoma de la Ciudad de Mexico. 2006. "Proyecto Educativo de la UACM."

Universidad Autónoma de la Ciudad de Mexico. n.d. "Programa de Educación Superior para Centros de Reinserción Social de la Ciudad de Mexico." https://portalweb.uacm.edu.mx/uacm/pescer/es-es/antecedentes.aspx.

Universidad Autónoma de la Ciudad de Mexico. n.d. "UACM Visión-Misión." Accessed November 25, 2022. https://uacm.edu.mx/inicio/institucion/mision_vision.

Wright, Deil S., and Jose Luis Mendez. 1997. *Para entender las relaciones intergubernamentales*. Mexico: Colegio Nacional de Ciencias Políticas Administración Pública.

4 ||| EDUCATION AND TRAINING IN AUSTRIAN PRISONS

ESSENTIAL PIECES IN THE REINTEGRATION PUZZLE

Introduction

Despite having many differences, prison systems around the world share numerous problems, including chronic overcrowding, tight budgets, and scarce human resources. These restrictive and difficult conditions often have detrimental effects on care as well as on support and treatment-oriented services and measures. The current state of affairs in most penal systems seems unfavorable for developments that will strengthen or expand a treatment-oriented penal system. However, it is precisely these unfavorable conditions that require these systems to adopt improvements that will help them fulfill their true mission.

Central here is that a core responsibility of any penal system is to prepare people for their return to society as comprehensively as possible, ensuring that they are both able to cope with life after prison and less likely to commit new offenses. Education in prison has the potential to bring about personal developments, improve perspectives, help prepare for life after release, and foster integration in order to counteract recidivism. Preparation for release, however, must be viewed holistically in order to be effective.

After a short description of the legal regulations concerning education in Austrian prisons, this chapter provides quantitative and qualitative data to spark a discussion about why efforts are needed to strengthen the complementary fields of education and training in prison. The next section will then elaborate on the benefits of combining education and training with practical application at work, and will also present some promising examples of innovations that accomplish this, such as e-learning. Finally, a holistic model will be presented, visualizing the diverse array of interventions necessary for consideration on the path toward release and integration. The focus presented here is in the context of Austria, but the chapter also draws on experiences collected in European cooperation, and the hope is that the arguments and models presented here may be of interest in other contexts and countries as well.

For the purpose of this contribution, the term "education" is used in a very broad sense to include basic education (i.e., basic language skills and arithmetic), secondary education, and postsecondary education, though the latter two unfortunately play a minor role in education in prison in Austria. The term "training," on the other hand, refers to measures aimed at improving general employment skills and vocational skills for specific jobs or industries (see, for example, Davis et al. 2014, 3). While the different levels of education and the various training measures generally provide a range of benefits and are geared toward different outcomes, in the prison context they share the common objective of improving the chances for rehabilitation and integration after release.

Austria and Its Prison System

The federal Republic of Austria is a landlocked country in central Europe, bordered by the Czech Republic and Germany to the north, Hungary and Slovakia to the east, Slovenia and Italy to the south, and Switzerland and Liechtenstein to the west, with a total area of 83,879 square kilometers—about the size of South Carolina. In early 2022, the population of Austria was around 8.98 million and growing due to a steady flow of people with non-Austrian citizenship. About 17.7 percent of inhabitants were reported to have citizenship in some other country (Statistik Austria 2022).

Based on the Austrian Constitution, Austria is established as a representative democracy in a federal system, and matters of criminal law and its execution are the responsibility of the federal government. The Austrian legal system has its origins in Roman law and is based on the civil law tradition, and all legal provisions must comply with the provisions of the constitutional laws. The supreme enforcement authority with respect to the prison system lies in the Federal Ministry of Justice and is mostly performed there by the Directorate General for the Execution of Sentences. Altogether, there are twenty-eight prisons in Austria; fifteen of these are court prisons connected to regional courts, similar to county jails in the

United States, where sentences up to eighteen months are served as well as pretrial detention. Court prisons are for people of all genders and ages. For those serving sentences beyond eighteen months, seven correctional facilities are dedicated to men, one to women, and another to juveniles. In addition, three correctional facilities serve to treat incarcerated people with a psychiatric diagnosis. Each Austrian prison has the capacity to house anywhere between 71 and 1,057 people, with most of them housing fewer than 500 (Austrian Ministry of Justice 2020a, 42).

As of April 1, 2022, there were a total of 8,599 people being held in Austrian correctional facilities (Austrian Ministry of Justice 2022). By comparison, the current numbers are relatively low, as the Covid-19 pandemic has impacted custodial standards. In 2019, for example, an average of about 9,200 people were detained in correctional facilities. Overall, in recent years, roughly 103 of every 100,000 people in Austria were being held in its prisons (Austrian Ministry of Justice 2020b, 146). About 60 percent are currently serving sentences, 19 percent are in pretrial detention, and 16 percent are in facilities for psychiatric treatment. Additionally, about 36 percent of the incarcerated people serving sentences serve one year or less, another 47 percent serve sentences between one and five years, and close to 7 percent serve sentences of more than ten years. In terms of demographics, 93.6 percent of the incarcerated people are male, while 6.4 percent are female; 98.75 percent are adults, while 1.25 percent are juveniles (between fourteen and eighteen years old). Remarkably, while a slim majority are Austrian citizens, an astonishing 49 percent hold citizenship in some other country, and two-thirds of these individuals are from non-European Union member states (Austrian Ministry of Justice 2022).

The Central Regulations on Training and Education in the Austrian Penitentiary System Act

The Austrian Penitentiary System Act, which came into force in 1969, provides a broad basis for educational measures, with a focus on basic education and vocational training. Notably, however, the legal provisions include conditions that allow for a great deal of room for interpretation and provide a rather minimal definition of training and education in Austrian prisons—apart from facilities for juveniles, where these restrictions do not apply. Section 48 of the Penitentiary System Act establishes a right to vocational training for incarcerated people "who have not learned a craft or cannot be employed in the trade they have learned." Unfortunately, this right is weakened by another passage that follows it, which explains that this only applies if and to the extent that this is possible within the term of a sentence and taking into consideration the facilities available within the institution.

According to Section 57, incarcerated individuals who lack the knowledge and skills regularly provided by elementary schools also have a right to appropriate or what the law refers to as "necessary" instruction. Again, this right is severely weakened because it only applies to "institutions in which this is compatible with the principles of economical and expedient administration in view of the average number of prisoners held there and the average duration of their sentences." Provided these conditions are fulfilled, one would assume that education courses are to be held regularly for all qualified people incarcerated in a given facility (§57). However, legal claims challenging decisions made by prison officials are unlikely to succeed, making it difficult to enforce these provisions.

Karl Drexler and Thomas Weger (2010), for instance, point out this difficulty. According to Drexler and Weger, though the cited caveats do not apply to juvenile facilities (§58 Abs. 5 Juvenile Court Act), they are quite decisive when it comes to people in adult facilities. It should also be noted that there is a right to participate in distance-learning courses set out in Section 57 (2), though this, too, is of importance only for a very small number of adults due to the advanced requirements, particularly regarding security demands. Distance learning often occurs in higher education or university studies as well, when available.

Apart from this particular regulation, however, Austrian penal law unfortunately does not address higher education at all. This may have been less of a shortcoming at the time of the development of the penal code in the late 1960s, but it presents a glaring omission today. Even if demand for higher education in prison might not be widespread, this gap should be filled. For Austria, no exact figures exist at present, but estimates and available data suggest that only about one-third of the prison population have any education or training beyond compulsory schooling (e.g., Austrian Ministry of Justice 2020b, 206), compared to about 82 percent of the general population between the ages of twenty-five and sixty-four (Statistik Austria 2019). Of course, this fact should be viewed as grounds for improving the educational level of incarcerated people. The high rate of incarcerated people from outside Austria, many of whom speak little to no German, makes this more difficult, however (Austrian Ministry of Justice 2020b, 206). Considering that the majority of sentences are short, another challenge could be the fact that general secondary or vocational secondary school terms in Austria usually last four to five years. Modularization of schooling probably would be helpful in the prison setting, allowing students to start a program inside prison and finish it outside, but this is only slowly developing in the Austrian school system.

In practice, demands for higher education appear to be supported by the prisons, provided that there are options available. Since none of the Austrian correctional institutions are currently equipped to offer these kinds of educational paths within their own facilities, however, the options are restricted to distance learning or to incarcerated people being granted day release to attend classes at regular schools, college, or universities.

A main reason for the rather narrow meaning of prison training and education and the focus on vocational training and basic education is found in the legal provisions in this respect provided by the Austrian Penitentiary System Act. Meanwhile, much has changed, not least the prison population, with a large increase in the number of noncitizens since about 2000 as well as a much higher educational level of the general population. The Penitentiary System Act, however, has not been adapted to reflect the numerous and diverse societal changes that have transpired since its enactment.

Figures and Observations

There is not a great amount of data available on the educational measures offered in Austrian prisons and on the number of participants. The security report of the Ministry of Justice for 2019 reports 3,116 participants in all education and training programs offered by prisons (Austrian Ministry of Justice 2020b, 217). Considering an average number of about 9,200 people detained by the Austrian justice system at any time, this seems like a relatively high level of participation. This may be a bit misleading, however, for several reasons. For one, 40 percent of these courses were language classes, which is largely due to the already mentioned fact that about half of all incarcerated people in Austria are foreign nationals, many of them without a working knowledge of German.

Another 40 percent of those participating in educational programs are subsumed into the category "diverse," which does not allow for much analysis, though it appears to include mostly limited vocational trainings such as forklift driving licenses, welding, and painting. Only a little more than 5 percent of students in educational programs in prisons are in a program that could be considered extensive vocational training, that is, those leading to an apprenticeship certificate. The final 5 percent concern a standardized computer literacy course where students can obtain a European Computer Driving Licence (ECDL). The available data for the year 2019 does not provide any information on enrollment in any kind of higher education, as these are part of the category "diverse" as well. Newly generated data for 2020 and 2021 also give some clue as to the marginal role of higher education in Austrian prisons currently. In both years and in all Austrian prisons altogether, a mere two students were enrolled in courses aimed at earning a high school diploma, two more in vocational secondary school, one in general secondary school, and three in college or university studies (Austrian Ministry of Justice 2022b). There is little doubt that the Covid-19 pandemic and the restrictions it spawned in the prison system reduced these numbers. Anecdotal estimates suggest that the pandemic may have caused a reduction of training and educational measures by 50 percent or even more. Still, even if the number of participants in higher education were to be tripled or even quadrupled in a more regular year, they would still remain rare.

It should also be noted that there are considerable differences in programming among the twenty-eight Austrian prisons, with some offering a broad range of measures and others hardly offering anything. There is quite a bit of room for improvement and development in the area of education and training provided in Austrian prisons. One relevant factor restricting educational and training measures is their subordination to work in prison, which is obligatory for juveniles as well as for adults serving sentences. As a rule, full-time education and training are considered to fulfill this requirement as well, although, apart from juvenile facilities, full-time educational or training offers are a very limited option and therefore not available to the majority of incarcerated people. The obligation to work is not enforced very strictly; in fact, the prison system is not able to provide a job to everyone in the system who wants one. Work, the thinking goes, allows an escape from boredom, an occupation, and even remuneration, although the payment is very little. Likewise, vocational training is mostly carried out during working hours and also typically provides an income. Often, however, potential candidates for vocational training programs must give up a better paying job to join a training course, and most often these jobs are not available anymore after completion of the training. On the other hand, many training courses and educational measures, such as basic education and language courses, are only offered during nonworking hours (§57 Penitentiary System Act) and do not provide the opportunity for an immediate income. The same is true for higher education, which is not even addressed in the Penitentiary System Act. With these pressures, people often decide against education and other, more basic training programs. Another somewhat symbolic problem of education and training in Austrian prisons is the very limited staff employed in this field.

Why Invest in Training and Education in the Penal System?

It is a fact that integration in our societies is largely dependent on integration into the labor market (e.g., Ramakers et al. 2017). Distance to the labor market means a high risk of marginalization, which again leads to poorer and riskier life conditions and, undoubtedly, a higher risk of entering a cycle of recidivism. The most relevant factors concerning chances in the labor market are education, training, and qualification (e.g., Bosch 2011, 28; Davis et al. 2014, 1; Hawley, Murphy, and Souto-Otero 2013, 12). Unfortunately, prison populations regularly underperform in these respects. Research has demonstrated how great the gap is between the majority of incarcerated people and the labor market (Hammerschick, Pilgram, and Riesenfelder 1997, 162). In fact, a growing distance from the labor market can already be observed for several years before imprisonment, and this most often continues after a sentence has been completed. If people released from prison succeed in finding and maintaining stable employment, their chances of staying out of the system are greatest. For example, research also shows that the chances are best for people with some qualification to offer, and that this group presents the lowest reconviction rates within four years after release (Hammerschick, Pilgram, and Riesenfelder 1997, 180).

Unfortunately, little research exists in the Austrian context to allow a deeper look into the value of diverse educational and training measures. Even internationally, more empirical research is needed to assess the efficacy of different kinds of programs. Nevertheless, there is, without a doubt, sufficient data to prove the potential value of training and education in correctional settings. Most often, the main research interest is the impact on recidivism rates. Of course, reducing the risk of recidivism must be a central aim for penal interventions, but other goals along the way—such as achieving stable employment or building self-esteem—may prove positive developments for measurement as well. Cathryn Chappell (2004), for instance, has arrived at positive findings with regard to a reduction of recidivism in a meta-analysis of studies on higher education measures (beyond secondary school) in the penal system.

In another meta-analysis, Lois Davis and colleagues (2014, 81) not only demonstrate positive impacts of training as well as education on recidivism rates, but also show that vocational training increases the chances for job placement and that correctional education in general is highly cost-effective. Stephen Steurer and Linda Smith (2003) describe positive effects of educational measures on recidivism rates, highlighting the importance of measures addressing life skills and job readiness. Wolfgang Wirth (2008) also shows positive effects of vocational trainings if suitable placement can be achieved afterward. In short, training programs should never be an end in themselves. For trainings to be most effective, there must be opportunities to take full advantage of them and maximize their utility. Considering their focus on labor market integration, this is naturally best served along with employment or at least further measures aiming at employment. Besides their qualities of counteracting recidivism, both training and education also offer chances for people to use their time in prison valuably in order to give rise to personal developments and improve outlooks. Most often, however, it will be important to have accompanying, connected, or subsequent measures in place to support students in prison as they realize their full potential through education.

Correctional systems in general have a mandate to prepare people for life after imprisonment, a goal that is also in the best interest of society as a whole (Council of Europe—Committee of Ministers 2020, 2; United Nations 2021, 14). If people successfully reintegrate, this also serves social cohesion and security on a societal level (United Nations 2021, 8). The Austrian prison system invests substantial resources into organizing and maintaining work opportunities inside its prisons. Most work offered in prison, however, is low-level, unskilled, and of a monotonous nature, such as packing or sorting. This means that most work in prison does not necessarily add value for the worker when it comes to preparation for a life after release. It is worthwhile, then, to think about ways to make better use of these investments.

Combining and Connecting Work, Training, and Education in Prison

One way to make better use of investments in work in prison is to effectively combine or connect work, training, and education. This calls for more integral organization, planning, and development. Helpful in this respect is a management system that is responsible for overseeing all three areas, as well as creating individual "development plans" for each client. This way, the needs and wishes of individuals with respect to education, training, and work can be coordinated with the possibilities and the competency needs observed at workshops and other areas of work in prison. According to this approach, work in prison becomes a potential beneficiary of training and education, as well as an opportunity to practice and deepen newly learned competencies. In this way, people serving sentences in prisons could be better trained and prepared for jobs while in prison; with a more educated workforce, the prison workshops could increase in quality and provide a more integrated experience for incarcerated workers. In fact, there is a general sense that Austrian prison workshops have lately seen decreasing levels of job readiness. To the contrary, work should become more of an opportunity to practice, develop, and deepen competencies relevant for professional integration after release.

This, however, does not apply equally to all kinds of education. Unfortunately, secondary and postsecondary education will rarely find immediate application or training opportunities in prison work. The potential of a connection is, above all, seen with respect to vocational training, which is of good use at work, as well as with respect to training on the so-called soft and basic skills needed in life in general and in professional life in particular. To a lesser degree, this is also true for basic (primary) general education, when, for instance, calculations are needed or documentation is to be done. Still, integrating higher education possibilities in prison in a way that also allows for student access to work and its benefits poses a significant challenge.

Strategies and efforts connecting or combining work, training, and education have the potential to continually engage more incarcerated people in a meaningful way and to better prepare them for release. To do this effectively, the planning stages must not only consider whether training or education should theoretically be organized before or along with work; they must also account for the unique needs of those living in each facility as well as the structures, opportunities, and requirements at the facility. The integrated approach counteracts possible competition between the three elements as well as institutional and individual preferences for work over education or training. This strategy may even help promote understanding and support of noneducational staff for training and education, providing opportunities to involve some of them as trainers or tutors as well.

Practical Examples of Combining and Connecting Training and Education with Work

One model successfully practiced in a few Austrian prisons since the 1970s involves intensive training courses for different trades (e.g., carpenters, cooks, bakers, and smiths), which award an apprenticeship certificate upon successful completion. These intensive courses condense the entire program of apprenticeship training, which usually lasts two to four years, into a span of only eight to twelve months. During this time, students engage full-time in both practical and theoretical instruction that is integrated into their work through a prison workshop. In some prisons, these trainings are carried out by prison staff, while in others there are partnerships with outside institutions. This type of training is based on Section 23 of the Austrian Vocational Training Act, which provides that persons beyond the age of twenty may be exempted from the general preconditions of apprenticeship training—such as several years of practical training and classroom instruction during that time—if they can prove that they have the abilities and knowledge necessary to carry out the profession in question, typically through a final examination. These trainings, though very demanding on participants, provide a high chance of job placement after release.

In addition, in its 2021 report titled "Integration of Learning and Working in Adult Prisons," the European Union–funded KEYS project identifies four basic models for integrating work with training and education. Important here are solutions that would adequately integrate trainings with work already being done by incarcerated people. The appropriate solution for any given facility must take into consideration the content of the training, the target group, the availability of staff, the facilities and equipment, time constraints, and security requirements. Each of these models carries with it different requirements for its planning and realization.

The first solution is to design trainings that can fit around and complement one's work schedule. On the one hand, trainings carried out this way must work harder to address the particular interests of the incarcerated person to incentivize their participation. On the other hand, the design of these trainings must ensure that participants are not too burdened when they are tired after work. Short modules of first aid courses, for instance, can quite easily be adapted to be carried out this way. The second model involves trainings that are integrated into or directly connected to the workplace. In KEYS, for example, a learning island was introduced into a prison workshop for carpenters, providing, among other things, learning material and tools for woodworking (KEYS 2021). As a model, learning islands take advantage of access to computers and learning software, and if the training is carried out by the prison staff responsible for the workshop, no additional staff is needed. This can be a very efficient model, though not applicable in every case. A third option envisions trainings related to the work carried out by incarcerated people during working hours, where this training cannot be integrated into work for various reasons. An example would be theoretical lessons for vocational training offered separately from work, like specific mathematics. One more model might see that incarcerated people are allowed to leave their workplace for several hours a week to participate in training or education, supplementing their professional competencies such as training on soft skills or language improvement.

Another valuable tool that can be combined with these models is self-directed learning—for instance, taking advantage of e-learning tools that already exist in Austrian prisons. This method offers the opportunity to address the needs of incarcerated people in a very individualized way, and it is suitable for a flexible application during either work or leisure time. Of course, this learning model does not suit all education programs, training regimens, or target groups, nor does it mean that there is no further need for support. On the contrary, self-directed learning works best when students feel guided and empowered, such as when instructors assign clear tasks and help students navigate individual goals (e.g., Hammerschick 2002, 16; Hawley, Murphy, and Souto-Otero 2013, 36). Motivational support is also important, so some element of human interaction should be ensured. To be sure, if self-directed learning is practiced simply by putting someone in front of a computer to work with software without assistance and instructions, this effort will likely fail and create frustration (e.g., Hammerschick 2019, 54). Staff must be available and prepared to support self-directed learning.

E-learning—in the sense of taking advantage of computers, suitable instructional software, the internet, and digital media—considerably broadens the options for training and education in prisons. In fact, this is the central argument regularly presented by e-learning trainers and tutors in European prisons, though there is still a lack of empirical data proving its value beyond this vocal support. Many jurisdictions in Europe, including Austria, take advantage of e-learning and internet use in prison. Most have found technical solutions that allow officials to restrict access to selected online sites (Hammerschick 2019, 49).

The Swedish prison system, for instance, has developed a distance-learning model with virtual classrooms that connect students and teachers all over Sweden via a closed network (i.e., not open to the internet) (Hammerschick 2019, 53). This allows prisons to offer a wide range of subjects otherwise not possibly covered by teachers at the individual prisons. Other systems like the German e-Lis-System, also used in Austrian prisons, only allow access to a central server, providing diverse learning software. For the connections, the internet is used in a tunneled way, which does not allow access to the open internet. There is, however, a "whitelist" of approved addresses, and access to other addresses can be granted after being cleared. A learning management system is also installed to support the e-learning organization, including group management and other features (Hammerschick 2019, 53).

From Imprisonment to Integration

High-quality training and education, including programs that lead to a formal certification, may in the end have little practical benefit if there are barriers hindering incarcerated students' maximum potential. Preparation for release must start upon one's entrance to prison, must be based on individualized plans, and must follow a holistic approach such as that visualized by figure 4.1.

This flowchart was first conceived during the European project KAMRA[1] (Hammerschick and Pilgram 2001), with partners from Austria, Germany, England, the Netherlands, Italy, and Portugal. It gives an overview of the decisions, pathways, phases, and activities relevant in preparation for release, especially for job placement. The elements are well known, but the quality of the model lies in the visualization of an "ideal"

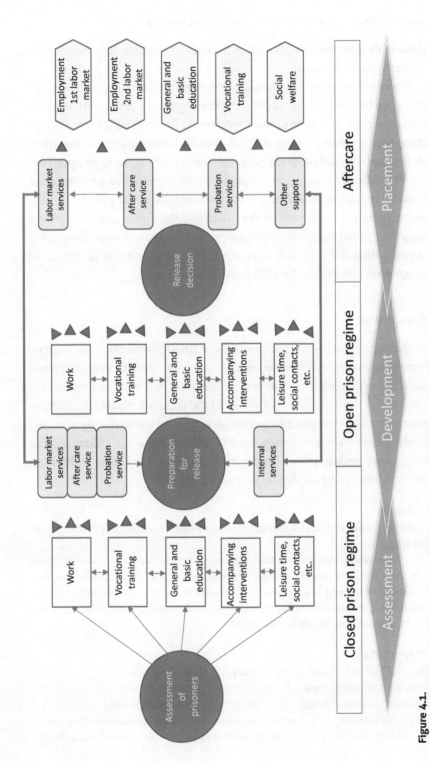

Figure 4.1.
Flowchart of a proposed holistic approach to preparation for release.

process or interplay of options and measures to be selected according to an individual assessment.

Correctional planning should merge with an integrational approach that goes beyond release. Ideally, the development phase—with its individualized combinations of work, vocational training, education, and accompanying measures such as social work and psychological or therapeutic support—would progress from a closed prison regime to an open one. As one's date of release approaches, the orientation toward job placement must be central, with available services from outside the prison reaching out to potential employees on the inside and starting or continuing their support toward release and placement. It is of utmost importance that support does not end with release but instead is ongoing at least until integration is complete for each incarcerated person.

Conclusion

Preparation for release is not a matter of a single intervention—it must be viewed as a complete, interconnected system of interventions with many potential improvements. Educational measures and training programs in the penal system are essential pieces of the complex puzzle of reintegration. They cannot replace comprehensive approaches to the organization of the penal system, but they must be part of them. Coordinating and combining work in prison on the one hand with training and education on the other can be a valuable step in this respect.

Notes

Many thanks to David Klingbacher at the Austrian Ministry of Justice for his support.

1. Komparative Analyse von Maßnahmen der beruflichen Aus- u. Weiterbildung von Straffälligen vor dem Hintergrund konzeptueller, sozialer und rechtlicher Rahmenbedingungen in den Ländern der EU (Comparative analysis of vocational education and training measures for offenders against the background of conceptual, social, and legal framework conditions in EU countries).

Works Cited

Austrian Ministry of Justice. 2020a. *Strafvollzug in Österreich*. Vienna.
Austrian Ministry of Justice. 2020b. *Sicherheitsbericht 2019*. Vienna.
Austrian Ministry of Justice. 2022a. "Verteilung des Insassinnen- bzw. Insassenstandes." https://justiz.gv.at/home/strafvollzug/statistik/verteilung-des -insassinnen-bzw-insassenstandes.2c94848542ec49810144457e2e6f3de9.de.html.

Austrian Ministry of Justice. 2022b. "Höhere Bildungsmaßnahmen im österreichischen Strafvollzug" (unpublished report).

Bosch, Gerhard. 2011. "Qualifikationsanforderungen an Arbeitnehmer—flexibel und zukunftsgerichtet." *Wirtschaftsdienst* 91 (13): 27–33.

Chappell, Cathryn A. 2004. "Post-secondary Correctional Education and Recidivism: A Meta-analysis of Research Conducted 1990–1999." *Journal of Correctional Education* 55: 148–67.

Council of Europe—Committee of Ministers. 2020. "Recommendation Rec(2006)2-rev of the Committee of Ministers to member States on the European Prison Rules." https://rm.coe.int/09000016809ee581.

Davis, Lois M., Jennifer L. Steele, Robert Bozick, Malcolm V. Williams, Susan Turner, Jeremy N. V. Miles, Jessica Saunders, and Paul S. Steinberg. 2014. "How Effective Is Correctional Education, and Where Do We Go from Here? The Results of a Comprehensive Evaluation." Santa Monica: RAND Corporation. https://rand.org/pubs/research_reports/RR564.html.

Drexler, Karl, and Thomas Heger. 2010. *Strafvollzugsgesetz: (StVG) : samt den wichtigsten, den Strafvollzug betreffenden Bestimmungen in anderen Gesetzen und Verordnungen* (2 Auflage) [Penal Law (StVG). Together with the most important provisions in other laws and ordinances relating to the execution of sentences (2nd ed.)]. Vienna: Manz.

Hammerschick, Walter. 2002. "Endbericht der Begleitforschung zum Ziel-3 Projekt ECDL via Telelernen für HaftinsassInnen." Vienna (unpublished research report).

Hammerschick, Walter. 2019. "Digitale Medien und E-Learning im Strafvoillzug." *Neue Kriminalpolitik* 31 (1): 46–57.

Hammerschick, Walter, and Arno Pilgram. 2001. "KAMRA—Komparative Analyse von Maßnahmen der beruflichen Aus- u. Weiterbildung von Straffälligen vor dem Hintergrund konzeptueller, sozialer und rechtlicher Rahmenbedingungen in den Ländern der EU." Vienna (unpublished research report).

Hammerschick, Walter, Arno Pilgram, and Andreas Riesenfelder. 1997. "Zu den Erwerbsbiografien und Verurteilungskarrieren Strafgefangener und Strafent-lassener, rekonstruiert anhand von Sozialversicherungs—und Strafregisterdaten." In *Jahrbuch für Rechts und Kriminalsoziologie '97: Arbeitsmarkt, Strafvollzug und Gefangenenarbeit*, edited by Walter Hammerschick and Arno Pilgram. Baden-Baden: Nomos.

Hawley, Jo, Ilona Murphy, and Manuel Souto-Otero. 2013. *Prison Education and Training in Europe: Current State-of-Play and Challenges*. European Commission.

KEYS. 2021. "Integration of Learning and Working in Adult Prisons." https://irks.at/forschung/social-inclusion/keys.html.

Penitentiary System Act (Bundesgesetz vom 26. März 1969 über den Vollzug der Freiheitsstrafen und der mit Freiheitsentziehung verbundenen vorbeugenden Maßnahmen, Strafvollzugsgesetz—StVG). 1969. Federal Law Gazette No. 144/1969.

Statistik Austria. 2021. "Bildungsstand der Bevölkerung." https://statistik.at/web
_de/statistiken/menschen_und_gesellschaft/bildung/bildungsstand_der
_bevoelkerung/index.html.

Statistik Austria. 2022. "Bevölkerungsstand und Bevölkerungsveränderung."
https://statistik.at/web_de/statistiken/menschen_und_gesellschaft/bevoelkerung
/bevoelkerungsstand_und_veraenderung/index.html.

Steurer, Stephen J., and Linda G. Smith. 2003. "Education Reduces Crime:
Three-State Recidivism Study; Executive Summary." CEA and MTCI. http://
antoniocasella.eu/nume/Steurer_2003.pdf.

Pilgram, Arno, and Wolfgang Stangl. 1996. "Kommentierung §20 StVG." In
Strafvollzugsgesetz, edited by Albert Holzbauer and Sepp Brugger. Vienna:
Verlag Österreich.

Ramakers, Anke, Paul Nieuwbeerta, Johan Van Wilsem, and Anja Dirkzwager.
2017. "Not Just Any Job Will Do: A Study on Employment Characteristics and
Recidivism Risks After Release." *International Journal of Offender Therapy and
Comparative Criminology* 61 (16): 1795–1818.

United Nations. 2021. "United Nations System Common Position on Incarceration."
https://unodc.org/res/justice-and-prison-reform/nelsonmandelarules-GoF
/UN_System_Common_Position_on_Incarceration.pdf.

Wirth, Wolfgang. 2008. "Qualifizierung-Vermittlung-Nachsorge. Eine
3-Säulen-Strategie zur beruflichen Wiedereingliederung von (ehemaligen)
Strafgefangenen." *Zeitschrift für soziale Strafrechtspflege* 44: 14–29.

5 ||| LEARNING BEHIND BARS

EDUCATION AND REINTEGRATION IN

DUTCH PRISONS

Introduction

For those of us invested in ensuring that prison spaces in our countries are as humane as possible, the words of the late Nelson Mandela provide true vision: "It is said that no one truly knows a nation until one has been inside its jails. A nation should not be judged by how it treats its highest citizens, but its lowest ones" (Mandela 1994). Fortunately, this sentiment largely reflects the priorities of Dutch society in the way it treats those under its custodial detention.

The Netherlands, a small but densely populated country of just over seventeen million, is often among the most progressive in Europe in its approach to solving many social problems. In a way, its flat landscape serves as a metaphor reflecting the notion that no barriers exist and that there is nothing to hide behind—hence its transparent character. Intentionally or not, the Dutch have often adopted a pragmatic approach when responding to social and political issues, rarely taking notice of any elitist undertones. The penal system in the Netherlands undoubtedly carries this unique DNA, emphasizing the collective responsibility of Dutch society to take care of its citizens who are falling behind. The Christian mindset of bringing back those who have strayed does to some extent resonate with the penal philosophy of the Netherlands, which justifies the substantial resources it invests in its criminal justice system by signaling a profound commitment to those in prison.

This chapter focuses on one fundamental aspect of the Dutch penal system: the educational opportunities offered to people inside Dutch prisons. It presents the results of qualitative research that took place in 2021–22, based on interviews conducted with government officials, staff members who work inside Dutch prisons, and academic researchers who teach in Dutch prisons. Some information also comes from Dutch government documents relating to education in prison. As a whole, the present study offers insights on valuable lessons that can be learned from the Dutch approach to incarceration while also reflecting on areas for improvement.

The Dutch Penal System

According to Jan Konings (interview by author, January 26, 2022), the senior policy advisor of reintegration and education at the Custodial Institutions Agency headquarters, there were 10,364 detainees in Dutch prisons as of January 2022. This is in close accord with earlier data relating that there are, on average, 10,732 persons in detention in the Netherlands on any single day (Ministry of Justice and Security 2021). Furthermore, according to a 2020 report from the Ministry of Justice and Security, 20 percent of detainees are serving sentences of two weeks, while another 45 percent serve between two weeks and three months, leaving only 35 percent of the total incarcerated population in the Netherlands serving longer than three months (Ministry of Justice and Security 2020). Because of these short timeframes for incarceration, providing sustained educational programs such as college are challenging but not insurmountable if planned carefully so that students can continue their studies upon release.

The Dutch penal system views education as an important step toward reaching the intended goal of reducing recidivism by means of justified incarceration. Punishment in the form of jail sentencing should be given in proportion to the seriousness of the crime committed and should not impose additional harm to the offenders. Imprisonment in the Dutch penal culture is therefore never simply the end of the equation, nor is it the end goal of incarceration. Rather, incarceration should mark the beginning of a process of assisting people to transform and reintegrate: to first serve their sentences and then learn how to turn a new page and strive to become better citizens. Education serves as the crucial factor in this process. Hence, offering people educational opportunities behind bars echoes the penal system's optimism of giving everyone a second chance. With the average cost of one prison bed occupancy close to 284 euros (or $291 USD) per day, the cost of incarceration is expensive in the Netherlands. Nevertheless, Dutch society believes that this is a price worth paying to focus on education and reintegration.

In the context of Dutch prisons, education can refer to a wide range of learning activities available to everyone, and these activities are built in as part of one's detention and reintegration (D-R) plan. These opportunities include basic education (including language and literary skills) or the most basic skills that any Dutch citizen would need in order to survive and function in society. Education also includes general work-related skills such as employment training, specific vocational training, and informal learning geared toward solidifying the personal and civic skills needed for active participation in society after serving one's sentence. Most of the content covered in the present study draws on data from Penitentiary Institution (PI) Vught, a correctional facility in the southern town of Vught, which has the largest educational program among all prisons in the Netherlands.

One of the limitations encountered when discussing educational opportunities in Dutch prisons is that each prison facility determines its own education budget. This, in turn, delimits the range and scale of education services offered to incarcerated people, such as, for example, the certificates or diplomas, the number of courses, and on what levels the courses can be offered. The number of staff available for education also varies from prison to prison. All of these factors make it difficult to generalize the overall situation among all Dutch prisons.

Nevertheless, there is no doubt that the Netherlands is committed to providing extensive educational opportunities in its correctional facilities. Within the EU, education has long been seen as a fundamental right for all people, no less for those people serving time in its prisons and jails. Article 14 of the Charter of Fundamental Rights of the European Union initially proclaimed on December 7, 2000: "Everyone has the right to education and to have access to vocational and continuing training." In a paper outlining the historical review of the EU and its vision for education in prison, Alan Smith gives credit to the Council of Europe, especially during the decade from 2000 to 2010. Smith praises the Council of Europe's work outlining the philosophy and principles of education in prison, work that continues to serve as the bedrock on which the good practices of the European Prison Education Association (EPEA) are based (Smith 2019). The EPEA is an organization made up of educators, administrators, governors, researchers, and other professionals committed to promoting and developing education and related activities in prisons throughout Europe in accordance with the recommendations of the Council of Europe.

In 2014, October 13 was designated the International Day of Education in Prison to mark the twenty-fifth anniversary of the Council of Europe's adoption in 1989 of a set of recommendations outlining the needs and responsibilities concerning the education of incarcerated persons (UNESCO Institute for Lifelong Learning 2019). To reify the new International Day of Education in Prison, various organizations around the world organized events to raise awareness, show solidarity, and strengthen the importance of the benefits of education in prison. In 2019, the UNESCO Institute for Lifelong Learning published the volume *Books beyond Bars: The Transformative Potential of Prison Libraries* (Krolak 2019), which is available in English, French, Spanish, and German. In addition, every two years, the EPEA holds its international conference in a different European country so that members and nonmembers can exchange best practices in the field of education in prison.

The Prison Education Consortium Netherlands initiated the "Changing Landscapes" project in 2017 to ensure that people incarcerated in Dutch prisons receive the best possible education, which will ideally help them refrain from committing crimes again or relapsing into substance abuse or addiction. The consortium consists of eight organizations, with EPEA Netherlands (EPEA-NL) serving as its leading partner. The overall purpose of this consortium of experts is to create an Innovative Plan for Prison Education by 2024 (Netherlands Helsinki Committee n.d.).

In the Netherlands, prisons are called penitentiary institutions (*Penitentiaire Inrichting*, or PIs). All Dutch prisons are financed, staffed, and managed as part of the Custodial Institutions Agency (Dienst Justitiële Inrichtingen) under the Ministry of Justice and Security (Ministerie van Justitie en Veiligheid). Currently, there are twenty-four PI facilities in the Netherlands, which implement various regimes of education. Staff members in the penitentiary facilities serve as guides, helping detainees[1] along the path of their rehabilitation.

To that end, when it comes to rehabilitation, the core difference between the Dutch and other common approaches lies in their interpretation of the purpose of incarceration. In the US penal system, for instance, sentencing serves mainly as a form of punishment and a deterrent, and the system is designed so that such a purpose is achieved. The Dutch criminal justice system, on the other hand, interprets incarceration as the beginning of a rehabilitation process. It believes in justified sentencing with the purpose of helping people by offering them a second chance to rebuild their lives so as to reduce recidivism. Imprisonment in the form of loss of freedom is already the biggest punishment in the Dutch penal system. Treating incarcerated people in a humane manner while offering them the rights all citizens deserve follows an important and principled logic. In the Dutch view, it is not necessary to add further harm beyond one's sentence.

What Is the Relation between Education and Reintegration?

When a detainee is admitted to a PI, the municipality where he or she originally came from is notified within two weeks, and the list of five essential elements (i.e., housing, work prospects, identity card, debt, and care/social network) is brought to the attention of the local municipality. This unique collaboration and support from the municipality contributes to the effectiveness of each person's reintegration process and the prevention of reoffending. Such crucial cooperation between the Dutch penal system and its 344 municipalities (within its twelve provinces in the Netherlands) provides one helpful model for other countries in tackling the problem of recidivism. Such mechanisms place a strong emphasis on multiple stakeholders to bear the collective responsibility of facilitating the reintegration process of a detainee.

Education in Dutch prisons remains one of the essential building blocks in an incarcerated person's D-R plan, and it is the right of all detainees in all Dutch prisons to receive an education if they choose. In any regular regime inside Dutch PI facilities, information about education opportunities is made known to all newly arrived detainees, often via their case manager during the intake conversation or through the Reintegration Center (RIC). After receiving advice (or approval, if necessary) from their case manager, detainees can decide whether or not to take advantage of the opportunity for education, and, if so, which pathways to start or follow. Each person has an individualized D-R plan, tailored to their specific needs and goals. To this end, potential students can start right away with basic education. As for vocational training, detainees are allowed to participate provided that such training is compatible with their D-R plan. Those in a PLUS program[2] can secure access to education beyond the basic levels with the advice and recommendation of their case manager and after seeking further approval from the multidisciplinary consultation, a health recommendation process.

It is also worth mentioning that within a given Dutch PI facility, apart from the personnel working as security officers and in catering, a large proportion of the staff members work directly with detainees. These include case managers, educators, legal officers, psychologists, therapists, administrators, and more—all of whom have been hired for the same reason and share one common goal: reducing recidivism by helping detainees in their process of rehabilitation. To achieve such a goal, staff members view jail time as the opportune moment to help equip people with the most effective skills for future employment and mindsets to help them return crime-free to Dutch society. No one, including prison security staff, bears arms. Hence, in theory, abuse of power is relatively rare in the Dutch system.

In Dutch PI facilities, a "traffic light" system has been adopted to encourage detainees to practice and maintain good behavior. Detainees may even be rewarded with promotion to the PLUS program, whereby additional privileges—such as the possibility to request certain education opportunities beyond a basic level—are allowed. Should a detainee decide to earn a basic education, two goals are woven into their D-R plan. First, a potential student starts training during detention and completes it with a diploma, certificate, or partial certificate. Second, taking up education allows a detainee to be more responsible with their life.

Types of Education in Dutch Prisons

In 2016, the Custodial Institutions Agency at the Ministry of Justice and Security published a memo stating its vision for education in Dutch PIs as well as the related policy frameworks. The memo was addressed to all directors and staff of the PI facilities within the Dutch prison system, including the teachers responsible for delivering education to the people incarcerated in them. Therefore, these serve as the leading policy guidelines concerning education in Dutch prisons. According to this memo, the Dutch government's vision of education consists of several key elements. Most important is that education must focus primarily on increasing a person's chances of finding work after detention. To this end, training focuses on the attainment of recognized certificates and diplomas, and every incarcerated person's D-R plan contains an individualized education plan. Structurally, the governmental departments that oversee education (Ministry of Education, Culture, and Science) and labor (Ministry of Social Affairs and Employment) coordinate regarding the supervision and progress of each student. In addition, incarcerated students learn independently, for the most part, but may receive the support of a teacher when necessary.

In addition, all facilities have access to the same educational offerings so that any person can continue with the same online teaching material should they be transferred to another facility. As a result, digital learning is used wherever possible.[3] Still, online access is very limited and restricted, and free internet access is still not possible for detainees. Some detainees may be allowed to use computers to study certain modules of digital materials for a specific course. But, as is often the case, this version of online learning refers simply to using a computer to study course content or programs that administrators have already uploaded onto the computer. On some occasions, detainees are allowed to go online for a very short duration to visit some course-related websites under close supervision, but such activities are rare and closely monitored.

The memo continues by outlining the policy frameworks for educational opportunities in Dutch prisons. To begin, basic education may be pursued by any incarcerated person and will be recorded in the education section of one's D-R plan. In addition, though education would ideally be attained in addition to work experience, if a schedule conflict cannot be avoided, education can be achieved during work hours, and the student will receive compensation if they cannot increase their working hours at another time.

In accordance with the government's vision stated above, education should primarily be linked to increasing one's opportunities in the labor market and to furthering social reintegration. Though liberal arts education is offered in some instances, the chief purpose of education within Dutch PI facilities is to encourage students to learn a specific skill that will hopefully increase their chances of finding employment opportunities after being released back to the community. To this end, a multidisciplinary consultation with the student's mentor or case manager assesses readiness and whether someone is motivated to prioritize reintegration.

The memo goes on to outline the three types of education available in Dutch correctional facilities: basic education, practical training, and vocational training. Basic education is offered in every PI and is available to everyone. This includes such staples as literacy education, Dutch language (reading, listening, speaking, and writing skills), English, mathematics, and computer skills (typing, word processing, data management, email, and the internet). Practical training, on the other hand, sees incarcerated people work twenty hours per week inside the prison facility, acquiring valuable employment skills and professional competencies. The ambition here is to map out these skills and competencies in a structured manner so that incarcerated people can build up an experience profile and eventually qualify for a certificate recognized by employers on the outside. Finally, vocational and so-called follow-up courses are only accessible to people in the PLUS program. In summary, the correlation between education and reintegration was reinforced and reiterated by the Custodial Institutions Agency within the Ministry of Justice and Security in the Netherlands.

PI Vught: Education for All

The present study now looks into the PI in the Dutch town of Vught as an instructive case. PI Vught is located in the southern Netherlands, near the border with Belgium, and lies just south of the industrial and administrative center of 's-Hertogenbosch. Situated on about thirty hectares (about seventy-four acres), the complex at PI Vught houses a total of eight distinct facilities: prison, house of detention, institution for systematic offenders, maximum security institution, terrorist department, controlled detainees' quarter, highly intensive specialist care, and penitentiary psychiatric center. According to Brigitte Verbeek, the Head of Education and Reintegration training, PI Vught currently houses about eight hundred male detainees, about half of whom are in psychiatric units (interview by author, January 11, 2022). In 2021, approximately eight hundred staff members (including security guards) were employed at the facility.

PI Vught has the largest educational program among all Dutch prisons in terms of staff members and teachers. Verbeek noted that ten staff members (eight of them full-time) currently work in PI Vught's education unit, serving the three hundred or so detainees who enroll in some education program in any given year, most in small groups of five or six students (interview by author, January 11, 2022). These staff members are a combination of both prison staff and outside educators, depending on the nature of the education involved. For example, for technical trainings such as welding and carpentry, instructors are usually brought in from the outside. On the other hand, Dutch-language trainings may be offered by a staff member permanently employed within a specific PI facility. Again, it is important to stress that budget limits and student demand help determine whether a PI facility will hire a permanent educator, regardless of the subject he or she will be teaching.

Education Components

Educational opportunities within PI Vught, as in most of the PIs in the Netherlands, include both basic education and vocational training. As mentioned earlier, basic education includes literacy education as well as general subjects such as English language, Dutch language, mathematics, and computer skills (including software such as Microsoft Office). Detainees can participate in any of these subjects at any time. For incarcerated people who wish to earn a certificate or diploma in English, Dutch, or mathematics, exams are offered three times a year to determine the level attained. Learning about civic duty and citizenship is also emphasized and available. In addition, basic education offerings include two safety, health, and environmental certification programs for contractors, called Safety Checklist for Contractors (Veiligheids Checklist Aannemers, VCA): Basic Safety VCA (without a diploma) and Full VCA (with a diploma). VCA is a mandatory certification process for anyone wishing to work in hazardous industrial environments within the Netherlands, and the examination is held about ten times each year.

Vocational education, including continuing education, is only accessible to incarcerated people in the PLUS program. As of 2022, there were four vocational courses available at PI Vught. First, the "General Entrepreneurial Skills" course (Algemene Ondernemers Vaardigheden, AOV) is suitable for detainees who believe they possess an entrepreneurial spirit or who used to run their own business prior to incarceration. Incarcerated people in Dutch PIs with approval can start with this vocational training after passing a mathematics test. To earn the AOV diploma, participants need an average of one year to pass all five modules.

Second, incarcerated people can pursue vocational training in welding to receive certification at MIGMAG levels 1 and 2 and TIG levels 1 and 2.[4] After successfully obtaining a diploma in welding, and in combination with the Basic Safety VCA, people will have one potential formal qualification for the labor market when they leave prison. Third, twice a year, PI Vught offers level 1 powder coating training, with a possibility to continue to level 2. Finally, incarcerated people may pursue certification for Hazard Analysis and Critical Control Points (HACCP), a food safety certificate specially designed for incarcerated people that plan to find work within Horeca (a catering business) or who work for an organization that produces, distributes, processes, or serves food in the hospitality industry. Training consists of seven e-learning modules and concludes with an online test.

In addition, people held at PI Vught may also follow a correspondence course of study through an external educational institution such as Leiden Educational Institutions (Leidse Onderwijsinstellingen, LOI), National Trade Academy (Nationale Handelsacademie, NHA), Dutch Language Institute (Nederlands Talen Instituut, NTI), or Open University (Open Universiteit, OU) if they meet certain conditions. As of February 2022, ten detainees in PI Vught were pursuing this self-study track.

Challenges Encountered

Despite the fact that PI Vught offers many educational opportunities to the eight hundred people incarcerated there, its education unit does face some tangible challenges. According to Verbeek, PI Vught's educational director, the relatively short sentence duration often affects the willingness and motivation of incarcerated people to take up educational opportunities (interview by author, January 11, 2022). This is particularly the case for those in pretrial detention, a group that tends to show little to no interest in taking up educational and vocational training opportunities. Some teachers also find it challenging to teach groups within the same class whose education levels vary. Cultivating motivation among incarcerated people to embrace educational opportunities can be challenging, but the reward for Verbeek and her team—witnessing someone in prison being awarded a certificate for the first time in one's life after successfully completing a training—makes all the hard effort worthwhile.

Despite the successful program structure, there is still room for improvement. For example, education within prisons should ideally fall under the supervision of the Ministry of Education, Culture, and Science rather than the Ministry of Justice and Security (Annet Bakker, interview by author, January 12, 2022). In addition, the course schedule for education in a PI needs more flexibility and should not be dependent on the daily regimen of the prison (Annet Bakker, interview by author, January 12, 2022). As for resources, the absence of regular internet access for people detained in Dutch prisons makes it impossible to provide education and training related to a more advanced level of information and communications technology, also limiting the scope of job-training opportunities in this field. Finally, as for the education itself, more practical skill-based training must be started on day one of detention, and gaps in the levels among incarcerated people attending the same education program or course must be bridged.

Conclusion

Within the EU, the Dutch criminal justice system follows the guidelines outlined by the Council of Europe in 1989. As for the educational opportunities offered to detainees, the Dutch penal system incorporates education into its penitentiary regime by making basic education available and accessible to all detained people. It sees education as a direct means to reduce recidivism and prevent crime, and it uses education to facilitate reintegration within and beyond its prisons. It allows people in prison who take up this opportunity to cultivate a sense of achievement and hope for a successful transition back to normal life after serving their sentences, with the ultimate goal of securing a certificate or diploma for their first time in their lives. It permits incarcerated people to see what they can achieve during their detention through education and vocational training, potentially even encouraging them to continue after release. In a broader sense, the Dutch penal system focuses on offering people a second chance. The Dutch approach is to focus on the person rather than the crime, looking at the circumstances leading to criminal behaviors and addressing the core reason for any crimes committed. Importantly, the Dutch system is geared toward social inclusion rather than exclusion.

In closing, Dutch prisons are not designed to function merely as carceral facilities that separate or isolate criminal offenders from other citizens. The penal philosophy of "punish and protect" emphasizes the initial loss of freedom for anyone convicted of breaking laws as a form of punishment, but incarceration must eventually yield constructive results for both the public *and* for those behind bars. There is no question that incarceration must be designed to hold incarcerated people accountable for their wrongful behavior. Nevertheless, serving time in a Dutch PI also allows the state to offer people a chance to reset, to rebuild their lives, and to strive to become better citizens after being released from prisons and returning to the community from which they originally came.

Notes

The author would like to thank the following people for their contributions to this research: Annet Bakker (Dutch prison teacher for more than thirty years, former chair of the European Prison Education Association [EPEA] from 2015 to 2021, and current board member of the Dutch EPEA branch); Brigitte Verbeek (Head of Education and Re-integration training at PI Vught, the Netherlands); Jennifer Doekhie and Joni Reef (assistant professors of Criminology, Institute of Criminal Law and Criminology at Leiden University, the Netherlands, and teachers of a Criminology course entitled "Inside Out" at PI Heerhugowaard, in which twelve university students learn alongside ten detainees attending the course inside the prison facility); Nathalie van Erkelens (case manager, Department of Detention and Re-integration at PI Almelo, the Netherlands, who oversees about twenty-eight cases within PI Almelo); Annemiek Nauta (case manager, Department of Detention and Re-integration at PI Almelo, the Netherlands, who oversees about twenty-four cases within PI Almelo); Jan (J. G.) Konings (senior advisor, Team Detention and Re-integration, Prison System, Custodial Institutions Agency, Ministry of Justice and Security, the Netherlands); John Adema (advisor, Capacity Management/Division Individual Cases, Custodial Institutions Agency, Ministry of Justice and Security, the Netherlands); Ada Kos (senior communication advisor, Corporate Communication, Custodial Institutions Agency, Ministry of Justice and Security, the Netherlands); and Joost de Looff (advisor analysis, Policy Department, Custodial Institutions Agency, Department of Justice and Security, the Netherlands).

1. Within the Dutch criminal justice system, terms such as "inmates" or "prisoners" are rarely used. Instead, the preferred term is "detainees."

2. A PLUS program is a program that awards detainees who exhibit good behavior while serving a jail or prison term. Once included in a PLUS program, detainees can be granted extended visiting hours and more free time for sports, to name a few advantages. It is an initiative whereby detainees must behave in order to earn these additional privileges. But detainees can also lose these privileges whenever they break the rules (e.g., using soft drugs).

3. Interestingly, education opportunities are also made accessible for Dutch people incarcerated outside of the Netherlands, though this article did not include this group in the present research.

4. MIGMAG (metal inert gas/metal active gas) and TIG (tungsten inert gas) are different processes involved in welding.

Works Cited

Education and Re-Integration Unit, PI Vught. 2022. "Onderwijs: Diploma's en Certificaten (2021)."

European Union. 2000. "Charter of Fundamental Rights of the European Union." https://fra.europa.eu/en/eu-charter/article/14-right-education.

Krolak, Lisa. 2019. *Books beyond Bars: The Transformative Potential of Prison Libraries*. UNESCO Institute for Lifelong Learning. https://uil.unesco.org/literacy/vulnerable-groups/books-beyond-bars-transformative-potential-prison-libraries.

Mandela, Nelson. 1994. *Long Road to Freedom*. New York: Little, Brown, and
    Company.
Ministry of Justice and Security. 2020. "Re-Intergratie: Succesvolle terugkeer van
    gedetineerden in de maatschappij." https://dji.nl/documenten/publicaties
    /2020/03/01/infographic-re-integratie-2020.
Ministry of Justice and Security. 2021. "This Is the Custodial Institutions Agency
    (DJI) in Facts and Figures." https://dji.nl/documenten/publicaties/2020/09/25
    /this-is-the-custodial-institutions-agency-dji-2021.
Ministry of Justice and Security—Custodial Institutions Agency. 2016. "Vision on
    Education." Internal memo.
Netherlands Helsinki Committee. "Changing Landscapes: Prison Education
    Consortium Netherlands." Accessed April 6, 2022. https://nhc.nl/programmes
    /criminal-justice-reform/prison-reform-probation/changing-landscapes-prison
    -education-consortium-netherlands/.
Smith, Alan. 2019. "The European Union and Prison Education: A Historical Review
    of the First Two Decades." *European Commission*. https://epea.org/wp-content
    /uploads/Smith-Alan-The-EU-and-Prison-Education-A-historical-review.pdf/.
UNESCO Institute for Lifelong Learning. 2019. "13 October: International Day of
    Education in Prisons." https://uil.unesco.org/13-october-international-day
    -education-prisons.

LISE ØEN JONES,
TORFINN LANGELID, TERJE MANGER,
PAAL BREIVIK, AND ARVE ASBJØRNSEN

6 ||| EVALUATING EDUCATION IN NORWEGIAN PRISONS

RESEARCH-BASED APPROACHES

Introduction: Historical Background

The first Norwegian house of corrections was established in Trondheim around 1630 (Lie 1935). From the very beginning, education has been an important part of the Norwegian prison system. The industrialization of Europe in the eighteenth and nineteenth centuries led to social unrest and poverty, and the situation in Norway was no exception. Prisons and penitentiaries became religious institutions where incarcerated individuals, in addition to being punished, were to be improved through work, spiritual guidance, and education. The education system and the penal system were closely allied, and the carceral schools were seen as part of the rehabilitation process (Hauge 1996; Schanning 2007; Sellin 1944).

In 1841, a government report on prisons was published. The report was very critical of the prison system, finding current sanctions an insufficient deterrent to crime (Commission til at Meddele Betaenkning Angaaende Strafanstalternes Bedre Indretning 1841). The ensuing Criminal Act of 1842 was based on the American "Philadelphia model," the cornerstone of which is solitary confinement. Other key elements were work and orderly lifestyle, as well as religious and ethical education and upbringing. The first prison facility established on this model opened in 1851 and was the first prison in Norway to operate based on clearly defined objectives and with a true focus on its educational mission. This was the first attempt to use education as an instrument of prison corrections (Langelid 2015; Langelid et al. 2009). Prison schools did their best to align with the regular school system. Until the mid-twentieth century, the prison system was responsible for all aspects of carceral sentences, including education, health, and chaplaincy services, named the "self-supply model" (Christie 1970).

Prison Education in Norway

Within the constraints of the prison system, incarcerated people in Norway have the same right to services and opportunities and the same obligations and responsibilities as the population at large. The Education Act (Ministry of Education 1998 [2014]) guarantees incarcerated Norwegians access to education just as it does for other citizens and residents (§13-2a). This includes seven years of mandatory primary schooling (age six to thirteen), three years of mandatory lower secondary schooling (age thirteen to sixteen), and three to five years of upper secondary schooling (age sixteen to nineteen). Upper secondary school is not mandatory, but it is a legal right, after completion of which young people can apply for general studies or vocational studies.

Adults also have the right to supplementary basic education and/or special education. The average incarcerated person in Norway is male,[1] has an average age of thirty-four, and has completed approximately eleven years of total education. About two-thirds of the incarcerated population hold Norwegian citizenship. In the Norwegian correctional system, incarcerated people are registered according to their citizenship; ethnicity or race is not included in the register.

Correctional services in Norway have now adopted the "import model" (Christie 1970) for delivery of services to incarcerated people (i.e., educational services in prison are delivered using the established school system), which is described in detail later in the chapter. Since 2008, education and training have been provided in all Norwegian prisons. Pursuant to the Corrections Act, incarcerated people are required to participate in activities during their term of incarceration, and the three options offered are prison work, education, or treatment programs for addiction, sexual behavior, anger, or violence (Ministry of Justice and Public Security 2018).

Educational funding for incarcerated students is budgeted and granted on a separate item in the state budget for education. In 2022, the subsidy granted approximately $8,000 USD for every incarcerated individual. On average, this translates to approximately seven teachers per hundred incarcerated individuals (Ministry of Education 2001 [2021]). Data from 2021 reveal that almost half (47 percent) of incarcerated adults have completed lower secondary education as their highest education level, just over one-third (35 percent) have completed upper secondary education, and almost one-fifth (18 percent) have completed some higher education (including single subjects and grades) (Eikeland et al. 2022).

All Norwegian prisons have established educational programs at the mandatory and upper secondary levels, including a faculty of formally qualified teachers. Incarcerated individuals also have access to any education beyond upper secondary school. Granted, prison teachers themselves do not generally have the requisite qualifications for teaching and supervising at this level, but the incarcerated students can take part in distance education or can even be offered day release to participate in courses on a nearby campus.

Higher education can be challenging to complete from prison due to the digital gap between the demands from colleges and universities and what the correctional services allow. Data from Ole-Johan Eikeland and colleagues (2021) show that half of incarcerated adults in Norway participate in education in some form. One-third of the incarcerated adults are in upper secondary education, 5 percent are taking higher education, and almost one in ten (9 percent) are participating in courses. These can include single subjects related to the curricula in upper secondary school or shorter independent courses. To date, the focus of our work has mainly been on upper secondary education, due to a separate line item in the fiscal budget, and it involves a large majority of the incarcerated population. Further assistance for incarcerated adults through upper secondary education, however, has important consequences for employability and further vocational and academic training.

The Import Model

Interestingly, it was the prison service and not the educational authorities that pushed for young people serving terms of incarceration to be given an education on par with other young people. In the 1960s, Kåre Bødal, director of the Juvenile Prison, argued that the responsibility for education in prisons should be taken over by the educational authorities. Bødal convinced the prison service and the educational authorities that incarcerated Norwegians had the same right and duty to secure an education as other young people in society (Langelid 2017). The Ministry of Church and Education issued a circular in October 1969 on education for young people in the prison service's institutions to this effect as well (Ministry of Church and Education 1969).

In a simple, theoretical model, criminologist Nils Christie summed up the idea that services offered in free society should also be offered in the prison system. In 1969, he launched the aforementioned import model, a model that is still in use today. Christie argued that this model opens up the system by placing all service functions, such as providing health, educational, and other services for the incarcerated population, outside prisons and in the hands of the welfare state (Christie 1970).

However, while the model was proposed by a researcher and advocated for by bureaucrats, it did not gain political support. Though Bødal and Christie argued that the welfare state should also include incarcerated people, the reality was a system where the right to an education was part of the services offered by the welfare state, but where many incarcerated people were denied these services when the state did not allocate sufficient funds for education in prisons. Where education did exist, young people were given priority. The principle of normalization (i.e., organizing a daily routine in prison that reflects the society outside the wall as much as possible) is also underlined in the name of a parliamentary report on the Norwegian Correctional Services: "Punishment that works—less crime—a safer society" (Ministry of Justice and Police 2008).

Schools had a central place in the development of the import model, which would, in the 1980s and '90s, include librarians, cultural workers, chaplains, health personnel, and representatives from the employment service. The import model was designed to have a transformative effect on the development of correctional services in Norway. Administrative cooperation between welfare agencies is now enshrined in law and in circulars and agreements between the correctional services and the "imported" agencies.

There will always be the potential for conflict between the policies of the individual agencies and the overarching goals of the correctional services. Nevertheless, the imported services have found an established place in the mission of Norwegian Correctional Services, and incarcerated people have thereby been given greater access to the same services afforded to other citizens. It is probably correct to say, as Christie assumed, that the import model has opened up the prison system. The different welfare agencies that operate in free society, such as those responsible for library services and health care, deliver their services in prison every day. Around five hundred workers collaborate with correctional services and develop a mutual understanding of how they can fulfill incarcerated people's right to these services (Fridhov and Langelid 2017).

Nordic Cooperation

Nordic cooperation has led to mutual consolidation and strengthening of educational programs. In 1999, the Nordic Council[2] adopted a recommendation on education in prison from a Nordic perspective. It was a political initiative aimed at ensuring that people in prison in the Nordic countries could enjoy the same public services as other members of society (Langelid 2017; Langelid et al. 2009).

Today, all the Nordic countries have enshrined into law the principle that incarcerated people have the same right to education as other citizens. The ensuing focus has been on strengthening vocational training (including the use of digital tools in educational programs), a greater emphasis on creative subjects, more thorough integration of incarcerated people who have immigrated to Norway, and the initiation of Nordic research in the field of prison studies. Indeed, the research collaboration on education in prison in the Nordic context was a completely new phenomenon. In 2009, it led to the first ever Nordic survey (Eikeland, Manger, and Asbjørnsen 2009). That report then led to greater interest in the issue of education for incarcerated people from politicians, decision-makers, correctional officials, educational authorities, and the media.

Rights to Education for Incarcerated People

According to the import model, because incarcerated people in Norway have the same right to education as other citizens, they have access to primary, lower secondary, and three-year upper secondary schooling. This includes adults who have not finished primary or upper secondary school, an important consideration for prison education given that around two-thirds of the prison population in Norway is age twenty-five or older. In terms of law, the rights to education for incarcerated people are stated both in the Education Act (Ministry of Education 1998 [2020]) and in the Execution of Sentences Act (Ministry of Justice and Public Security 2001 [2021]). Importantly, incarcerated people are viewed as citizens of society with the same rights as other citizens, a significant contrast with the situation of incarcerated people in many other countries, including the United States.

The development of education in prisons has been influenced by conventions and recommendations from the Council of Europe and from

EU programs (Smith 2019). The Council of Europe's recommendations in *Education in Prison* (Council of Europe 1990) came to have a great influence on education in prisons in Norway and throughout Europe. The document contained seventeen recommendations and was used more or less as a textbook on how education in prisons should be organized in the different European countries. Key here is the overriding goal that education in prison should have the same status as education outside prison.

The EU has contributed to the development of education in prison in Europe through its education programs, and many schools have gained a new perspective on their own teaching, while at the same time offering partners new knowledge and competence (Langelid 2015, 320–28). According to the European Commission, various actors are responsible for providing education in prisons. In many countries, the ministries of education and justice take the lead. In addition, voluntary organizations offer education and training, and EU-funded projects play an important role in securing resources for organizing and implementing education in prison (Hawley, Murphy, and Souto-Otero 2012). Not all countries have a statutory right to education in prison, as exists in the Nordic countries. The European Convention on Human Rights (article 2) states, "No person shall be denied the right to education" (Council of Europe 1950). The problem is that while the members of the Council of Europe have signed the European Convention for the Protection of Human Rights, not all of them enforce it.

Rights of Incarcerated Noncitizens

One-third of the prison population in Norway are from countries other than Norway, and these noncitizens have the same right to education as Norwegians. This is especially important to note at a time when a recent report from the EU points out that the prison systems of Europe are in crisis (Hawley, Murphy, and Souto-Otero 2012). The prison population in the twenty-seven member states comprises 640,000 people and the capacity utilization is 105 percent. In a Nordic context, the capacity utilization is often around 85–90 percent. Many people enter prison with a poor education, and that lack of qualifications makes it difficult for them to find a job or a place in further education upon release.

Linda Gröning (2014) states that national and international laws contain a general prohibition against discrimination, whereby everyone—including incarcerated people serving a sentence in a Norwegian prison—shall have equal access to education. Furthermore, as a human right, access to education applies to everyone, including those serving a prison sentence, irrespective of nationality (Gröning 2014). The number of incarcerated people in Nordic prisons from other countries has been increasing rapidly, posing several major linguistic, cultural, and social challenges.

Nordic researchers conducted a survey on this issue, interviewing people from Somalia, Russia, Poland, Iraq, and Serbia who were being incarcerated in Nordic countries. As a whole, the incarcerated individuals of foreign nationality were motivated by the opportunity for education and training. Nevertheless, the survey found that they were often not aware of their rights. The final report contains a number of recommendations for improving the situation of foreign incarcerated people in Nordic prisons, as they were shown to experience many barriers to gaining an education (Westrheim and Manger 2013).

Though the Ministry of Education and Research stated in its ensuing white paper, "The Ministry favors guaranteeing the right to education and training for foreign prisoners, so that they are better able to continue their education or work in their native countries" (2007, 39), some problems arose concerning the universal right to education. For example, despite the clarity found in international law and in much of Norwegian national law, the Education Act states that the right to education is contingent upon the applicant having legal residence in the country. This condition applies both to youth and adults. Høstmælingen and colleagues (2013) and Gröning (2014) state that, based on the source statutes, "there is no basis for claiming that Norway is bound by criminal law to ensure a certain level of educational provision for either adult prisoners or for prisoners who are to be deported after serving their sentences" (Høstmælingen, Steen, and Kjeldegaard-Peders 2013, 183; Gröning 2014). Instead, they both refer to the principle of nondiscrimination.

The question is "whether it is lawful under the provisions relating to the right to education to treat foreign prisoners who are to be deported from Norway after serving their sentences differently from Norwegian prisoners. Pursuant to the European Convention on Human Rights, it is, in principle, unlawful to discriminate between people in comparable situations based on nationality" (Høstmælingen, Steen, and Kjeldegaard-Peders 2013, 15–16; see also Gröning 2014, 183–88). The principal argument for the import model in 1969 was that incarcerated people should not forfeit their civil rights. As a human right, the right to education applies to everyone, including those serving a prison sentence and irrespective of nationality (Høstmælingen 2004, 311).

White Paper 2004–2005 on Education in Prison

In light of the research-based evaluation, the government presented a white paper on education in prison in 2005 (Ministry of Education and Research 2005). This is the first ever white paper in this field, and it is unique in the European context. It is a sign that the education in correctional services is now on an equal footing with other areas of the welfare society. The white paper highlighted the right to education for incarcerated people, and, in addition to the Education Act and the Execution of Sentences Act, referred to international conventions and recommendations such as Article 2 of the First Protocol of the European Convention on Human Rights, the UN International Covenant on Economic, Social, and Cultural Rights, and two recommendations from the Council of Europe: *Education in Prison* (1990) and *The European Prison Rules* (2006).

Strategies for Highlighting Education in Prisons

A focus on information was and still is an important strategy for drawing attention to education in prisons. Myriad conferences have been held bringing together correctional services, educational authorities, and other relevant agencies represented. Irritation and discord were gradually replaced by understanding between the different personnel groups. A circular entitled the "Circular on Administrative Cooperation Between the Education and Training Sector and the Norwegian Correctional Services" (Ministry of Justice and Police and Ministry of Education and Research 2008) played an important part in the normalization process and in clarifying the rights of incarcerated citizens. This circular is based on the principle that incarcerated people have the same rights and duties as the rest of the population. The circular identifies who is responsible for the different areas at national, regional, and local levels.[3]

Another strategy was research and evaluation. In this area, the county governor of Hordaland managed to secure a research and development agreement with the Bergen Cognition and Learning Group at the University of Bergen, which, together with educational consultants at Eikeland Research and Education, have carried out surveys of the prison population's educational background, needs, and wishes since 2003. During its consideration of the national budget for 1998, the Storting, Norway's parliament, requested that the government take the initiative on a research-based evaluation of education in prison. The evaluation covered a broad area: education for women, education for minority language speakers, and education for incarcerated people serving short sentences, as well as an evaluation of how well the public administration worked in this field at the central, regional, and local levels. All the reports were sent to those involved in correctional services, to the Storting and to Nordic partners. A summary report was also sent to all the ministries of education and ministries of justice in Europe (County Governor of Hordaland 2005).

A third strategy involved experimental and developmental work. Several national projects in this area were initiated to follow up the white paper. One innovative project involved validation of the prior educational attainment of incarcerated people. This validation is important for the prison population, as many of them do not have formal certification of competence, but they do have know-how that they have picked up in the "school of life." Another project involved further developing cooperation between the schools and vocational workshops of prisons in Norway. Workshops have long been the most important activity offered by correctional services. More apprenticeship contracts within vocational training have been completed, and more incarcerated people have taken craft certificate exams and practical training.

Yngve Mathisen's cookbook *Ærlig mat i Halden fengsel* (Decent food in Halden Prison) (2012) is a good example of strong cooperation between schools and workshops in prison. Sixteen incarcerated people, five teachers, and two workshop officers took part in the project. One of the students even translated the book into English. A third edition of the book has now been printed, bringing the total print run to thirty-five hundred, and it has received excellent reviews in food magazines. At the incarcerated people's request, part of the profits go to the Wayback Foundation, which is dedicated to ensuring that formerly incarcerated people can live a life without crime, drug abuse, or alcohol abuse after their release.

Norwegian research has shown that incarcerated people are interested in education (Eikeland, Manger, and Asbjørnsen 2013; Manger, Eikeland, and Asbjørnsen 2013). They see education as important when it comes to coping with life and changing their future. For some incarcerated people, education in prison has helped give them a new voice—a voice that has been liberating in a system otherwise characterized by control.

Research on Prison Education by the Bergen Cognition and Learning Group

As previously mentioned, since 2003 the Bergen Cognition and Learning Group, located at the University of Bergen, has conducted research on prison education in Norway. This research program has had three strands. The first has been assessment of needs and wishes for education among the incarcerated population in Norway, as well as how the available programs have been designed to meet these needs and priorities. The second strand has focused on challenges that incarcerated people face regarding education, such as reasons for pursuing education, maintaining academic motivation, and overcoming barriers to education in the prison context. The third strand has been further analysis of vulnerable groups, such as incarcerated students with learning impairments, young incarcerated persons, incarcerated women, and those with foreign citizenship. Here, we discuss strands one and two in more detail.

Strand One: Assessment of Needs and Wishes for Education

The first strand of this important research agenda has had a clear focus on the analysis of needs and desires for education among the people incarcerated in Norway (Eikeland, Manger, and Asbjørnsen 2010, 2013, 2016; Eikeland, Manger, and Diseth 2006; Eikeland and Manger 2004). The prison population in Norway is rather small compared to many other countries, with an average total prison population of 3,646 (Kriminalomsorgen 2020) and an annual incarceration total of approximately 12,500. Sentences are also rather short, and up until 2016 the average sentence was approximately 101 days. After the introduction of electronic control (e.g., ankle monitors) for the least serious crimes—those with sentences of less than six months—the average time served in prisons has actually increased.

The first survey, conducted in 2003, documented a lack of access to education resources in thirteen of the forty-seven prison institutions in Norway, in addition to a substantial deficit in education level among the incarcerated adults. The highest level of education completed was comparable to what was seen in the general population approximately thirty years earlier, and the general increase in competence building in the community at large had not benefited the incarcerated population. This assessment resulted in a political initiative to ensure educational access to all prisons in Norway. Due to the previously discussed import model (Christie 1970)—where the responsibility for providing services to the incarcerated was delegated to local school authorities under the direct supervision of the county governor in Hordaland County—there was already an organization for effective implementation of the new system. With a visible line item in the fiscal budget earmarked for prison education, access to education was established rather quickly.

Later surveys in 2005 and 2007 documented that a large segment of the incarcerated population expressed a desire for vocational programs in their upper secondary school programs, as well as vocational continuing education for those enrolled in academic programs (Eikeland, Manger, and Diseth 2006). Because they demand fewer resources, academic programs had been prioritized. This deficit was addressed later, but resource-intensive programs (those requiring access to advanced workshops and specially qualified teaching personnel) will only be available for a small number of students.

Motivation for Education

People's motives for education in prison are formed through reflections about the future and a desire to better cope with life after release (Manger et al. 2010). In our first studies of incarcerated persons' motives for starting an education, three motive categories were identified: 1) future planning, 2) social reasons and escapism, and 3) competence building (i.e., learning for the sake of learning). The first factor, future planning, explained more than the two other factors combined (Manger, Eikeland, and Asbjørnsen 2013; Roth and Manger 2014). This factor and the third motive category stem from clear educational intentions—in contrast to the second one, which is rooted in social reasons (i.e., being with others) or a need to get away from something less attractive, such as prison work and prison routines. No significant difference in scores was found between respondents with low and high levels of education on the future planning factor, which demonstrates an external motivation, but those with a relatively high level of education were more motivated than others to acquire knowledge and skills, reflecting an intrinsic motivation.

In a later study that included everyone enrolled in education programs in Norwegian prisons, researchers explored incarcerated adults' academic motivation structure from the theoretical perspective of self-determination theory (SDT). Data analyses supported that a five-factor model—including intrinsic motivation, three types of extrinsic motivation (identified regulation, introjected regulation, and external regulation), and amotivation—yielded the best fit with the data provided by incarcerated people (Manger et al. 2020). SDT suggests that incarcerated students who are intrinsically motivated are not only acting autonomously but also participating in education because it is interesting or fun. In contrast, extrinsic motivation means that the activity is instrumentally important to personal goals and identities. Incarcerated students in this study who exhibited all three forms of extrinsic motivation were acting under a high or moderate level of external pressure.

Incarcerated students may deviate from traditional students in some ways, but not to such a degree that would necessitate an alternative conceptualization of academic motivation. Indeed, they describe their motivations according to the conceptual structure of the model. The studies also found that incarcerated people from Norway (Manger, Eikeland, and Asbjørnsen 2016) and from other countries such as Albania, Poland, and Lithuania (Eikeland, Manger, and Asbjørnsen 2017) who participated in education in Norwegian prisons had a relatively high score on both intrinsic motivation and all three forms of extrinsic motivation.

Although extrinsic motivation refers to the performance of an activity for instrumental reasons, a large body of empirical evidence suggests that both intrinsic motivation and autonomous types of extrinsic motivation are associated with successful outcomes (e.g., Carasoli, Nicklin, and Ford 2014). In the perspective of SDT (Ryan and Deci 2000), the Prison and Probation Service and the school inside each prison are required to ensure that ideal environmental factors develop and do not undermine students' internal and external academic motivation.

Strand Two: Challenges to Education in Prison

The average person incarcerated in Norway terminated their formal education after the first year in upper secondary education, or high school. Approximately one in four has reading and spelling impairments, one in three report signs and symptoms that correspond to a diagnosis of attention-deficit and hyperactivity disorder (ADHD), and one in nine of those serving longer sentences (secure remand) has been found to have serious cognitive developmental impairments (Søndenaa et al. 2008).

Formal Education and School History for Learners in Prison

Just about one in three incarcerated adults have completed the Norwegian equivalent of high school. The school system in Norway is regulated according to the Educational Act (Ministry of Education 1998 [2020]), which requires ten years of mandatory education (primary school and lower secondary school), starting at age six, and continuing with three years of voluntary upper secondary education. Although the three years of upper secondary education are voluntary, this is an entitled and free right that has been established as a norm for young people and which forms the basis for vocational training or serves as preparatory school for college and university training. Following the secondary school reform that was initiated in 1994, approximately three out of four Norwegians complete secondary education before the age of twenty-five. In addition, roughly one in three has graduated from or taken at least some college or university coursework. However, an estimated 5 percent have not completed any formal education that can be documented and thus have not completed the mandatory first ten years in public school (Statistisk sentralbyrå 2017).

By comparison, half of the incarcerated adults reported completing the tenth grade of obligatory education as their highest formal education, about one in three has completed upper secondary school, and roughly one in seven has completed some higher education. Most striking, perhaps, is that approximately one in ten has not completed *any* formal education (Eikeland, Manger, and Asbjørnsen 2013, 2016; Eikeland, Manger, and Diseth 2006). Thus, the average incarcerated student shows a formal educational level comparable to Norway writ large in the 1970s.

Reading and Spelling Impairments

As a part of the ongoing evaluation of the prison education programs in Norway, we have been monitoring participants' self-reporting of reading and spelling skills, as well as their self-reports of reading and spelling impairments. The findings have been quite stable; approximately one in four have reported that they experience reading and spelling issues. However, we have also noted that it seems to be easier to report reading and spelling problems of this kind if there is a moderated alternative to dichotomous yes/no questions, and in later studies we have applied three- to five-point scales to address these issues[4] (see, for example, Asbjørnsen et al. 2014a, 2017; Asbjørnsen, Jones, and Manger 2008; Asbjørnsen, Manger, and Jones 2007).

In 2007, we conducted a research project regarding reading and spelling skills among incarcerated people in Norway (Jones 2012), where we also had the opportunity to screen for reading impairments in a subsample of the participants. In general, the prevalence of illiteracy was low, and although technical reading skills were established, they were found to be immature and essentially comparable to what is normally seen in seventh grade in Norway. They did show lower scores on reading comprehension compared to what could be estimated from their reading speed, and the reading scores were mostly associated with attention skills more than with a phonological deficit.

In addition to readings skills, the test battery included word decoding, nonsense words, and orthographic skill through word dictation and proof-reading exercises. On all these tests, the mean scores were low and equivalent to a standard deviation of approximately 1.5 below average compared to the norm group, which included students in their first year in higher education (Strømsø et al. 1997). However, self-reported data also disclosed that the participants estimated their reading skills to be above average and comparable to what is reported among undergraduate students. Moreover, very few of the incarcerated participants reported "large difficulties" in comparison to difficulties "to some extent" (Jones et al. 2011).

Not reporting a high degree of difficulty despite the low scores of their overall mean test results may be explained by the incarcerated person's frame of reference. If they find reading the headline of a newspaper sufficient, they may not perceive their reading skills as low. Furthermore, how the incarcerated participants perceive their difficulties may also be influenced by whom they compare themselves with. According to Leon Festinger (1954), the academic self-concept is formed when people compare their own level of achievement with the achievement of others in their comparison group.

Attention Deficits and Hyperactivity

Attention-deficit and hyperactivity disorder (ADHD) is a formal diagnosis of a neurocognitive deficit with a childhood onset (DSM-V/ICD-10). Symptoms cluster around lack of impulse control, impaired attention and distractibility, emotional lability, and agitated behavior and hyperactivity. The prevalence estimates of this disorder in the general population across countries varies between 2.5 and 17.8 percent in children. The symptoms seem to decline with age, but about half of those will have persisting symptoms into adulthood (Skounti, Philalithis, and Galanakis 2007). Internationally (Appelbaum 2008; Dalteg, Gustafsson, and Levander 1998; Eme 2008; Farooq et al. 2016; Ginsberg, Hirvikoski, and Lindefors 2010; Gudjonsson et al. 2009; Gunter et al. 2008; Lahey et al. 2002; Román-Ithier et al. 2017; Rösler et al. 2004), as well as nationally (Asbjørnsen et al. 2014b, 2017; Asbjørnsen, Manger, and Eikeland 2015; Brevik et al. 2020; Rasmussen, Almvik, and Levander 2001), many studies have concluded that the prevalence of ADHD is markedly increased in many incarcerated populations (Young et al. 2015).

As a result of our research, we have identified a few screening tools that seem to be working well in identifying and studying the prevalence of ADHD among the incarcerated. For several studies, we have been using either the short form of the Wender Utah Rating Scale (WURS-25) (Retz-Junginger et al. 2002; Rösler et al. 2004) or the Adult Self-Report ADHD-Scale (ASRS) (Kessler et al. 2005, 2007) as part of our questionnaire surveys among the incarcerated adults in Norway. The short form of the WURS consists of twenty-five questions where the respondents answer the items with reference to behavior as a child in school. The results show good compliance with a clinical diagnosis of ADHD (Retz-Junginger et al. 2002) as a retrospective assessment of early starting symptomatology.[5]

In our studies among incarcerated adults in Norway, approximately one in three people show signs equivalent to ADHD either on the WURS-25 or the ASRS. This is important information for the planning of educational activities and for counseling programs in prison. However, it should be noted that the symptoms described as ADHD, in an incarcerated sample, may also be a consequence of several other conditions that may be frequently seen among incarcerated adults. Emotional problems and depressive conditions, for example, can often manifest in agitated behavior and restlessness, impaired concentration skills, and emotional lability, particularly in men, and may occasionally be mistaken as symptoms of ADHD (Möller-Leimkühler et al. 2004; Zierau et al. 2002). Minor head trauma and mild traumatic brain injuries may also give similar symptomatology, as well as drug abuse and, ironically, abstinence from drug abuse. The cause of the symptoms may not be vital for the educator, but the consequent effects on the incarcerated student can be valuable to consider when planning educational curricula or activities.

Research-Based Tools for Assessment and Counseling: Self-Report Instruments

The Norwegian version of the self-report instrument Adult Reading Questionnaire (ARQ), developed by Margaret Snowling and colleagues (2012), has been used in national surveys in Norway since 2015. The ARQ as a screening procedure was devised to identify poor reading and writing skills, as well as word-finding problems and common signs associated with dyslexia, without leaning solely on the phonological skills as a core deficit in reading difficulties (Smythe and Everatt 2001; Snowling et al. 2012; Vellutino et al. 2004). Other aspects embedded in the questionnaire are literacy, language skills, and organizational skills, as ADHD is often reported as a comorbid condition with reading impairments (Snowling et al. 2012). The questions in the scale are related to how difficulties appear to those who have such difficulties. In addition to questions about reading and writing, it also includes questions concerning attention. Four of the questions are control questions, one of which provides a definition of dyslexia and then asks "Do you think you have such difficulties?" The authors of this study reported good psychometric properties of the scale and decent predictive properties, as the questions at large could be used to identify adults at risk of dyslexia in a normative sample.

One of our main questions was whether a translated checklist could also be used in a language with very different orthography compared to English. Due to the transparent orthography of Norwegian, we would expect that more reading-impaired adults have developed compensatory reading and writing strategies. Accordingly, we included the ARQ in a survey study on incarcerated adults, and we experienced that we were able to collect good-quality normative data on the ARQ. Basically, the psychometric properties of the questionnaire were equal to what was published by Snowling and colleagues (2012) but with a few exceptions, which could be related to an increased prevalence of signs of ADHD among the incarcerated adults that were not seen in a normative community-based sample (Asbjørnsen et al. 2016). When we repeated the study among undergraduate students who were not incarcerated (Asbjørnsen et al. 2021), the factor solution was nearly identical to what was reported in the study by Snowling and colleagues (2012). As a result of this research, a new screening tool for reading impairments is available for educators working in prisons, one that is easy to use and gives meaningful information for application in counseling and educational planning during incarceration and for transfer to educational programs outside prison following release.

Barriers to Education and Practical Implications

In a lifelong learning perspective, perceived barriers to education during incarceration can be crucial for incarcerated people's reintegration. In her seminal work *Adults as Learners* (1981), K. Patricia Cross suggests that obstacles or barriers to education can be classified under three headlines: institutional, situational, and dispositional. Institutional barriers are policies, procedures, or exclusion criteria that systematically disadvantage certain groups of people. Situational barriers are those that arise from one's situation in life at any given point, such as family life and physical environment at a particular time. Dispositional barriers are related to the attitudes and self-perceptions about oneself as a learner (e.g., reading and writing problems).

Although our assessments have contributed to the political initiative to ensure access to education in all prisons in Norway, every prison has a highly diverse population, which must be considered when educational activities are being organized. Findings from the parts of the studies applying to incarcerated persons who were not participating in educational activities indicate that there are a number of factors preventing them from becoming involved. Our own analyses revealed barriers such as lack of information about educational opportunities, substandard practical arrangements, and inadequate access to software and the internet, which were collectively categorized under the first main factor: institutional barriers.

A second set of barriers reflected an assessment of the individual's general situation or environment, which is consistent with the concept of situational barriers: the idea that education is not worth the effort in the present situation or that it will not lead to a better life following release. Finally, dispositional barriers, resulting from the individual's difficulties in reading and writing or mathematics, or lack of concentration, also surfaced (Manger, Eikeland, and Asbjørnsen 2019).

In comparison with individuals pursuing an education in the outside community, the institutional barrier of inadequate access to computer equipment and the internet places incarcerated people at a competitive disadvantage. Thus, the conflict between essential prison security routines and the need of incarcerated persons to use computer equipment in their studies must be resolved. Among the inadequate practical arrangements that constitute an institutional barrier, there is also the fact that the Norwegian Correctional Services may transfer someone to another prison in the middle of an educational situation or just before an exam, leading to an interrupted or aborted educational program. The criminal administration system and the schools themselves must ensure that incarcerated persons are allowed to complete the education program they are undertaking. If we take seriously the Norwegian criminal justice administration's ambition that the day of release starts on the day of imprisonment (Ministry of Justice and Public Security 2017), every incarcerated person should be offered a career plan developed in cooperation with a career counselor. The aim should be to evaluate the skills of every incarcerated individual serving a short sentence and then draw up a plan that would also motivate incarcerated students to continue with education or work after release.

It is a matter of concern that so many young incarcerated persons come to prison needing basic compulsory education, especially upper secondary education. Among the characteristics of the prison system is that it places humans in a situation associated with uncertainty about their detention situation and future. Dorien Brosens and colleagues (2015) found that incarcerated people in Belgium who do not participate in vocational orientation programs are particularly confronted with situational barriers, which, according to the authors, include that they may have just arrived in prison or that they do not know when they will be released.

Many people incarcerated in Norway serve short sentences of under four months, with the consequent paradox that the very fact of a short sentence becomes a barrier to participation in education. A short sentence can perversely become a stepping stone to further criminality, especially for young people who do not receive their entitled access to mastery experiences in school or work during incarceration. Thus, it is important to ensure from the start of incarceration that every person can gain new skills through education or other activities, and that ongoing educational programs should not be interrupted by imprisonment. This will require close collaboration with the school system from which the persons have come and to which they will be returning after release.

The high prevalence rates of reading, writing, and mathematics difficulties among incarcerated people suggest that these may be the most important dispositional barriers to study (Jones et al. 2012; Manger, Eikeland, and Asbjørnsen 2019). Younger persons are more likely to perceive dispositional barriers compared to other groups. One explanation may be that younger students have more recent experiences of failure in school, which has influenced their perceptions. Likewise, incarcerated persons with no formal education at all perceived more dispositional barriers than the other groups. This may partly reflect that learning difficulties may have been a cause of a lack of previous education. Research indicates that reading disabilities among incarcerated people are often primarily environmental- and experience-based (Samuelsson, Herkner, and Lundberg 2003), which highlights the importance of education in prison to help with these problems, through efforts such as good library services and general access to literature.

In the end, it is the criminal administration system that is responsible for carrying out a sentence involving the loss of freedom, while the educational system is responsible for providing the education to which those who are incarcerated have a legal right. However, in the meeting of the two systems, situations can arise that are detrimental to high-quality education. For example, there seems to be a move toward a tightening of security in prison by correctional services (Norwegian Correctional Service 2020). One of the arguments made is that this is a necessary move because of changes in the prison population. There are, for example, more sentences being carried out in the community (e.g., with ankle monitors), and the population that opted for these measures is among the segment with few or no security issues. The consequence is a point of view aiming to strengthen security measures.

During the same period, more complex and streamlined approaches within different educational programs have been developed nationally. These approaches are strongly supported by different web-based resources. The changes, based either on the law regarding the execution of sentences or on the educational act, are not proportional. Accordingly, we can forecast at least two diverging developments. First, there may be a gap within education for incarcerated people who do not meet the standards developing within mainstream education. This will create obstacles for the newly educated when it comes to meeting the demands of school and work life, putting them at a competitive disadvantage when released. The second development is potentially more positive. Responsible parties will invest in technical solutions that give learners access to mainstream educational tools. Such an improvement will give the newly released job applicant and education seeker better opportunities.

Education and prison are ruled under different laws, but the criminal administration system and the educational authorities must, as much as possible, work toward eliminating the disparity between traditional educational programs and programs offered for incarcerated students. Both systems should also cooperate with various authorities in the community with a view toward facilitating the transition between prison and the community, helping incarcerated individuals draw up and implement their plans.

Through years of focusing on incarcerated students' needs and learning challenges, the awareness of the need for increased competence among teachers and prison staff has also evolved. In collaboration with the County Governor of Vestland, our research group established a continuing education course titled "Correctional Education as Learning Environment." How incarcerated people's educational needs are met and how teachers motivate them may be factors that influence their choice in educational activity. Especially when incarcerated students participate despite their reading and spelling difficulties, robust support from teachers and adequate educational activity are important factors.

Conclusion

Dissemination of our research includes several measures proposed since the national surveys were first completed in 2004. The practical implications of the research include better coherence between educational needs and available programs, increased awareness of the individual educational needs of the incarcerated adults, continuing higher education programs for teachers and policymakers, and continuing political focus on the issue. In addition to publishing academic papers, we have also written research reports for practitioners in the correctional field and policymakers after every survey. Moreover, the Bergen Cognition and Learning Group has presented research data at national and international conferences and workshops. Through our research work, we have developed a new screening tool for reading impairments available to educators working in prisons.[6] The tool is easy to use and gives meaningful information for counseling and educational planning during incarceration and for transfer to educational programs outside of prison following release.

Incarcerated students' reading and writing difficulties indicate that one should aim for a systematic approach to screening procedures to uncover their difficulties. This may contribute to a more research-based practice that can help administrators plan for effective educational programs in line with the needs of incarcerated people, and it may also develop a common frame of reference for teachers in charge of such testing. In addition, systematic standardized testing may also increase visibility of incarcerated people's levels of reading and writing skills. Consequently, this may affect the allocation of resources for education in prison. Strengthening reading and writing skills may have positive implications for their ability to continue their education. It may also have implications for motivation to participate in educational programs during incarceration and for planning future steps toward increased competence after release.

Notes

1. Men make up 95 percent of the prison population in Norway.

2. The Nordic Council is the official body for formal interparliamentary cooperation. Formed in 1952, it has eighty-seven members from Denmark, Finland, Iceland, Norway, Sweden, the Faroe Islands, Greenland, and Åland (norden.org).

3. The circular is now being revised, because it needs to be clearer and strengthen the tasks for both the correctional services and the school authorities.

4. "Not at all" or "never occurring" to "serious problem" or "always."

5. The ASRS has been developed by the World Health Organization as a screening tool for ADHD in adults. The short form consists of six questions focusing on the main symptoms as they appear in established diagnostic manuals. The responses show high concordance rates with clinically diagnosed ADHD in adults (Brevik et al. 2020; Kessler et al. 2007), confirming that it is a valid and reliable screening tool.

6. Norwegian version of ARQ.

Works Cited

Appelbaum, Kenneth L. 2008. "Assessment and Treatment of Correctional Inmates with ADHD." *American Journal of Psychiatry* 165 (12): 1520–24. http://psychiatryonline.org/data/Journals/AJP/3877/08aj1520.pdf/.

Asbjørnsen, Arve E., Lise Ø. Jones, and Terje Manger. 2008. *Innsatte i Bergen fengsel: Delrapport 3: Leseferdigheter og grunnleggende kognitive ferdigheter*. Fylkesmannen i Hordaland. https://oppikrim.no/siteassets/dokument/publikasjonar/delrapport -3-2009.pdf/.

Asbjørnsen, Arve E., Lise Ø. Jones, Ole-Johan Eikeland, and Terje Manger. 2016. "Spørreskjema om voksnes lesing (SLV) som screeninginstrument for leseferdigheter : erfaringer fra bruk i en surveyundersøkelse blant norske innsatte." *Norsk tidsskrift for logopedi* 62 (3): 14–25. http://norsklogopedlag.no /tidsskriftet.

Asbjørnsen, Arve E., Lise Ø. Jones, Terje Manger, and Ole-Johan Eikeland. 2021. "Can a Questionnaire Be Useful for Assessing Reading Skills in Adults? Experiences with the Adult Reading Questionnaire among Incarcerated and Young Adults in Norway." *Education Sciences* 11 (4): 154.

Asbjørnsen, Arve E., Terje Manger, and Lise Ø. Jones. 2007. *Leseferdigheter og lesevansker.* Fylkesmannen i Hordaland (Bergen). https://oppikrim.no/siteassets /dokument/publikasjonar/delrapport-1-2007.pdf/.

Asbjørnsen, Arve E., Terje Manger, and Ole-Johan Eikeland. 2015. "Symptoms of ADHD Are Related to Education and Work Experience among Incarcerated Adults." *Journal of Prison Education and Reentry* 2 (1): 18–30.

Asbjørnsen, Arve E., Terje Manger, Lise Ø. Jones, and Ole-Johan Eikeland. 2014a. *Norske innsatte: Lesevansker og oppmerksomhetsvansker.* Fylkesmannen i Hordaland (Bergen: Fylkesmannen i Hordaland). https://oppikrim.no/siteassets /dokument/publikasjonar/rapport-2-2014.pdf/.

Asbjørnsen, Arve E., Terje Manger, Lise Ø. Jones, and Ole-Johan Eikeland. 2014b. *Norske innsatte: Lesevansker og oppmerksomhetsvansker.* Fylkesmannen i Hordaland.

Asbjørnsen, Arve E., Terje Manger, Lise Ø. Jones, and Ole-Johan Eikeland. 2017. *Norske innsatte: Kartlegging av lesevansker og oppmerksomhetsvansker 2015.* Utdanningsavdelinga, Fylkesmannen i Hordaland (Bergen). https://oppikrim.no /siteassets/dokument/publikasjonar/rapport-2-2017.pdf/.

Brevik, Erlend Joramo, Astri J. Lundervold, Jan Haavik, and Maj-Britt Posserud. 2020. "Validity and Accuracy of the Adult Attention-Deficit/Hyperactivity Disorder (ADHD) Self-Report Scale (ASRS) and the Wender Utah Rating Scale (WURS) Symptom Checklists in Discriminating between Adults with and without ADHD." *Brain and Behavior* 10 (6).

Brosens, Dorien, Liebeth De Donder, Sarah Dury, and Dominique Verté. 2015. "Barriers to Participation in Vocational Orientation Programmes among Prisoners." *Journal of Prison Education and Reentry* 2 (2): 4–18.

Carasoli, Christopher P., Jessica M. Nicklin, and Michael T. Ford. 2014. "Intrinsic Motivation and Extrinsic Incentive Jointly Predict Performance: A 40-Year Meta-analysis." *Psychological Bulletin* 140 (4): 980–1008.

Christie, Nils. 1970. "Modeller for fengselsorganisasjonen" [Prison organization models]. In *I stedet for fengsel,* edited by Rita Østensen, 70–78. Oslo: Pax forlag.

Commission til at Meddele Betaenkning Angaaende Strafanstalternes Bedre Indretning. 1841. Beretning om Beskaffenheden af Norges Strafanstalter og Fangepleie samt Betaekning og *Indstilling om en Reform i begge, efter fremmede Staters Mönster / afgivne af den under 10 Septbr. 1837 nedsatte Commission til at meddele Betaenkning angaaende Strafanstalternes bedre Indretning m. V.* Christiania: Chr. Grøndahl.

Council of Europe. 1950. "Convention for the Protection of Human Rights and Fundamental Freedoms." Council of Europe Treaty Series 005. http://conventions .coe.int/Treaty/EN/Treaties/html/005.htm.

Council of Europe. 1990. *Education in Prison. Recommendation no. R (89) 12 Adopted by the Committee of Ministers of the Council of Europe on 13 October 1989 and Explanatory Memorandum. Legal Affairs.* Strasbourg: Council of Europe.

Council of Europe. 2006. *European Prison Rules.* Council of Europe Publishing.

County Governor of Hordaland. 2005. *Research-based evaluation of education in Norwegian prisons. Recommendations from the group nominated to monitor the evaluation of education in Norwegians prisons. Report no. 1.* (Bergen).

Cross, K. Patricia. 1981. *Adults as Learners: Increasing Participation and Facilitating Learning.* San Francisco, CA: Jossey-Bass.

Dalteg, Arne, Per Gustafsson, and Sten Levander. 1998. "Hyperaktivitetssyndrom vanligt bland interner: ADHD inte bara en barnpsykiatrisk diagnos" [Hyperactivity syndrome is common among prisoners: ADHD not only a pediatric psychiatric diagnosis]. *Läkartidningen* 95 (26–27): 3078–80. https://lakartidningen.se/wp-content/uploads/OldPdfFiles/1998/17933.pdf/.

Eikeland, Ole-Johan, and Terje Manger, eds. 2004. *Evaluering av fengselsundervisninga, Kompendium med oppsummeringskapitla frå forskingsrapportane Fylkesmannen i Hordaland, Utdanningsavdelinga, Evaluering av fengselsundervisninga.* Bergen: Fylkesmannen i Hordaland.

Eikeland, Ole-Johan, Terje Manger, and Åge Diseth. 2006. *Utdanning, utdanningsønske og rett til opplæring.* Fylkesmannen i Hordaland (Bergen, Norge). https://oppikrim.no/siteassets/dokument/publikasjonar/utdanningskvalitet-laringstrategier-og-motivasjon.pdf/.

Eikeland, Ole-Johan, Terje Manger, and Arve E. Asbjørnsen, eds. 2009. *Education in Nordic Prisons: Prisoners' Educational Background, Preferences, and Motivation.* English ed. Vol. 508, TemaNord. Copenhagen: Nordic Council of Ministers.

Eikeland, Ole-Johan, Terje Manger, and Arve E. Asbjørnsen, eds. 2010. *Innsette i norske fengsel: Kompetanse gjennom utdanning og arbeid.* Fylkesmannen i Hordaland. https://oppikrim.no/siteassets/dokument/publikasjonar/rapport-1-2010-kompetanse-gjennom-utdanning-og-arbeid-fmho.pdf/.

Eikeland, Ole-Johan, Terje Manger, and Arve E. Asbjørnsen, eds. 2013. *Nordmenn i fengsel: Utdanning, arbeid og kompetanse.* Fylkesmannen i Hordaland, Utdanningsavdelinga (Bergen). https://oppikrim.no/siteassets/dokument/publikasjonar/rapport-3-2013.pdf/.

Eikeland, Ole-Johan, Terje Manger, and Arve E. Asbjørnsen, eds. 2016. *Norske innsette: Utdanning, arbeid, ønske og planar.* Fylkesmannen i Hordaland (Bergen: Utdaningsavdelinga Fylkesmannen i Hordaland). https://oppikrim.no/siteassets/dokument/publikasjonar/rapport-2-2016.pdf/.

Eikeland, Ole-Johan, Terje Manger, and Arve E. Asbjørnsen, eds. 2017. *Innsatte fra Albania, Litauen og Polen: Utdanning, arbeid, ønske og planer.* Fylkesmannen i Hordaland. https://oppikrim.no/siteassets/dokument/publikasjonar/rapport-1-2017.pdf/.

Eikeland, Ole-Johan, Terje Manger, Arve E. Asbjørnsen, and Lise Ø. Jones. n.d. "Nordmenn i fengsel: Utdanning, arbeid og kompetanse." Statsforvalteren i

Vestland, Utdanningsavdelinga, Bergen. Unpublished manuscript, last modified April 9, 2022.

Eme, Robert F. 2008. "Attention-Deficit/Hyperactivity Disorder and the Juvenile Justice System." *Journal of Forensic Psychology Practice* 8 (2): 174–85.

Farooq, Romana, Lisa-Marie Emerson, Sue Keoghan, and Marios Adamou. 2016. "Prevalence of Adult ADHD in an All-Female Prison Unit." *ADHD Attention Deficit and Hyperactivity Disorders* 8 (2): 113–19.

Festinger, Leon. 1954. "A Theory of Social Comparison Processes." *Human Relations* 7 (2): 117–40.

Fridhov, Inger M., and Torfinn Langelid. 2017. "Importmodellen i norsk fengselsvesen." *Nordisk Tidsskrift for Kriminalvidenskab* 104 (3): 29.

Ginsberg, Ylva, Tatja Hirvikoski, and Nils Lindefors. 2010. "Attention Deficit Hyperactivity Disorder (ADHD) among Longer-Term Prison Inmates Is a Prevalent, Persistent and Disabling Disorder." *BMC Psychiatry* 10 (1): 112.

Gröning, Linda. 2014. "Education for Foreign Inmates in Norwegian Prisons: A Legal and Humanitarian Perspective." *Bergen Journal of Criminal Law and Criminal Justice* 2 (2): 164–88.

Gudjonsson, Gisli, Jon Fridrik Sigurdsson, Susan Young, Anna Kristin Newton, and Marius Peersen. 2009. "Attention Deficit Hyperactivity Disorder (ADHD). How Do ADHD Symptoms Relate to Personality among Prisoners?" *Personality and Individual Differences* 47 (1): 64–68.

Gunter, Tracy D., Stephan Arndt, Gloria Wenman, Jeff Allen, Peggy Loveless, Bruce Sieleni, and Donald Black. 2008. "Frequency of Mental and Addictive Disorders among 320 Men and Women Entering the Iowa Prison System: Use of the MINI-Plus." *Journal of the American Academy of Psychiatry and the Law* 36 (1): 27–34. http://jaapl.org/content/36/1/27.full.pdf.

Hauge, Ragnar. 1996. *Straffens begrunnelser*. Oslo: Universitetsforlaget.

Hawley, Jo, Ilona Murphy, and Manuel Souto-Otero. 2012. *Survey on Prison Education and Training in Europe—Final Report Order 23 of the DG Education and Culture Framework Contract 02/10-Lot 1*. European Commission/GHK (Brussels/Birmingham). https://op.europa.eu/en/publication-detail/-/publication/6480d344-75e7-4573-b860-1f62f1edc6c3#.

Høstmælingen, Njål. 2004. *Internasjonale menneskerettigheter*. Oslo: Universitetsforlaget.

Høstmælingen, Njål, Hanne Steen, and Astrid Kjeldegaard-Peders. 2013. *Notat om menneskerettslig regulering av rett til opplæring i norske fengsler for utenlandske fanger som skal sendes ut av landet etter endt soning*. Edited by Justis- og beredskapsdepartementet [Ministry of Justice and Security]. Oslo: International Law and Policy Institute.

Jones, Lise Ø. 2012. "Effects of Reading Skills, Spelling Skills and Accompanying Efficacy Beliefs on Participation in Education: A Study in Norwegian Prisons." Department of Biological and Medical Psychology, University of Bergen.

Jones, Lise Ø., Arve E. Asbjørnsen, Terje Manger, and Ole-Johan Eikeland. 2011. "An Examination of the Relationship between Self-Reported and Measured Reading and Spelling Skills among Incarcerated Adults in Norway." *Journal of Correctional Education* 62 (1): 26–50.

Jones, Lise Ø., Jeanette Varberg, Terje Manger, Ole-Johan Eikeland, and Arve E. Asbjørnsen. 2012. "Reading and Writing Self-Efficacy of Incarcerated Adults." *Learning and Individual Differences* 22 (3): 343–49.

Kessler, Ronald C., Lenard A. Adler, Michael J. Gruber, Chaitanya A. Sarawate, Thomas Spencer, and David L. Van Brunt. 2007. "Validity of the World Health Organization Adult ADHD Self-Report Scale (ASRS) Screener in a Representative Sample of Health Plan Members." *International Journal of Methods in Psychiatric Research* 16 (2): 52–65.

Kessler, Ronald C., Lenard Adler, Minnie Ames, Olga Demler, Steve Faraone, E. V. A. Hiripi, Mary J. Howes, Robert Jin, Kristina Secnik, Thomas Spencer, T. Bedirhan Ustun, and Ellen E. Walters. 2005. "The World Health Organization Adult ADHD Self-Report Scale (ASRS): A Short Screening Scale for Use in the General Population." *Psychological Medicine* 35 (2): 245–56.

Kriminalomsorgen. 2020. *Kriminalomsorgens årsstatistikk 2019*. Kriminalomsorgsdirektoratet. https://kriminalomsorgen.no/getfile.php/4768782.823.77npnkalujumpt/Kriminalomsorgens+%C3%A5rsstatistikk+2019.pdf/.

Lahey, Benjamin B., Rolf Loeber, Jeffrey Burke, and Paul J. Rathouz. 2002. "Adolescent Outcomes of Childhood Conduct Disorder among Clinic-Referred Boys: Predictors of Improvement." *Journal of Abnormal Child Psychology* 30 (4): 333–48.

Langelid, Torfinn. 2015. *Bot og betring?: Fengselsundervisninga si historie i Noreg.* Oslo: Cappelen Damm akademisk.

Langelid, Torfinn. 2017. "The Development of Education in Norwegian Prisons." In *Scandinavian Penal History, Culture and Prison Practice*, edited by P. Scharff Smith and T. Ugelvik, 225–47. Palgrave Studies in Prisons and Penology. London: Palgrave Macmillan.

Langelid, Torfinn, Marianne Mäki, Kaj Raundrup, and Svenolov Svensson, eds. 2009. *Nordic Prison Education: A Lifelong Learning Perspective*. Vol. 536, TemaNord: Nordic Council of Ministers.

Lie, Magnus. 1935. *Waisenhusstiftelsen i Trondheim gjennom 300 år.* Waisenhusstiftelsen i Trondheim (Trondheim).

Manger, Terje, Jørn Hetland, Lise Ø. Jones, Ole-Johan Eikeland, and Arve E. Asbjørnsen. 2020. "Prisoners' Academic Motivation, Viewed from the Perspective of Self-Determination Theory: Evidence from a Population of Norwegian Prisoners." *International Review of Education* 66 (4): 551–74.

Manger, Terje, Ole-Johan Eikeland, Åge Diseth, Hilde Hetland, and Arve E. Asbjørnsen. 2010. "Prison Inmates' Educational Motives: Are They Pushed or Pulled?" *Scandinavian Journal of Educational Research* 54 (6): 535–47.

Manger, Terje, Ole-Johan Eikeland, and Arve E. Asbjørnsen. 2013. "Effects of Educational Motives on Prisoners' Participation in Education and Educational Desires." *European Journal of Criminal Policy Research* 19 (3): 245–57.

Manger, Terje, Ole-Johan Eikeland, and Arve E. Asbjørnsen. 2016. *Norske innsette: Utdanningsmotivasjon og hinder for utdanning i fengsel.* Fylkesmannen i Hordaland, Utdanningsavdelinga (Utdaningsavdelinga Fylkesmannen i Hordaland). https://oppikrim.no/siteassets/dokument/publikasjonar/rapport-1-2016.pdf/.

Manger, Terje, Ole-Johan Eikeland, and Arve E. Asbjørnsen. 2019. "Why Do Not More Prisoners Participate in Adult Education? An Analysis of Barriers to Education in Norwegian Prisons." *International Review of Education* 65 (5): 711–33.

Mathisen, Yngve. 2012. *Ærlig mat i Halden fengsel* [Decent food in Halden Prison]. 2nd ed. Halden: Lutefiskakademiet.

Ministry of Church and Education. 1969. "Education for the Young Incarcerated People in Correctional Facilities" [Undervisning for unge innsatte i fengselsvesenets anstalter]. *Rundskriv 6 As L 1969 24.10.69 (2869 As L 69).* Oslo.

Ministry of Education. 1998 [2020]. "Lov om grunnskolen og den vidaregåande opplæringa (Opplæringslova)" [Act relating to primary and secondary education and training (The Education Act)]. Oslo: Lovdata.

Ministry of Education. 1998 [2014]. "Lov om grunnskolen og den vidaregåande opplæringa (Opplæringslova)" [Act relating to primary and secondary education and training (The Education Act)]. Oslo: Lovdata.

Ministry of Education. 2001 [2021]. Prop. 1 S. "(2021–2022) Proposisjon til Stortinget (forslag til stortingsvedtak)." https://regjeringen.no/contentassets/1c6c5ffc45744233b0d8d3313d127dc8/nn-no/pdfs/prp202120220001_kddddpdfs.pdf/.

Ministry of Education and Research. 2005. St.meld. nr. 27 (2004–2005). "Om opplæringen innenfor kriminalomsorgen. 'Enda en vår' " [White paper no. 27 (2004–2005). Education and training in the correctional services. "Another spring"]. Oslo.

Ministry of Justice and Police. 2008. St. melding 37 2007–2008. "Straff som virker— mindre kriminalitet—tryggere samfunn—(kriminalomsorgsmelding)" [White paper 37 2007–2008. Punishment that works—less crime—a safer society]. Oslo.

Ministry of Justice and Police and Ministry of Education and Research. 2008. "Rundskriv om forvaltningssamarbeid mellom opplæringssektoren og kriminalomsorgen fra Justis-og politidepartementet og Kunnskapsdepartementet" [Circular on administrative co-operation between the education and training sector and the Norwegian Correctional Services]. Oslo. https://regjeringen.no/no/dokumenter/rundskriv-g-12008-om-forvaltningssamarbe/id543821/.

Ministry of Justice and Public Security. 2001 [2021]. "Act Relating to the Execution of Sentences etc. (The Execution of Sentences Act)."

Möller-Leimkühler, Anne Maria, Ronald Bottlender, Anton Strauß, and Wolfgang Rutz. 2004. "Is There Evidence for a Male Depressive Syndrome in Inpatients with Major Depression?" *Journal of Affective Disorders* 80 (1): 87–93.

Norwegian Correctional Service. 2020. *Annual Report 2020.* Oslo: The Norwegian Correctional Services. https://kriminalomsorgen.no/getfile.php/4852079.823.amjubkaqlqkaql/%C3%85rsrapport+2020+-+samlet2.pdf/.

Rasmussen, Kirsten, Roger Almvik, and Sten Levander. 2001. "Attention Deficit Hyperactivity Disorder, Reading Disability, and Personality Disorders in a Prison Population." *Journal of the American Academy of Psychiatry and the Law* 29 (2): 186–93.

Retz-Junginger, Petra, Wolfgang Retz, Detlev Blocher, Heinz-Gerd Weijers, Götz-Erik Trott, Paul Wender, and Michael Rösler. 2002. "Wender Utah Rating Scale (WURS-k): Die deutsche Kurzform zur retrospektiven Erfassung des hyperkinetischen Syndroms bei Erwachsenen" [Wender Utah Rating Scale: The short version for the assessment of attention-deficit hyperactivity disorder in adults]. *Nervenarzt* 73 (9): 830–38.

Román-Ithier, Jan C., Rafael A González, María C. Vélez-Pastrana, Gloria M. González-Tejera, and Carmen E. Albizu-García. 2017. "Attention Deficit Hyperactivity Disorder Symptoms, Type of Offending, and Recidivism in a Prison Population: The Role of Substance Dependence." *Criminal Behaviour and Mental Health* 27 (5): 443–56.

Rösler, Michael, Wolfgang Retz, Petra Retz-Junginger, Georges Hengesch, Marc Schneider, Tilman Supprian, Petra Schwitzgebel, et al. 2004. "Prevalence of Attention Deficit-/Hyperactivity Disorder (ADHD) and Comorbid Disorders in Young Male Prison Inmates." *European Archives of Psychiatry and Clinical Neuroscience* 254 (6): 365–71.

Roth, Beate Buanes, and Terje Manger. 2014. "The Relationship between Prisoners' Educational Motives and Previous Incarceration, Sentence Length, and Sentence Served." *London Review of Education* 12 (2): 209–20. https://files.eric.ed.gov/fulltext/EJ1160352.pdf/.

Ryan, Richard M., and Edward L. Deci. 2000. "Intrinsic and Extrinsic Motivations: Classic Definitions and New Directions." *Contemporary Educational Psychology* 25 (1): 54–67.

Samuelsson, Stefan, Birgitta Herkner, and Ingvar Lundberg. 2003. "Reading and Writing Difficulties among Prison Inmates: A Matter of Experiential Factors Rather Than Dyslexic Problems." *Scientific Studies of Reading* 7 (1): 53–73.

Schanning, Espen. 2007. *Menneskelaboratoriet. Botsfengslets historie.* Oslo: Scandinavian Academic Press/Spartacus Forlag.

Sellin, Thorsten. 1944. *Pioneering in Penology. The Amsterdam Houses of Correction in the Sixteenth and Seventeenth Centuries.* Philadelphia: University of Pennsylvania Press.

Skounti, Maria, Anastas Philalithis, and Emmanouil Galanakis. 2007. "Variations in Prevalence of Attention Deficit Hyperactivity Disorder Worldwide." *European Journal of Pediatrics* 166 (2): 117–23.

Smith, Alan. 2019. *The European Union and Prison Education—Cooperation, Innovation, Policy Support: A Historical Review of the First Two Decades.* https://epea.org/wp-content/uploads/Smith-Alan-The-EU-and-Prison-Education-A-historical-review.pdf/.

Smythe, Ian, and John Everatt. 2001. "A New Dyslexia Checklist for Adults."
  In *The Dyslexia Handbook 2001*, edited by Ian Smythe. Reading: British Dyslexia
  Association.
Snowling, Margaret J., Piers Dawes, Hannah Nash, and Charles Hulme. 2012.
  "Validity of a Protocol for Adult Self-Report of Dyslexia and Related Difficulties."
  Dyslexia: An International Journal of Research and Practice 18 (1): 1–15.
Søndenaa, Erik, Kirsten Rasmussen, Tom Palmstierna, and Jim Aage Nøttestad. 2008.
  "The Prevalence and Nature of Intellectual Disability in Norwegian Prisons."
  Journal of Intellectual Disability Research 52 (12): 1129–37.
Statistisk sentralbyrå. 2017. "Befolkningens utdannigsnivå." Last modified June 15,
  2017. https://ssb.no/utniv.
Strømsø, Helge, Bente E. Hagtvet, Solveig A. Lyster, Anne-Lise Rygvold. 1997. *Lese-
  og skriveprøver for studenter på høyskole- og universitetsnivå* [Reading and spelling
  tests for students in higher education]. Oslo: Institutt for spesialpedagogikk.
  Universitetet i Oslo.
Vellutino, Frank R., Jack M. Fletcher, Margaret J. Snowling, and Donna M. Scanlon.
  2004. "Specific Reading Disability (Dyslexia): What Have We Learned in the Past
  Four Decades?" *Journal of Child Psychology and Psychiatry* 45 (1): 2–40.
Westrheim, Kariane, and Terje Manger, eds. 2013. *Educational Background,
  Preferences and Needs: A Qualitative Study of Prisoners from Iraq, Poland, Russia,
  Serbia and Somalia.* Vol. 1/2013: Fylkesmannen i Hordaland.
Young, Susan J., Debby Moss, Ottilie Sedgwick, Moshe Fridman, and Paul Hodgkins.
  2015. "A Meta-analysis of the Prevalence of Attention Deficit Hyperactivity
  Disorder in Incarcerated Populations." *Psychological Medicine* 45 (2): 247–58.
Zierau, Finn, Anne Bille, Wolfgang Rutz, and Per Bech. 2002. "The Gotland Male
  Depression Scale: A Validity Study in Patients with Alcohol Use Disorder." *Nordic
  Journal of Psychiatry* 56 (4): 265–71.

SILVIA LUKÁČOVÁ,
DOMINIKA TEMIAKOVÁ,
AND MAREK LUKÁČ

7 ||| WHO BENEFITS MOST FROM CORRECTIONAL EDUCATION?

A VIEW FROM SLOVAKIA

Introduction

The education of incarcerated people fulfills an important resocializing function, as it enables them, even during a prison sentence, to acquire qualification or requalification and enhance their prospects in the labor market once they have completed their sentence. Nevertheless, some scholars (e.g., Coates 2016; Warner 2007) have increasingly argued in favor of going beyond an instrumental perception. In this view, the education of incarcerated people is not aimed at merely acquiring the qualifications necessary for employment; rather, it is to further the broader goal of humanization through the cultivation of the individual. Such a philosophy is adopted, and its scope applied in, for instance, many Scandinavian countries (see, for example, Langelid et al. 2009).

But is this how it works in practice? The main goal of this chapter is to use original research conducted by the authors to uncover answers to the question of whether correctional education is truly oriented toward positive and desirable changes on the part of incarcerated students, or whether it brings more benefits to the prison system itself. The following introductory section provides some information regarding the conditions under which research is carried out in Slovak prisons and the restrictions that Slovak researchers face in this specific sphere. In 2005, several legal norms were amended in the Slovak Republic with the aim of changing the philosophy from a passive reception of activities by incarcerated people to a system that actively uses their abilities, as well as efforts aimed at resocialization. Paradoxically, this revision of the penal codes also brought about the renaming of institutions from "correctional-educational institutions" to "facilities for serving sentences withholding of freedom," a phrase still used today. For better comprehension of how formal and informal education of incarcerated students works, this chapter provides an overview of the legislation covering education in prison in Slovakia. At the end of the chapter, the authors present the findings of their research regarding how incarcerated women evaluate education, as well as what teachers have to say about education behind bars. The findings suggest that this education is truly formalized to such an extent that it no longer reflects the real needs of people who are incarcerated or the communities they are supposed to reenter after serving their sentence.

We believe it is important for teachers to be specially trained in two key areas related to working with incarcerated students: understanding how conditions for teaching differ in prison generally and learning how to teach incarcerated adults in particular (their learning needs, motivations, individual life stories, aspirations). The lack of teacher training in these areas can increase the risk that education in prison becomes a formality. When this occurs, the rules and regulations of those running the prison and school come first, while individual learning needs and aspirations of incarcerated students are relegated to the background. This situation is not unique to Slovakia, as was shown by the research results of a project focusing on select European countries ("Skillhubs" 2020). To combat this, teachers' university education should include competence in teaching adults, specifically those in total institutions.

A growing emphasis on lifelong education could be reflected in undergraduate training of teachers who, in their careers, come across adult learners more and more frequently. Educational instruction in formal as well as informal settings is often not adapted to the learning needs of incarcerated people; rather than being innovative, it is often recycled based on existing and functioning partnerships with a limited spectrum of educational institutions. Present-day education of people who are incarcerated in Slovakia does not provide students in prison with many opportunities to continue in higher education, and the informal education offered does not always reflect their needs.

Limitations of Research on Education in Slovak Prisons

As of 2020, there were 10,519 people in prison in Slovakia (total pretrial and convicted), or 0.19 percent of the country's total population of almost 5,456,000, yielding an incarceration rate of 192 per 100,000 people. Since

2016, the number of incarcerated people has slightly increased. Out of the twenty-seven European Union (EU) countries, Slovakia has the second-highest prison population rate (Fair and Walmsley 2021). Therefore, insufficient prison capacity is a major problem of the Slovak prison service ("Aktualizovaná Koncepcia" 2011). As for education, incarcerated people with primary and some secondary education represent the largest group of incarcerated people in the Slovak Republic (more than 70 percent). According to the data provided in the Yearbooks of the Prison and Court Guard Corps (*Ročenky Zboru väzenskej a justičnej stráže*) (2015–20), only 6 percent of all incarcerated people in Slovakia were enrolled in any type of educational program or activity between 2015 and 2020.

The process of research in closed, total facilities is difficult in almost any context. For this reason, the attention of Slovak authors (e.g., Jusko, Temiaková, and Papšo 2018; Vanková 2018) is usually focused on people released from prison, a concession to the large-scale unavailability of currently incarcerated subjects in the research field. Research taking place in Slovak prisons is regulated by the Prison and Court Guard Service (hereinafter Guard Service) and is still vastly insufficient and incomplete. Penological research was systematized by the Guard Service on January 1, 2016, when it founded an analytical-research unit, a body for applied penological research studying those serving a prison sentence at the General Directorate. In connection with this, the Guard Service drafted a document entitled the "Conception of Applied Penological Research for 2016 to 2026 and the Long-Term Focus of Analytical Research within Prison and Court Guard Service."[1] That document states, "Applied penological research is to, by means of theoretical, analytical, research, and publication activities, contribute to the formation of legislation and criminal policies from the viewpoint of their functionality, meeting goals, and care for the staff who actually carry out these policies" (Prison and Court Guard Service 2016, 7).

In this paradigm, there are typically two ways that research is carried out: either the Guard Service carries out their own research projects or research is carried out through approved partnerships with other institutions. In some specific cases, however, a third way is possible: research can also be carried out by university students. In such cases, this cooperation is based on agreements, and the topics of the final works must be authorized by the Guard Service, though they should ideally correspond to the research objectives defined in the aforementioned formulation.

The Guard Service justifies this control over research by making several claims: that research carried out by university students used to be uncoordinated; that the results lacked added value, as the topics were not defined by the needs of the Guard Service; that the outcomes were not applicable in meeting the defined goals of applied penological research; that results were not verifiable; and that final products either went unpublished or their publication was atomized in various university periodicals without the possibility of a critical review on the part of the Guard Service. We are, however, convinced that any scrupulous research in the penitentiary context is always meaningful. The primary role of the Guard Service, as with any other national institution, is not to subvert or overrule any research findings, just as the researcher's goal is not to undermine the facility.

Prior to the existence of this conception, the Guard Service stated that research, provided it had been approved, could only be carried out *without* direct contact with people who were currently incarcerated. This placed the researcher outside the prison environment and determined that the only methodological tool available would be the questionnaire. The reasons are obvious, as the Guard Service was concerned about personal data protection and the ethical aspect of carrying out such research. Nevertheless, the Conception of Applied Penological Research does not include any such restriction; on the contrary, it states that "cognition of reality is to be based on reliable quantitative and qualitative data" (2016, 14). It does, however, add that "statistical findings are also a tool for studying and clarifying phenomena of the prisoner reality." It is thus unclear to what extent such specifically defined conditions in the Slovak Republic also allow, in certain circumstances, quantitative research requiring direct contact with incarcerated respondents.

As such, it is not surprising that, under such narrowly defined conditions, Slovakia lacks adequate research regarding the education of incarcerated people, the extent to which it reflects social and individual educational needs, and the extent to which it contributes to social rehabilitation and effective reentry. There are a small number of papers available on the education of incarcerated people (e.g., Kováč and Šírová 2008; Lukáčová et al. 2018; Španková and Grenčíková 2012; Temiaková 2015, 2021), and several focus specifically on aspects of social welfare and social work (e.g., Papšo 2011; Vanková 2018, 2019, 2020). That is why the present research, aimed at providing at least partial insight into how education of the incarcerated is carried out in Slovak prisons, is based mainly on research by Silvia Lukáčová and colleagues (2018) and Dominika Temiaková (2021).

The Nature of Education in Prison in Slovakia

In the Slovak Republic, prison sentences are executed by the Guard Service, which performs significant and irreplaceable tasks. Beyond protecting society from criminal activity, the Guard Service also plays a difficult but meaningful role: supporting the social reintegration of incarcerated people, almost all of whom will return to society one day. For incarcerated people, the potential benefits of education are clearly important. Regardless of public opinion concerning the education of incarcerated adults, the commonly held claim that educating people in prison is purposeless has no place in any modern society. In response to these critiques, efforts to educate incarcerated people during their time in prison must require observable educational goals across a broad range of activities, including education, work, and leisure activities.

Interventions may include both individual and group forms of treatment. Individual treatment may include educational counseling, work, spiritual activities, leisure activities, or interest activities carried out with a single incarcerated person. Moreover, group forms of treatment may consist of community meetings carried out for the purposes of education, spiritual service, work, or for culturally edifying activities, as well as community activities such as self-government of incarcerated people. Self-government is the way prison life is organized in those facilities with minimum security and in open blocks, with the aim of minimizing the negative influences of the prison sentence on the personality of the incarcerated person by simulating the conditions of everyday life outside prison. What is key is making sure the incarcerated persons share responsibility for the conditions of the prison sentence in the area of employment and work performance, cultural and educational activities, and discipline and order (Notification of the Ministry of Justice of the Slovak Republic No. 368/2008 Coll.). An elected incarcerated person oversees each area and also attends regular meetings with the teacher or the head of the open block.

In Slovakia, education in prison can be divided into two relatively distinct classifications. Though they are not defined legislatively, they nevertheless designate education as a legitimate aspect of penitentiary treatment. The first classification is penitentiary education, or informal education, and the second is the subsystem of more formal secondary and higher education often referred to as "second-chance education." In practice, it is possible to list differences between these in terms of organization, duration, personal support, outcomes, and, especially, goals; however, in legislative terms, they are considered part of a compact system of education in prison.

Education of incarcerated people as a means of intervention in Slovakia is defined by several documents, namely, Act No. 475/2005: Coll. on the Serving of Prison Sentence,[2] Act No. 368/2008: Notification of the Ministry of Justice of the Slovak Republic[3] (publishing the Order for the Serving of Prison Sentence, amended and annexed by Regulation No. 500/2013),[4] and the Order of the General Director of the Prison and Court Guard Service No. 7/2009 on Education and the Organization of Leisure and Interest Activities of the Charged and Incarcerated.[5]

Act No. 475/2005 Section 32 defines education of incarcerated people as a set of activities based on active participation of people in prison aimed at their integration into society in accordance with their personal and social needs. Notification of the Ministry 368/2008 defines the following forms of education in prison: comprehensive education, cultural and sport activities, social education, and free use of the library. Unlike the others, comprehensive education falls into the category of formal education aimed at achieving a particular level of educational qualification, and what some might call "second-chance education." Of those who have the opportunity, most incarcerated adults acquire full secondary general education or full secondary vocational education (upper secondary). And, though technically available as of April 2022, no students are currently attending higher education, for reasons explored in the following section. The remaining forms of education in prison can be classified as informal education.

Formal Education: A Second Chance in Prison

By definition, education in prison of the formal type must be organized in a way that allows for incarcerated people, on finishing their education, to be issued official documentation proving the completion of their studies by an accredited institution. The law also accounts for the negative effect of the stigma of a prison sentence on civilian life, which is why it must not be stated on the certificate that it was acquired during their term of incarceration. Even though Slovak legislation does not explicitly refer to "second-chance education," the law claims that "those convicted who have the predispositions to do so will be enabled to acquire primary education, secondary vocational education, full secondary education, or participation in other forms of education that will allow them to acquire, or increase, their work qualification" (Act No. 475/2005: Coll. on the Serving of Prison Sentence, §32, Point 2). The law does not explicitly prescribe the form of education the incarcerated student must take, which means that the school in question can opt for a full-time, part-time, or evening schedule. The school must, however, consider the individual characteristics of the incarcerated student and the distinct conditions under which such education is carried out.

Programs aimed at the completion of a discrete level of education are provided by external educational institutions (most often primary schools and secondary vocational schools). The teaching process is controlled by the teacher, based on methodological principles of educating children and youths rather than on the principles of adult education. Most often, teachers use methods that are typical for educating children, as they are not specifically trained to teach adult learners. In formal education of adults, cognitive and psycho-motoric educational goals (knowledge and skills) are primarily followed. Second-chance education is predominantly of an instrumental nature, with the aim of increasing the level of education and the chances of finding one's place in the labor market. It does not specifically focus on the education of adults—that is, on fulfilling effective educational goals—because it is presumed that the personality of an adult has been fully formed. However, the education of adults should always be of a resocializing nature; our legislation also considers rehabilitation through education to be one of the fundamental functions of incarceration.

According to the Notification of the Ministry No. 368/2008, incarcerated students may complete primary education, take a requalification course or a course aimed at increasing or broadening their qualification, be trained in selected study programs, or study at a secondary school. The educational facility providing the instruction sets up classrooms of various types in the detention center, and the allocated workplace is to be a "permanently set-up closed space where regular educational activities take place, which follows the school's educational program it is part of" (Act No. 596/2003: Coll. on State Administration in Education and School Self-Government).[6] The school is also in charge of providing the materials and equipment for the classrooms and workshops.

From a legislative standpoint, the system of second-chance education in detention facilities for adults is designed to be humane and comprehensive. Apart from legislation related to the fulfillment of prison sentences, there is also Act No. 245/2008: Coll. on Education and Training,[7] allowing primary and secondary schools to participate in this education. A detention facility itself may initiate an educational program by approaching a primary or secondary school with an education proposal. In response, if it accepts, the school is obliged to develop individual study plans approved by the head teachers, ensuring quality (§26). Secondary vocational education is also an option for incarcerated students who have not completed lower secondary education or are unable to provide evidence of its completion, such as a certificate (§62 Art. 4). Completion of primary education in detention facilities is carried out through a course aimed at finishing lower secondary education within a total of eighty hours. Upon conditional release, the incarcerated student can continue their studies and complete them based on an individual study plan drawn up by the secondary school in question (Act No. 245/2008 Coll. on Education and Training, §26).

A detention center can also enable and facilitate incarcerated students in Group A[8] to study in a part-time university program, as long as they are not housed in maximum security facilities (Act No. 475/2005 Coll. on Serving of Prison Sentence, §32). According to statistical data, however, university education is not carried out to its potential. For example, most recently, university education was attended by only three incarcerated people in an open block in the form of individual part-time studies back in 2007. Similarly, between 2015 and 2020, only seventeen incarcerated people have participated in higher vocational education.

Apart from these basic statistical data, there is not much information available about the higher education of incarcerated persons in Slovakia. No analyses or research has been carried out to explain why incarcerated people do not participate in higher education. In reality, there is almost nothing known in this area. One could only assume that it is caused by a lack of tradition of higher education within disadvantaged groups of the population, a strong tradition of vocational education, and the markedly industrial character of the national economy.

As has already been mentioned, legislation enables incarcerated persons to participate in higher education, which means it falls upon the penal institutions to arouse greater interest in it. It is of paramount importance, therefore, that universities focus on incarcerated people and start cooperating with prisons to provide greater educational opportunities.

More focus must be placed on issues such as access to university educa-tion, recreating a university environment inside the prison regime, and the mechanisms of targeted support for people in prison as they work toward a higher education qualification. Financing the education of incarcerated people is also a significant issue, as students in Slovakia are charged for part-time studies at secondary school and at university. Access to online content and other critical educational resources is a problem as well.

Second-Chance Education: Who Uses It and How?

Almost half of all incarcerated women and men (49.4 percent) have com-pleted secondary education (International Standard Classification of Edu-cation [ISCED] 3 or 4). In 2020, the percentage of incarcerated people who had completed primary education stood at 38.5 percent. It is among this category of incarcerated people that there is the most incentive to par-ticipate in second-chance education. However, there is also a significant percentage of incarcerated people with incomplete primary education: the average of the past four years is 7.5 percent of the total number of in-carcerated people. In fact, the Guard Service reports that approximately 2 percent of incarcerated persons are illiterate.

A course aimed at acquiring lower secondary education (consisting of eighty lessons, ideally at primary schools) has been designed for in-carcerated people with incomplete primary education. Such an offering represents a significant opportunity for them to complete their primary education in the school system as a prerequisite for continuing to second-ary education. Figure 7.1 shows the levels and types of formal education in which incarcerated adults (not counting pretrial) in Slovakia participate.

Regarding the education system in Slovakia in general, compulsory education lasts ten years. What is also compulsory is the final year of pre-school (preprimary) education, which means that children are obliged to attend kindergarten from age five as a preparatory year before they start attending primary school. Primary schools then offer compulsory general education for children from the age of six. When they have completed their primary education, students can continue on to secondary school, either at a comprehensive (grammar) school or a vocational school. This level lasts between three and five years, depending on the level of education (ISCED 3 and 4). For those students who failed to complete their primary education, there are programs of lower vocational education (ISCED 2C)

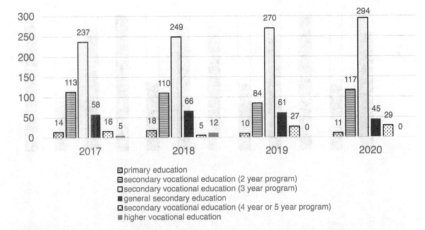

Figure 7.1.

Participation of incarcerated adults in Slovakia (not counting pretrial) in the formal system of education between 2017 and 2020. Data processed based on the 2019 *Almanacs of the Prison and Court Guard Service* (2020, 58), 2018 (2019, 53), 2017 (2018, 55) and 2016 (2017, 57).

they can take at secondary vocational schools. One can only start higher education provided they have passed a school exit exam ("Maturita"[9]), by which general or vocational secondary education is completed.

As shown in figure 7.1, the most numerous group (on average approximately two hundred fifty incarcerated students per year) took part in a three-year course of study at a secondary vocational school. Such education gives the graduates a vocational qualification, which allows them to perform activities in jobs according to the program they completed at secondary school. However, vocational study does not allow them to continue in higher education. The second-largest group was incarcerated students at secondary vocational schools in a two-year study program (lower secondary vocational education). From 2017 to 2021, there were some incarcerated students (an average of fifty-seven per year) who studied in secondary comprehensive schools (upper secondary general education).

Likewise, figure 7.2 shows the ratio between the total number of incarcerated individual groups according to education and those who, in the given group, participate in formal education. It illustrates the space in which the given groups of incarcerated people participate in education. Notably, the figure contains two pieces of statistical data regarding the groups of incarcerated adults: those whose level of education falls within the target group that could participate in the given education program

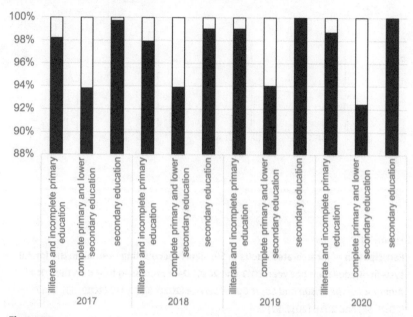

Figure 7.2.

Participation of incarcerated adults in Slovakia in formal education in comparison to the cohort of the incarcerated regarding their education level between 2017 and 2020. Data processed based on the 2020 *Almanacs of the Prison and Court Guard Service* (2021, 57, 63), 2019 (2020, 58), and 2018 (2019, 53).

(the black part), and the group participating in the respective program (the white part). This figure points to the great gap between the ratio of incarcerated adults who could be educated and those who are actually taking part in education.

The most frequent groups participating in corresponding levels of formal education are those with incomplete primary and secondary education who are completing their schooling in primary (approximately 2 percent) or secondary education (approximately 6 percent). Nevertheless, in the past four years, their share has been roughly between 8 and 10 percent of total students. Between 2016 and 2020, on average, 6 percent of incarcerated persons took part in programs aimed at completing secondary education (finishing with the Maturita exam), which would allow them to commence higher education (postsecondary and university).

It is not easy to explain this gap, as there are no research data regarding barriers to education for incarcerated adults; in the present research, only the barriers for incarcerated women, not men, were studied. One could

imagine myriad explanations, including insufficient offerings in some facilities, disinterest in some groups of incarcerated people who may not
wish to further their education, or systemic barriers such as disallowing
participation in education for various reasons. Many of these incarcerated
people have a low initial education or a negative experience with education, which may be the reason why they do not consider education important. They have never experienced education as a tool for a better life
(e.g., in society, at work), so education is not a priority or a value for them.

The range of second-chance education providers in Slovak prisons is
quite heterogeneous. The incarcerated student population, likewise, is a
group with widely differing educational needs, which should be reflected
in the methodological processes of second-chance education. In this context, Faye Taxman (1998) aptly claims that while formal education programs in prisons are available, they are uniform and have no regard for the
individual educational needs and preferences of the incarcerated student.
For education in prison to be effective, the programs of study must take
into consideration the specific needs of incarcerated students (e.g., low
self-esteem and aspirations, difficulties with studying, addiction to substances) (Inmate Education 2002).

Unlike some systems in other countries, formal education in Slovak
penitentiaries is carried out on an ad hoc basis, based on contracts, agreements, and the willingness of schools and the Guard Service to cooperate.
There is no national model and no network of schools offering systematic
education, so the offer of formal education and its focus differs depending
on the region. This is exemplified by the fact that, since 2009, incarcerated
people in several detention facilities have been provided with the opportunity to complete their secondary comprehensive education at grammar schools and secondary vocational schools. One example is the study
program Business in Crafts and Services (completed with the Maturita
final exam and graduation from four or five years of study at secondary
schools); there are also study programs for butchers, cooks, gardeners,
carpenters, painters, industrial electricians, mechanical engineers, and
others (Aktuality 2020). These programs are not, however, offered in all
penitentiary facilities throughout the country. The frequency of enrollment in the individual study programs by incarcerated people is closely
connected to the potential of the local labor market. The opportunity to
work while serving a prison sentence is an important part of penitentiary
treatment in Slovakia.

Informal Education of the Incarcerated

Informal education in detention facilities mainly takes the form of requalification courses and mostly includes scheduled events, such as discussions, lectures, and quiz games. Dame Sally Coates points to the importance of informal education in the penitentiary environment when she claims that "education in prison should provide individuals with skills they need to broaden their potential. . . . It is one of the pillars of effective re-socialization. Education should build the social capital and increase the welfare of incarcerated prisoners" (2016, 3).

As stated by Notification 368/2008, publishing the Order for the Serving of Prison Sentences ($45), these developmental events are co-organized by professional employees of the facility, attorneys, and other qualified persons, sometimes joined by interest, civic, religious, or other associations. At the heart of these events are artists, sports figures, scientists, and other luminaries, though lectures or discussions can also be given by a qualified incarcerated person.

Participation in most educational activities depends on the particular security group in which the incarcerated person is placed. In facilities with a minimum level of security, incarcerated people in Groups A and B may freely attend a wide range of activities, while for those in Group C it is the prison's education coordinator[10] who decides each person's participation. Similarly, in facilities with a medium level of security, only those in Group A may participate freely, while those in Group B are approved for a limited set of activities, and those in Group C may participate as the education coordinator allows. Finally, in facilities with a maximum level of security, the participation of those in Groups A and B is governed by legislation as appropriate, while the incarcerated in Group C are not eligible for these activities (Notification No. 368/2008, publishing the Order for the Serving of Prison Sentence).

In short, out of nine internal differentiating groups, seven—or the vast majority of incarcerated people in Slovakia—are directly allowed by legislation to organize and participate in educational, character-building, or leisure activities. In addition, the participation of incarcerated people in educational activities is compulsory in the case of facility-wide activities designed to present facility regulations (e.g., routine and regimented activities, clothing and hygiene, meals, correspondence). Regarding the range of educational activities offered, from 2017 to 2020 a total of 540

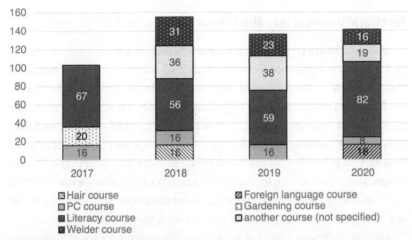

Figure 7.3.
Participation of the incarcerated population in Slovakia in requalifying courses between 2017 and 2020. Data processed based on the *2020 Almanacs of the Prison and Court Guard Service* (2021, 62), 2019 (2020, 58), 2018 (2019, 53).

adult incarcerated people participated in requalification courses,[11] most of them (155) in 2018. The offering of requalification courses and the numbers of incarcerated adults who attended them are presented in figure 7.3.

Since 2020, the highest participation has been in the literacy course. If incarcerated people are assigned to a literacy course according to Act No. 475/2005 (§32), they are obliged to regularly attend it. In spite of this, only 30–40 percent of incarcerated people who are functionally illiterate participate in the literacy course each year. Between 2018 and 2020, the most frequented courses were computer courses, construction courses, and "other courses" (i.e., those not specified in the statistics).

Although there is data available regarding the number of informal educational activities held each year, this data does not specify the numbers of incarcerated adults participating in activities like discussions, lectures, and quizzes, among others. Nevertheless, thousands of such events are carried out each year, with some of the most common being activities focused on alcohol and drug use, health and hygiene, general (unspecified) education, social services, and social welfare. Although these activities are those most frequently attended by the incarcerated and are a necessary, edifying, and even pleasant way to pass time in prison, they cannot be considered a replacement for educational activities with added value, which incarcerated people could significantly utilize on their release from prison.

Teachers' Insights into the Prison and Education Systems

Many scholars are trying to determine whether, in a total institution such as a prison, it is possible to freely teach and achieve a quality education comparable to a standard education on the outside. Unique, albeit methodologically limited, findings regarding the view of teachers on academic education of incarcerated students was the subject of research by Silvia Lukáčová and colleagues (2018). This qualitative research was carried out by means of grounded theory[12] and took place at a secondary school, with researchers interviewing teachers who teach traditional students at school in the morning and incarcerated students in the afternoon. This way, it was not necessary to coordinate the research with the Guard Service.

The research was aimed at evaluating the competencies of secondary school teachers who, apart from teaching traditional students, also taught incarcerated men in a detention facility in a three-year program of study. The information obtained can be useful to help understand how a total institution influences the actual process of education. This is especially true when focusing on its main actors: school as an external institution entering the total environment; teachers trained to work with children and youth in a free environment; and prison as a total institution with a set of strict rules that define and maintain it. The conditions of the organization and the course of education were determined by the rules set within the facility's regime, while the school tried to adjust the content and the conditions of education to meet these.

These important findings (Lukáčová et al. 2018), though unpublished, are relevant here. The majority of conclusions resulted from teachers' statements that the influence of the facility's regime on education was most significant in the following areas.

Selection of incarcerated participants in education: For the research in question, adult incarcerated students were selected for education by the facility, while the most important criterion was not the intellectual ability of the incarcerated people or their individual educational needs, but rather security (e.g., flight risk, aggressive behavior). Consequently, the students selected were also assessed by the school according to the duration of their sentence, so that there was as high a chance as possible for them to successfully complete their education before they were released. Peter—a teacher of Slovak, English, and civics—said, "We only accept those. . . . who can manage to finish" (Lukáčová et al. 2018). The selection process of the participants in education is thus subordinated to the needs and possibilities of the prison and school (which might deepen the differing approach of all incarcerated people to education). Paradoxically, an incarcerated person who does not meet the requirements of the prison facility and school might have limited access to education. There are, however, other educational and counseling activities available. Those who advise incarcerated people and determine the opportunities of their personal development should take this into consideration.

Selection of the study program: Unfortunately, the educational programs offered were not created with the interests and needs of incarcerated people in mind but were determined primarily by the needs of the prison (e.g., vocational programs for builders, electricians, or other jobs directly related to working inside the facility). Accordingly, two- and three-year programs that focused on practical skills took precedence, as they were less demanding regarding the content of education. Again, Peter stated, "You know, for them, practical training is more interesting and useful; if he becomes a skilled welder, he will find a job; but not knowing the Slovak language won't be a serious issue" (Lukáčová et al. 2018).

Selection of the form of studies: The choice of the part-time form of education was influenced by the facility's effort to have education interfere in the regime as little as possible, to avoid any disruptions in the prison's daily routine, and not to place increased demands on the wardens (such as accompanying the teacher in the facility). The part-time form of study made it possible to carry out education en bloc, with teachers changing as little as possible during the day, since any move or change is very closely monitored.

On the other hand, there was an emphasis on self-education of the students, which is more difficult in prison. The students are not allowed to freely decide on the time for education and self-study, and they are barred from using resources typically considered necessary for studying (e.g., study room, library with specialized literature, internet access). The prison regime clearly states the conditions of confinement such as place, time, and duration, so the space for self-study is limited. Ormond Simpson relates an apt comment: "Permanent noise of TVs and music from the neighboring cells, doors banging, bars being locked and unlocked make necessary concentration on studying much harder" (2003, 210). Apart from a lack of privacy, incarcerated persons might find themselves in a situation where they are not fully capable of attending the education for the entire allocated time interval, due to their duties resulting from the institution's regime (Maunsell, Downes, and McLoughlin 2008).

Teaching materials and equipment: This area, typically decided by the school, was ultimately subjected to the approval of the facility due to security concerns. The school itself was responsible for providing teaching aids, but, due to the facility's rules, these were limited (in the theoretical subjects) to an overhead projector, a flash drive, and CDs. Anything a teacher wanted to use that was not included on the list of approved teaching aids was subjected to authorization and inspection. A broader array of teaching aids is thus limited by bureaucracy that teachers are not always prepared to go through. Another teacher, Miro, offered this observation: "To have a computer available takes a whole range of things to be approved. . . . It is administratively demanding if I want something [outside the approved list]" (Lukáčová et al. 2018). Thus, according to the teachers, it was not possible to use the full range of teaching aids in the classroom in prison as it was in a traditional school setting. Moreover, for reasons of space, workshops were not equipped for practical training in the same way as in school, and, again, emphasis was placed on security and the inspection of work tools. Textbooks were not very widely used; teachers tended to make photocopies of materials to give out to their students.

Moreover, lacking access to the internet is a particular problem. The prison regime does not allow internet access, even in the classroom, and teachers can only bring their own laptops if there is no internet connection built in. This problem fully manifested during the pandemic, when face-to-face lessons were canceled. Our ongoing (as yet unpublished) research into education in prison during the pandemic has provided information about primary school teachers working with incarcerated students to complete their lower secondary education. In the experience of Zuzana, a teacher, schools had to change to a distance-learning form of teaching without the use of online education and, when facilitating the content of education of individual subjects, had to rely solely on the distribution of study material in print by means of an employee of the facility. Zuzana went on to state, "Luckily, they have their own education coordinator. I communicated with her online and sent her all the materials; she sent us feedback. . . . I got as far as the front desk so we could exchange some stuff but, really, all went on in a distance form."

Relationships between teachers and incarcerated students: The relationship between teachers and incarcerated students was considerably influenced by the information embargo, meaning that teachers had no information regarding the civilian or prison life of incarcerated students and were banned from asking them directly about it. Thus, they felt unsure, especially when encountering new students. As Jozef, a teacher, noted, "[Teaching during] the first year is the worst, as I only meet them at that point and I have no idea what I can say; you really have to weigh every word." According to the teachers, facility administrators justified this to the teachers by citing the risk of manipulation by the incarcerated (Lukáčová et al. 2018). As a result, relationships between the teachers and their incarcerated students remain impersonal and formal, ostensibly in order to prevent potential problems.

Self-study: Another problem arose when prison authorities did not allow incarcerated students to freely choose the time for individual study. According to the teachers, the conditions in the facility were not adequate for self-study: it could only take place in the cells, where the learners were disturbed by their cellmates. In the prison library, study materials were not available for the learners. This was one of the reasons the teachers did not assign incarcerated students any homework. Another was insufficient material for the students, as available resources were considerably restricted. Paper, for instance, is a precious commodity, since it can be used to make cigarettes, which are used as a means of payment among incarcerated individuals. As Ján, a teacher, recalled, "You give them books, because you have some; not new, used books, and, after a while, you find out there are pages missing." As a consequence, incarcerated students were given no homework assignments, as the teachers realized the conditions for studying outside of class were considerably limited. Thus, teachers had higher expectations for the teaching process and for navigating the content in person, as the only time their students had a chance to acquire knowledge was during lessons.

Apart from these areas, in which teachers were able to detect the influence of the facility's regime on the teaching process, it was also interesting to find that the form and degree of influence was assessed and interpreted differently by the teachers of theoretical subjects and the masters of practical training. Several components of the teaching process garnered varying characteristics depending on whether they were part of theoretical or practical lessons. In the part-time form of studies, the extent of education is reduced, which naturally creates pressure on the course content as well the self-study capabilities of the incarcerated learners. Reduction mainly impacted theoretical subjects, as teachers agreed that for incarcerated persons practical education is more useful, as it enhances their prospects in the labor market when they are released from prison. That is why the curriculum for practical education was not reduced: in order to provide those who take the course with enough practical vocational skills. That was also why the necessary reduction in the part-time form of studies affected theoretical education, which was justified by the teachers with appeals to the greater importance of practical education, less time allocated for the lessons, low level of education and knowledge on the part of the students, and limited conditions for self-study.

Another difference between theoretical and practical education was the perception of how demanding the teachers' preparation for the lessons was. On a daily basis, before and after the lessons, the masters of practical training had to pay close attention to the inspection of the work tools and divert time to record-keeping. Creating adequate time and conditions for vocational education (e.g., preparation and use of material, configuring technology for teaching) was significantly constrained, as it was impossible to equip the facility with the same equipment as a regular trade school (Kasáčová and Kosová 2006).

The differentiated nature of theoretical and practical education was also reflected in the varied levels of teaching activities. Unlike theoretical lessons, where the incarcerated students mostly passively accepted the mediated educational content, practical education was aimed at managing and maintaining the required technological methods when working with material, which is often a tangible finished product. This caused higher demands on the activity of both the incarcerated student (through their more difficult learning environment) and the teacher (through their more difficult teaching environment). In practical training, the teacher often had to opt for an individual approach, manifested through more intense interaction with the student. As a practical training instructor, Jozef, stated, "Anything we start to do, I take the drawing and I first do it myself, then they start, but never mind I have showed them everything, demonstrated it all. I have to keep coming back to it; I never stop."

These differences between the theoretical and practical lessons, as expressed by the teachers, were of critical significance in assessing the various experiences of those educating incarcerated students. On the one hand, the teachers of theoretical subjects assessed teaching in the prison environment highly positively, which was mainly connected to a higher level of discipline of the incarcerated students during lessons (in comparison to that of their students at school). For example, as Peter related, "So, tomorrow morning I'm going to teach in prison, I look forward to it much more than if I was going to spend the time with my [traditional students]. Because, you know . . . , it is easier to teach them; you don't have to tell anyone to be quiet . . . and pay attention; they sit there and look back at you." On the contrary, teachers of practical courses considered the education of incarcerated students to be very demanding and expressed a lower level of satisfaction compared with teaching in a regular school. As Jozef, who was in charge of practical training in machine maintenance, stated, "When I get [to school], I finally see normal people . . . you get that good feeling from work in comparison to [prison]."

Differing approaches and attitudes toward several key components of education in prison—the incarcerated students themselves, the preparation for the teaching process, and the effective communication of the subject matter—were all recorded depending on whether the teacher taught a practical or theoretical subject. These generalizations, however, only result from the data that came directly from the teachers. Sandra Mathews (2000), too, argues that it is difficult to understand why some teachers describe teaching incarcerated students as a valuable and productive activity while others think of it as frustrating and often manage to stay only a short time. Therefore, when assessing teachers' work, their activity in class, and other duties, it is necessary to consider a great number of additional factors that the available methodology did not previously allow for in the research.

In addition, there is some potential for teachers to be important agents of change in the organizational culture of the prisons where they teach by means of transforming the lives of the students who benefit from their effort. For example, Susannah Bannon (2014) claims that teachers have the potential to positively influence the lives of the incarcerated simply by teaching them, and that this is an important source of their satisfaction with their work. Teachers are those who bring a piece of freedom into an unfree environment. The classroom could be one of those few places within a prison where free discussion in relatively safe surroundings could take place, unhindered by the presence of correctional personnel (Yates and Frolander-Ulf 2001). Even so, the findings of Lukáčová and colleagues (2018) suggest that the current system of education in prison in Slovakia does not provide teachers with sufficient space to fully participate in the complete resocialization of the incarcerated, since they are solely limited to subject matter education. According to the authors of this study, the teachers who were surveyed claimed that all they were expected to do was teach the subject matter and that it was undesirable to establish anything other than formal relationships with the students.

It turns out that, as a result of strict internal prison rules, an environment conducive to learning is not currently possible in Slovak prisons (Gehring and Puffer 2004). So far, we have presented only information regarding the educational process as experienced by the teacher, but the views of the incarcerated learners could provide a more complete insight. While it is difficult to acquire information from students due to the data-gathering challenges described earlier, some interesting findings were presented in research carried out by Dominika Temiaková (2021). This research provides a unique view on the value preferences toward education, motivation, and the areas of education as seen by incarcerated adult women.

Value of Education for Incarcerated Women in Slovakia

From the statistics of the Guard Service, it follows that, on average, out of all incarcerated persons in Slovakia, only 6 percent participated in formal or informal education between 2015 and 2020. By comparison, "a 2012 survey of prison education and training in Europe showed that, in a majority of the European Union, the participation of inmates in prison education and training was lower than 25 percent" (Crowley 2019, 9). There might be several reasons for this disparity, from accessibility and admissions procedures to attitudes of incarcerated people themselves toward education.

Using a questionnaire developed by the author, one recent quantitative study aimed to identify the preferences of incarcerated women (Temiaková 2021). The target group included one hundred eighty-six adult incarcerated women in Slovakia, a third of the total incarcerated women in the country. The respondents were presented with fifteen values and asked to select each value's level of importance on a four-point scale.[13] The selection included the following: basic modern materialistic values (e.g., money, work, travel, and art); modern idealistic values (i.e., integrative values such as friends, relationship with a partner, and children); and traditional values (i.e., a sense of order represented through such values as tolerance, justice, and dignity, as well as conservative values such as health, family, education, freedom, and religious affiliation in the form of faith in God).

The results showed that, among the fifteen values, the highest scores were awarded to conservative values (with health scoring above all), integrative values focused on interpersonal relationships and family structures (with family coming in second and children fourth), and traditional values reflecting a sense of order (freedom third, justice sixth, and dignity seventh). The lowest scores were given to materialistic and spiritual values (travel in last place, art fourteenth, and faith in God thirteenth). Interestingly, education was ranked tenth among the fifteen values. Considering the level of education achieved, the education value paradoxically received the lowest scores among incarcerated students *with* a primary education (Temiaková 2020).

Thus, education placed rather low in the value rankings by the incarcerated women surveyed. Similar data were recorded among incarcerated women in Bulgaria in a survey carried out by Pepka Boyadjieva and colleagues (2010). Not only was education ranked low by incarcerated students with a primary education, but it also placed tenth out of fifteen among all respondents, regardless of their education level. There are several possible reasons for this, including that many incarcerated women might not realize the need for and importance of education since a majority of them have never experienced the benefits of it on the outside. This low ranking might also have been caused by prematurely leaving school and the related negative experience with education and frequent problems with studying, which then led to further frustration and discouragement from continuing education. This is further evidenced by research carried out in Slovenia (Vermeersch and Vandenbroucke 2009), where the incarcerated people who were surveyed stated loss of motivation, drug addiction, and problems with studying as reasons for leaving school prematurely. Admittedly, the actual value preferences of incarcerated women might differ from those they stated or those that are socially desirable, which is one of the limitations of quantitative research in this environment.

Motivation for Education

Temiaková (2021), too, tried to uncover the reasons incarcerated women participated in education. Based on theoretical sources (Knowles, Holton, and Swanson 2005; Turek 2008) and the outcomes of partial surveys (Hladílek 2009; Šauerová 2013; Španková and Grenčíková 2012), the fac-

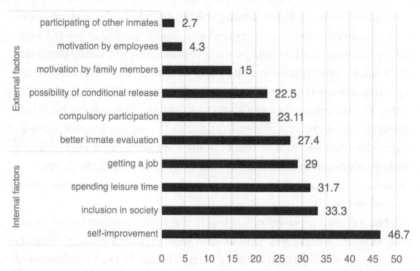

Figure 7.4.
Stated motivations of incarcerated women for participating in educational programs in Slovakia (in percentages).

tors of motivation for incarcerated adults were, in the questionnaire, categorized as factors of either external or internal motivation. On the one hand, factors of external motivation are ones such as fulfilling expectations of other people (e.g., family, friends, employees of the Guard Service) and systems (e.g., duty, possibility of conditional release, better evaluations, participation of other incarcerated people). On the other hand, factors of internal motivation are ones such as compensating for failing in education for the purposes of succeeding in professional life and adapting in social and cultural life, believing in the importance of education, interconnection of education and interests, true interest in cognition, escaping from problems resulting from adverse life circumstances, spending free time, and establishing social contacts.

Overall, as figure 7.4 indicates, Temiaková (2021) finds that the factors of internal motivation were noted by respondents more frequently than factors of external motivation. The greatest number of respondents identified self-improvement as their primary goal, followed by better inclusion in society upon their release from prison, education as a way of spending leisure time, and education as a means to finding a job upon release. In contrast, the most frequent external factors were better evaluation and compulsory participation in education as one of the preconditions for conditional release. In the open variant of the same question, where the respondents could provide "a different reason (please specify)," they most frequently stated things such as "great personal interest," "I'm into it," "I want to learn," and "this is how I feel about it, I don't do it for any gain"—all strong evidence of these respondents' internal motivation toward education.

Available Education and the Interests of Incarcerated Women

From Temiaková's (2021) research, a clearer picture has emerged about which informal educational activities garnered high levels of participation by incarcerated women in Slovakia in 2016 and in what frequency.[14] The offering of educational activities mostly included discussions, lectures, and quizzes in the following areas: culture (e.g., discussions and lectures by well-known personalities from the cultural and social spheres or presentations by music school students), health (e.g., first aid, sexually transmitted diseases, addictions), environment (e.g., nature, sustainability), social life (e.g., prevention of domestic or spousal abuse, the importance of family in society, legal topics), and religion and spirituality (e.g., spiritual services, discussions about religion).

In general, the respondents assessed the range of available educational activities in the facility rather positively. It was graded as sufficient by 39 percent, out of which 13 percent labeled it as completely sufficient and almost 26 percent as partially sufficient. However, 20 percent expressed their dissatisfaction and evaluated the slate of offerings as insufficient. The most numerous group of respondents could not (more than 30 percent) or would not (almost 10 percent) express their views. Of those who took part in the educational activities with any frequency, the array of educational offerings was found to be completely sufficient according to only 8 percent, sufficient to 21 percent, and insufficient to 14 percent, while as many as 20 percent of the respondents did not provide their opinion.

Interestingly, the higher the education level completed by the incarcerated student, the more they graded the offered educational activities as unsatisfactory. In other words, the demand for more educational activities seemed to grow with increasing level of education. From the viewpoint of age, the youngest respondents (those aged nineteen to twenty-one) assessed the offerings as being least satisfactory (20 percent), compared with those aged twenty-six to thirty (almost 25 percent of this age group) and women aged thirty-one to forty-five years (approximately 20 percent). Thus, Temiaková (2021) found that most incarcerated respondents aged twenty-six to forty-five wanted to receive more education but also rated the educational activities currently available as unsatisfactory.

Additionally, it turned out that the longer the prison sentence, the more the educational opportunities offered were considered insufficient by respondents. As many as 40 percent of the women serving a long prison sentence (i.e., longer than ten years) assessed the current educational offerings as insufficient. Temiaková (2021) explains this by stating that the more time the women spent in prison, the more they recognized the need for education not only as one of the few means of self-realization and a tool of enhancing their prospects in the labor market, but also as a worthwhile way to both spend their leisure time in prison and facilitate their social life upon release. Moreover, taking their long sentence into consideration, they were better able to evaluate the education offered in prison.

When comparing the education offerings with the respondents' preferences,[15] it turned out that the most preferred area of education was language courses (almost 50 percent). The second most sought after by incarcerated women was a course in computer skills (43 percent), followed by education focused on interpersonal communication (almost 29 percent). The lowest interest expressed by respondents was in such topics as political events (less than 5 percent), while six respondents specified other areas, such as psychology, art, construction, or the automobile industry (in relation to the job they did prior to starting their prison sentence). The respondents also stated that they would prefer sports activities or handicrafts, suggesting that various clubs or interest groups would be popular.

Respondents were also interested in topics they could utilize in their future job when released from prison, though there was also obvious interest in topic areas that did not relate to work life and that were connected to their role as a parent, for example. Were the educational opportunities provided by the facility to be compared with the preferences of the incarcerated women who participated in the study, it could be stated that, in spite of the proclaimed interest of the respondents in participating in, for instance, requalification courses—as the research might suggest, at least since 2016 (*Ročenka Zboru* 2016, 57)—not a single incarcerated woman has taken a requalification course. There might be two reasons for this disconnect: either the respondents were not really interested in such educational activities (and their responses in the questionnaires are of socially desirable nature) or such education was not previously available.

The situation is rather paradoxical, as worldwide trends emphasize the need for complementary programs for incarcerated women designed to prepare them for the process of reintegration into society. As stated by Marie Panayotopoulos-Cassiotou (2008, 9–10), a former member of the European Parliament, these women should have access to a wide range of specialized education adapted to the requirements of the labor market. She also calls on member states "to invest more in the development of programs aimed at increasing the level of literacy, lifelong education, and specialized training in prisons, adjusted to the requirements of the labor market and that could lead to the acquisition of a certificate." It is also necessary to create educational opportunities in the field of foreign languages, computer courses, and courses focused on social and work life.

Conclusion

The discussion about the education of incarcerated people is, in Slovak professional and academic circles, minimal. To a certain extent, it is also dependent on the limited access of the researchers to accurate and transparent data in a total institution. The present chapter strives to contribute to answering the question of whether the education of incarcerated people in Slovakia is truly aimed at positive changes on the part of the incarcerated person, or, rather, contributes to fulfilling the function of the prison apparatus. It can be concluded from the research available in this area that the education incarcerated people are provided does not reflect their educational needs and is instead focused on carrying out only those activities defined by law and necessary for the functioning of prison.

According to research by Temiaková (2021), the availability of informal education (such as requalification courses) is not based on the educational needs of incarcerated individuals, who showed interest in areas of education other than what they were offered. Similarly, Lukáčová and colleagues (2018) claim that the situation is similar in formal school education, carried out in order to utilize the opportunity of mutually beneficial cooperation between a specific facility and a secondary school. The relationships between teachers and students are set by the regime so that they are formal and exclusively defined within the educational setting. The course of education is subordinated to the needs of the prison, and the limits placed on the educators are in service to the regular functioning of the prison regime (i.e., time, form, and means). When arranged this way, the system of education is designed to disrupt the prison regime as little as possible. Accordingly, educators of people who are incarcerated in Slovakia cannot, on principle, become partners in education when their role is reduced to merely passing on knowledge.

Nevertheless, it is necessary to keep asking questions regarding the possibilities of education in the process of reintegrating incarcerated people and to provide an adequate theoretical and empirical response. Undoubtedly, education has great power to help incarcerated people achieve their true potential. It would, however, also require changes in the approach of prisons to education, which would no longer merely be a form of conditioning the incarcerated, as discussed by Julia Braggins and Jenny Talbot (2005), but, rather, would become part of the whole prison approach toward teaching, one in which learning is viewed as an activity where everyone is "involved in working towards a common goal" (55).

We are convinced that education in Slovak prisons needs change. The necessary change should reflect not only the goals of the penal system but also the educational needs of incarcerated students and their teachers. In the end, these more isolated goals should be integrated into the complex goals of the social reintegration of the imprisoned person, the fulfillment of which will benefit the whole society. The education of incarcerated people, therefore, should become an important part of the discussion about the humanization of the prison service, with a particular emphasis on expanding the rights of the incarcerated individual in education. To achieve this, however, it would be necessary to allow researchers to go behind prison walls to conduct not only quantitative but primarily qualitative research that would help them better discern what exactly is occurring in the mutual process of teaching and learning, including the various aspects that influence these processes. Only by carrying out research is it possible to accurately assess data and the systems that create such realities without merely supporting the status quo. Instead, research can be used to change the status quo and to offer answers to the question of "Why?" rather than just "How?"

Notes

The authors would like to thank the Prison and Court Guard Service of the Slovak Republic for the opportunity to carry out this research. This chapter is the output of Project APVV-18-0018: "Teaching at Second Chance Schools from the Perspective of a Teacher and Adult Learner," funded by the Slovak Research and Development Agency.

1. (Slovak) Koncepcia aplikovaného penologického výskumu na roky 2016 až 2026 a dlhodobá orientácia analyticko-výskumnej činnosti v podmienkach Zboru väzenskej a justičnej stráže.

2. (Slovak) Zákon č. 475/2005 Z. z. o výkone trestu odňatia slobody.

3. (Slovak) Vyhláška Ministerstva spravodlivosti Slovenskej republiky č. 368/2008 Z.z.

4. (Slovak) Vyhláška Ministerstva spravodlivosti Slovenskej republiky č. 500/2013 Z.z.

5. (Slovak) Rozkaz generálneho riaditeľa Zboru väzenskej a justičnej stráže č. 7/2009 o vzdelávaní a organizovaní záujmových aktivít a aktivít vo voľnom čase obvinených a odsúdených.

6. (Slovak) Zákon č. 596/2003 Z. z. o štátnej správe v školstve a školskej samospráve, §19, Art. 7.

7. (Slovak) Zákon č. 245/2008 Z.z. o výchove a vzdelávaní (školský zákon).

8. Incarcerated people who have been convicted serve their sentences in differentiated ways. External differentiation (facilities according to their security level: minimum, medium, and maximum) is a matter for the court. Internal differentiation (classification of individual security levels into groups—A: open block, B: semi-open block, C: closed block, and D: block of life sentences) is determined by the prison director or main warden based on the psychological assessment, behavior, and attitudes of the incarcerated persons toward their duties and the prescribed program. In this sense, individuals in Group A follow a moderate regime: they are allowed freer movement and given the possibility to participate in a broader range of prison activities. Group A can be subjected to a minimum, medium, or maximum security (minimum standing for A) prison sentence in an open block organized in the form of self-government.

9. "Maturita" is a shortened version of "maturitná skúška" (the highest type of qualifying exam), ending the studies of four- and five-year programs at secondary vocational schools and grammar schools (upper secondary general and upper secondary vocational education—ISCED 3A).

10. In the Slovak system, there is the position of "pedagogue," which is close to that of a correctional educator. This is a staff member employed by a prison facility, in charge of the educational, cultural, and leisure activities of incarcerated persons.

11. Requalification courses are part of further education, outside formal school education, carried out as part of an accredited education program and are aimed at acquiring partial or full qualification—the professional ability to perform one or more tasks in a different profession to that which the person acquired in school education.

12. The research was carried out as part of the dissertation work entitled "Second-Chance Education during the Serving of a Prison Sentence" (2015).

13. The four values were "very important," "rather important," "rather unimportant," and "not at all important."

14. With regard to the frequency of adult incarcerated women participating in each, the research showed that in the observed period in 2016 in the prison where the study was conducted, 53 (38.1 percent) of the female respondents attended at least one discussion, while 83 (59.7 percent) never attended one; 87 (62.6 percent) of the female respondents attended at least one lecture, while 52 (37.4 percent) never attended one; and 86 (61.9 percent) of the female respondents attended at least one quiz, while 53 (38.1 percent) never did so. Considering the fact that some respondents took part in some educational activities more than once, the total number of participants in the activities is much higher than the number of the respondents (186). The discussions were attended 217 times, lectures 519 times, and quizzes 252 times.

15. Respondents were asked to choose from a list of fourteen thematic areas with the option to select several options or add their own.

Works Cited

"Aktualizovaná Koncepcia väzenstva Slovenskej republiky na roky 2011 až 2020" [Updated prison concept of the Slovak Republic for the years 2011 to 2020]. 2011. Word document. https://rokovania.gov.sk/download.dat?id=652860CC0E7747759B46B0007659A290-46CD640EB3E92AF122AADA4A511B12D5.

Bannon, Susannah. 2014. "Why Do They Do It? Motivations of Educators in Correctional Facilities." *Saint Louis University Public Law Review* 33 (2): 301–15.

Boyadjieva, Pepka, Valentina Milenkova, Galin Gornev, Kristina Petkova, and Diana Nenkova. 2010. *The Role of Bulgarian Educational Institutions for Promotion of Access of Adults to Formal Education.* Sofia: Institute of Sociology/Bulgarian Academy of Sciences.

Braggins, Julia, and Jenny Talbot. 2005. *Wings of Learning: The Role of the Prison Officer in Supporting Prisoner Education.* London: The Centre for Crime and Justice Studies.

Coates, Dame Sally. 2016. *Unlocking Potential: A Review of Education in Prison.* London: Ministry of Justice. https://assets.publishing.service.gov.uk/government/uploads/system/uploads/attachment_data/file/524013/education-review-report.pdf/.

Crowley, Martha, ed. 2019. *The Rehabilitation and Social Reintegration of Women Prisoners: Implementation of the Bangkok Rules.* Bangkok: Penal Reform International and Thailand Institute of Justice. https://cdn.penalreform.org/wp-content/uploads/2019/05/PRI_Rehabilitation-of-women-prisoners_WEB.pdf/.

Fair, Helen, and Roy Walmsley. 2021. "World Prison Population List, Thirteenth Edition." *World Prison Brief.* London: ICPR. https://prisonstudies.org/sites/default/files/resources/downloads/world_prison_population_list_13th_edition.pdf/.

Gehring, Tom, and Margaret Puffer. 2004. *Integral Correctional Education: Three Explanatory Essays.* San Bernardino: California State University Center for the Study of Correctional Education. https://coe.csusb.edu/documents/ICEEssays.pdf/.

Hladílek, Miroslav. 2009. *Kapitoly z obecné didaktiky a didaktiky vzdělávání dospělých.* Prague: UJAK.

John Howard Society of Alberta. 2002. *Inmate Education.* https://silo.tips/download /inmate-education-john-howard-society-of-alberta.

Jusko, Peter, Dominika Temiaková, and Peter Papšo. 2018. "Education of the Convicts Serving Their Prison Terms in the Slovak Republic." *Hungarian Educational Research Journal* 8 (4): 70–79.

Kasáčová, Bronislava, and Beata Kosová. 2006. "Kompetencie a spôsobilosti učiteľa – európske trendy a slovenský prístup." In *Profesijný rozvoj učiteľa,* Kolektív autorov, 34–49. Prešov: MPC.

Knowles, Malcolm S., Elwood F. Holton, III, and Richard A. Swanson. 2005. *The Adult Leader: The Definitive Classic in Adult Education and Human Resource Development.* Amsterdam: Elsevier.

Kováč, Andrej, and Lea Šírová. 2008. Vybrané aspekty teórie a praxe vzdelávania odsúdených. In *AEDUCA festival '07,* 1–9. Olomouc: Univerzita Palackého. http:// ua-ed.narod.ru/AEDUCA_2008/index.html.

Langelid, Torfinn, Marianne Mäki, Kaj Raundrup, and Svenolov Svensson, eds. 2009. *Nordic Prison Education: A Lifelong Learning Perspective.* Copenhagen: Nordic Council of Ministers.

Lukáčová, Silvia, Marek Lukáč, Ivana Pirohová, Eduard Lukáč, and Lucia Hartman-nová. 2018. "Prison Education in Slovakia from the Teacher's Perspective." *Journal of Prison Education and Reentry* 5 (1): 63–79.

Mathews, Sandra. 2000. "Each Day Is a Challenge: Paving the Way for Success in the Prison Classroom." *Journal of Correctional Education* 51 (1): 179–82.

Maunsell, Catherine, Paul Downes, and Valerie McLoughlin. 2008. *National Report on Lifelong Learning in Ireland.* Dublin: St. Patrick's College.

Panayotopoulos-Cassiotou, Marie. 2008. *Správa o osobitnej situácii žien vo väzení a o dosahu uväznenia rodičov na sociálny a rodinný život* [Report on the situation of women in prison and the impact of the imprisonment of parents on social and family life] (2007/2116[INI]). Dokument na schôdzu Európskeho parlamentu. https://europarl.europa.eu/doceo/document/A-6-2008-0033_SK.html#title1.

Papšo, Peter. 2011. *Resocializácia odsúdených vo výkone trestu odňatia slobody.* Banská Bystrica: Univerzita Mateja Bela.

Prison and Court Guard Service. n.d. *Aktuality.* Accessed on April 7, 2022. https:// zvjs.sk/sk/aktuality/.

Prison and Court Guard Service. 2016. *Koncepcia aplikovaného penologického výskumu na roky 2016 až 2026 a dlhodobá orientácia analyticko-výskumnej činnosti v podmienkach Zboru väzenskej a justičnej stráže* [Conception of applied penological research for 2016 to 2026 and the long-term focus of analytical research within prison and court guard service]. Bratislava: Zbor väzenskej a justičnej stráže. https://old.zvjs.sk/files/field/koncepcia_penologickeho_vyskumu .pdf/.

Ročenky Zboru väzenskej a justičnej stráže [Yearbooks of the Prison and Court Guard Corps]. 2015. Bratislava: Zbor väzenskej a justičnej stráže. https://zvjs.sk /sk/vyrocna-sprava.

Ročenky Zboru väzenskej a justičnej stráže [Yearbooks of the Prison and Court Guard Corps]. 2016. Bratislava: Zbor väzenskej a justičnej stráže. https://zvjs.sk /sk/vyrocna-sprava.

Ročenky Zboru väzenskej a justičnej stráže [Yearbooks of the Prison and Court Guard Corps]. 2017. Bratislava: Zbor väzenskej a justičnej stráže. https://zvjs.sk /sk/vyrocna-sprava.

Ročenky Zboru väzenskej a justičnej stráže [Yearbooks of the Prison and Court Guard Corps]. 2018. Bratislava: Zbor väzenskej a justičnej stráže. https://zvjs.sk /sk/vyrocna-sprava.

Ročenky Zboru väzenskej a justičnej stráže [Yearbooks of the Prison and Court Guard Corps]. 2019. Bratislava: Zbor väzenskej a justičnej stráže. https://zvjs.sk /sk/vyrocna-sprava.

Ročenky Zboru väzenskej a justičnej stráže [Yearbooks of the Prison and Court Guard Corps]. 2020. Bratislava: Zbor väzenskej a justičnej stráže. https://zvjs.sk /sk/vyrocna-sprava.

Rozkaz generálneho riaditeľa Zboru väzenskej a justičnej stráže č. 7/2009 o vzdelávaní a organizovaní záujmových aktivít a aktivít vo voľnom čase obvinených a odsúdených.

Šauerová, Markéta Švamberk. 2013. "Motivace odsouzených mužů ve výkonu trestu k účasti na celoživotním vzdělávání." In *Vzdělávání dospělých: Příležitosti a úskalí v globalizovaném světě,* edited by Jaroslav Veteška and Jarmila Salivarová, 141–60. Praha: Educa Service.

Simpson, Ormond. 2003. *Student Retention in Online, Open, and Distance Learning.* London: Kogan Page.

"Skillhubs: Transnational Prison-Up Skilling Guidance and Training Model." 2020. http://skillhubs.eu/wp-content/uploads/2019/01/Research-Report-with-project -guidelines.pdf/.

Španková, Jana, and Adriana Grenčíková. 2012. Význam vzdelávania vo výkone trestu odňatia slobody. *Aktuální otázky sociální politiky—teorie a praxe,* VI: 99–106.

Taxman, Faye S. 1998. "Reducing Recidivism through a Seamless System of Care: Components of Effective Treatment, Supervision, and Transition Services in the Community." *Treatment and Criminal Justice System Conference, 1998.* Washington: Office of National Drug Control Policy. https://ojp.gov/pdffiles1 /Digitization/171836NCJRS.pdf/.

Temiaková, Dominika. 2015. *Penitenciárna a postpenitenciárna edukácia dospelých.* Banská Bystrica: Belianum.

Temiaková, Dominika. 2020. "Value Orientation of Convicted Women in Slovakia in Relation to Their Age and Education." *Ad Alta: Journal of Interdisciplinary Research* 10 (2): 321–25.

Temiaková, Dominika. 2021. *Vzdelávanie žien v penitenciárnych podmienkach.* Nitra: UKF.

Turek, Ivan. 2008. *Didaktika.* Bratislava: Iura Edition.

Vanková, Katarína. 2018. "Social Curatorship in Provision of Social Services in Post-penitentiary Care." *Journal of Social Sciences Research* 4 (12): 571–81.

Vanková, Katarína. 2019. *Postpenitenciárna starostlivosť v kontexte sociálnej práce a sociálnych služieb*. Nitra: UKF.

Vanková, Katarína. 2020. *Penitenciárna a postpeniteciárna starostlivosť v teórii a praxi*. Nitra: UKF.

Vermeersch, Lode, and Anneloes Vandenbroucke. 2009. *The Access of Adults to Formal and Nonformal Adult Education*. Leuven: Higher Institute for Labour Studies. https://lirias2repo.kuleuven.be/bitstream/handle/123456789/266442 /R1338_Country_report_SP5.pdf?sequence=2.

Vyhláška Ministerstva spravodlivosti Slovenskej republiky č. 368/2008 Z.z.

Vyhláška Ministerstva spravodlivosti Slovenskej republiky č. 500/2013 Z.z., ktorou sa mení a dopĺňa vyhláška Ministerstva spravodlivosti Slovenskej republiky č. 368/2008 Z. z., ktorou sa vydáva Poriadok výkonu trestu odňatia slobody.

Warner, Kevin. 2007. "Against the Narrowing of Perspectives: How Do We See Learning, Prisons and Prisoners?" *Journal of Correctional Education* 58 (2): 170–83.

Yates, Michael D., and Monica Frolander-Ulf. 2001. "Teaching in Prison." *Monthly Review* 53 (3). http://monthlyreview.org/2001/07/01/teaching-in-prison.

Zákon č. 245/2008 Z.z. o výchove a vzdelávaní (školský zákon).

Zákon č. 475/2005 Z. z. o výkone trestu odňatia slobody.

Zákon č. 596/2003 Z. z. o štátnej správe v školstve a školskej samospráve.

8 ||| PREPARING FOR RELEASE

ACADEMIC AND VOCATIONAL EDUCATION FOR INCARCERATED PERSONS IN POLISH EXECUTIVE CRIMINAL LAW

Introduction

In the lives of most Poles, education plays an important role. It is no surprise, then, that the Polish legislature lists education among the measures necessary for the effective functioning of the penal system. Not only does education help incarcerated people develop useful life habits and strengthen a sense of responsibility for their actions; it also reduces the negative behaviors associated with persistent inactivity and isolation in prison. Still, implementing any measure of penitentiary programming, such as education or work, will only be effective if the incarcerated person is committed to making the most of it.

In Poland, which has a population of roughly 38 million (*World Population Review* n.d.), there are about 72,000 incarcerated people in its prisons (*World Prison Brief* n.d.). Though these numbers have gone down since their Cold War peak, its population rate of 195 incarcerated people per 100,000 citizens is almost twice the European Union average (*Landgeist* n.d.; *World Prison Brief* n.d.). As of 2019, there were 130 penitentiary facilities in Poland, including 46 pretrial remand centers and 84 prisons, of which 24 are high-security facilities (*Prison Insider* n.d.). While education is widely available for anyone who desires it, as of 2017 only 2.1 percent of incarcerated people in Poland avail themselves of one of these programs, while as many as 48.6 percent of incarcerated people perform some sort of work, either paid or unpaid (*Prison Insider* n.d.).

This chapter will discuss the twin issues of education and employment of incarcerated people in Poland as effective interventions in carceral settings. There will also be examples of how the educational system functions in the isolation of prison.

Background

At its most basic, incarceration consists of the forceful confinement of a person in a closed and guarded prison or other detention center for the time specified in one's sentence.[1]

In Poland, there are three types of penal institutions: closed, semi-open, and open. These type distinctions correspond to various rights and obligations of the people held in them, including the degree of isolation both internally and externally, as well as the use of different rehabilitation and reintegration methods. Into these different settings are apportioned four distinct populations: juvenile offenders, first-time offenders, repeat offenders, and military offenders. Additionally, the Polish legislature has designated three different systems for carrying out terms of incarceration: programmed rehabilitative, therapeutic, and the ordinary system. In order to correctly place a sentenced person in the appropriate type and population of prison, and to select the appropriate punishment regime, each is classified according to statutory criteria (Executive Criminal Law of 1997, Art. 82).

At its core, the penitentiary system in Poland is designed to provide rehabilitative resources as part of its mandate. In every penal institution and pretrial detention center, regardless of the type and population, a convicted person is statutorily entitled to serve their imprisonment in a dignified way. The Executive Criminal Law (ECL) of 1997 includes an open catalog of protected rights for incarcerated people, including education work, cultural and athletic activities, and contact with family and the outside world. These are designed to prepare a currently incarcerated person for a life outside prison, thus helping newly released people avoid reoffending (Dawidziuk 2013, 138). Violation of these rights gives a convicted person the legal right to pursue claims in court and, consequently, to potential financial liability on the part of the State Treasury (Civil Code Act of April 23, 1964, arts. 24 and 448).

Likewise, to discuss effective penitentiary measures, it is also necessary to consider appropriate living conditions for inmates. The Polish legislature has issued detailed guidance concerning requirements for the living conditions of incarcerated persons (Executive Criminal Law of 1997, Art. 110). In penitentiary units, though cells may be single- or multi-person, the area of each cannot be smaller than 3 square meters (32 square feet) per person. Even this standard, however, is among the lowest for European countries. For instance, the minimum area is 10 square meters (107 square feet) in Norway, Iceland, Greece, and the Netherlands; 9 square meters (96 square feet) in Belgium and Italy; 8 square meters (86 square feet) in Croatia; 7 square meters (75 square feet) in Germany; and 6 square meters (64 square feet) in Romania, Bulgaria, and Spain (Dawidziuk 2013, 90).[2] There must also be adequate furnishings in living quarters—including beds, tables, cupboards, stools, and other items—and this also includes standards for lighting, air supply, and seasonally adjusted temperature.[3]

Every human being benefits from natural light and fresh air, and these are especially critical for incarcerated persons, both for mental health and because they help deter the spread of infectious diseases (Dąbkiewicz 2015, 494). In addition, hygiene products must be provided, and their use is encouraged as a practice for helping to maintain personal dignity. In fact, all elements that make up the social and living conditions in penitentiary units should meet the standards of respect for inherent human dignity and humane treatment of the incarcerated (Dawidziuk 2013, 72). With this important background in mind, I turn to the two most effective measures of reintegration available to the incarcerated in Poland: education and employment.

Education in Polish Prisons

Undoubtedly, one of the most important rehabilitative measures for incarcerated people is education, both formal and vocational. Polish legislation expressly provides access to education for those serving a term of incarceration. Indeed, the educational process itself is one of the essential elements of penitentiary measures, allowing incarcerated people to receive a more robust preparation for life outside prison. Most people who are incarcerated have lower educational attainment than the average Polish citizen, and many have not even completed primary school (Juwa 2013, 131). Since so many do not have an acquired profession, great importance is attached to education during the rehabilitation process (Hołda et al. 2017, 225).

Educating people who are incarcerated allows for the mitigation of some of the most adverse effects of serving a prison sentence in the first place. It has both educational and therapeutic features, in addition to improving mental health (Kuć 2007, 123). Undoubtedly, education contributes to enlarging one's knowledge base and expanding one's intellectual perspectives and has long been used in the penitentiary system to contribute to shaping a person's character. The provision of education, especially (but not limited) to people who are incarcerated when they are young, helps create conditions for effective social readaptation (Postulski 2017).

At the primary level, education in penal institutions is compulsory, while secondary (middle and high school) education and vocational courses are available on a voluntary basis (ECL 1997, Art. 130, §1). Unlike programs in other contexts that outsource education entirely, the compulsory primary element of this requirement is organized by prison administration (Postulski 2017). Importantly, the requirement is also compulsory for incarcerated juveniles or temporary detainees under eighteen years of age (Constitution of the Republic of Poland, Art. 70, para. 1; Juwa 2013, 119–20). Educational offerings may be provided entirely or partially, and when a training is offered at a reduced price, the costs are covered by the prison. This is especially important for incarcerated people who have not developed marketable job skills or who need remedial education. Teaching is conducted in schools and in continuing education centers located on the premises of penal institutions. Training courses commissioned by the governors of the facilities as well as statutorily mandated vocational courses may be implemented by these continuing education centers at penal institutions or by external organizations. Regarding temporary detainees, they may participate in education when it is conducted in a separate department of the facility and is not prohibited for security reasons.

In Poland, secondary education and vocational preparation, however, are generally the most important arenas for education in prison. Obtaining further education in this setting will help incarcerated persons better adapt to life in society after leaving prison (Szymanowski 2017, 307). Likewise, basic vocational schools are popular among incarcerated persons because they are believed to offer the best chance of acquiring professional skills and gaining employment immediately after one's sentence. Employment in school workshops and practical vocational training are compulsory for juveniles if they are included in the mandatory curriculum. In the prison setting, practical vocational training can even be combined with work. Unfortunately, this type of hands-on training is often severely hindered due to the lack of equipment and up-to-date teaching materials in prisons (Jaworska 2012, 323–24).

People nearing probation qualify for all types of educational programs and vocational qualifying courses if there are no less than six months left before their release, allowing them enough time to complete an educational program before the end of their sentence. The goal of acquiring general knowledge and professional qualifications may be realized, for example, through general competence courses, vocational skills courses, or vocational certification courses, which may be valuable for people serving shorter sentences and seeking certification as chefs or mechanics, for instance. Admission is based on recruitment, though there are no entrance exams or interviews for the first semester of study. Final decisions for admittance are made by the penitentiary commission, and all admitted students must obtain a medical certificate stating that there are no health restrictions to commencing education.

According to the set of regulations entitled "On the Manner and Mode of Education in Penal Institutions and Pre-trial Detention Centers" (Rozporządzenie Ministra Sprawiedliwości), to maintain minimum enrollment, the number of students in the first semester should be at least twenty, ensuring that, with attrition, there will be no fewer than ten students in each consecutive semester (§15). Significantly, the time devoted to education must not interfere with other activities and obligations required by the facility.

When approving an incarcerated student for an educational program, the penitentiary commission (ECL 1997, Art. 2) takes into account, among other factors, the following criteria: prior education, prospects and willingness to learn, previous work experience in a particular profession, the need to guarantee order and security in the penitentiary unit, time remaining until early probation or the end of the sentence, and any psychological evaluations performed (MMEPD §12). The aforementioned calculus will be of fundamental importance for educating incarcerated students, especially in determining any potential reasons for not referring an incarcerated person to any forms of education due to developmental concerns.

There are many situations, all of which are outlined in pertinent regulations, in which the penitentiary commission might reject the possibility of participating in education, but these restrictions only apply to noncompulsory education. Among these situations are refusal to attend school, safety-threatening behavior, deterioration of health preventing participation in classes, inability to repeat a semester because the course is no longer offered, failure to advance for consecutive semesters, breaks in education longer than 50 percent of the time provided for lessons in the semester in the event of transport ordered by the prosecutor's office, or failure to return from a temporary permit to leave the facility (ECL 1997, Art. 131a).

The largest groups that enroll in education in prison are juveniles and those serving a sentence of imprisonment for the first time, with obvious overlap between the two. Priority in gaining admittance to secondary school and vocational courses is given to those who do not have a profession, are unable to practice it after serving their sentence, or are under the age of twenty-one (i.e., juvenile offenders). The principle here is that by prioritizing the education of the most vulnerable, the penitentiary system is fulfilling its court-directed goal of elevating and rehabilitating individuals.

This focus on the education of juveniles is also consistent with developed international standards. For example, according to the principle of humane treatment, an incarcerated youth who does not have sufficient funds may use the necessary textbooks and learning aids at the expense of the facility (Szymanowski 2017, 309). Likewise, a juvenile who conscientiously fulfills the obligations of a student is entitled to a fourteen-day leave after one year of education, if such a break has not already accrued from the completion of a separate work program. Furthermore, during a leave, incarcerated students may exercise the same privileges and are afforded the same relief as an incarcerated worker during their leave (ECL 1997, Art. 132–33).

From the point of view of curriculum and pedagogy, education offered in a penal institution should be consistent with education systems operating outside prison (Kuć 2017, 159). The schools functioning at penitentiary units are public schools, and the teachers are subject to the same requirements as their counterparts outside the prison walls. Many of the students achieve good academic results, which is confirmed by external examinations. Schools organized within penitentiary units educate at all levels, and if the prison has signed an agreement with a university, it is even possible to study in any field specified in the agreement. The appropriate level of education in a penal institution is influenced not only by legal regulations but also by organizational issues, the level of overcrowding, and financing (Szymanowski 2017, 309).

An incarcerated person who graduates from school while serving their sentence obtains a diploma from the school just like an ordinary student on the outside. Moreover, any notation on the school certificate stating that it was obtained while serving a sentence of imprisonment is prohibited. Such a notation would have a negative impact on the perception of the graduate who, after leaving the penitentiary unit, will have to present documents confirming their education and qualifications, as these documents are generated according to commonly used templates.

It is also possible for a student to take final exams at a penal institution if the student is released before the end of the school year or training course; if they are released before the confirmation of a degree or certification, they receive a certificate confirming their attendance at the school (On the Organizational Bylaws for Serving an Imprisonment Penalty [OBSIR] 2016, §42). In the event of serious circumstances preventing an incarcerated student from fulfilling their obligation to be educated, it is possible to temporarily release them from this obligation. It is worth emphasizing that educational activities are not only theoretical lessons that teach, for example, mathematics; they also provide a transfer of ethical values from which a person can derive appropriate social models that can be applied toward integrating more fully into society. To this end, incarcerated persons may attend any religion or ethics classes they choose as well.

Education of incarcerated individuals may also take place outside a penal institution if students meet the generally applicable requirements for public education, maintain good behavior, and do not pose a security threat to the community (ECL 1997, Art. 131, §1). The main reason for conducting education outside penitentiary units derives from limitations in organizing a sufficient number of public schools to conduct classes. To help with this issue, private schools are also allowed to provide education in penitentiaries where appropriate (Hołda et al. 2017, 226). In practical terms, the consent to receive education outside the prison is granted by the governor of the particular penal institution. Before this consent is given for the first time, a criminological and social risk assessment should be prepared. The same conditions are necessary if an incarcerated student wishes to take examinations or participate in other educational activities outside the prison.[4]

The goal of allowing incarcerated students to learn outside the walls of a penal institution hinges on striving to integrate education in prisons with the regular education system. Thanks to this, incarcerated students have the opportunity to receive contact with the outside world, which in their case is very important (Kuć 2007, 122). In an open or semi-open penal institution, it is possible to allow participation in education outside the prison, but in a closed penal institution participation is possible only on the premises (Szymanowski 2017, 272). The director of the prison may, where justified, suspend or limit group classes in certain situations (ECL 1997, Art. 247). It should be noted that the teaching staff of the school collaborates with the administration of the prison through monthly meetings that involve the exchange of information or discussions on organizational matters (MMEPD, §9). Finally, incarcerated individuals may also be educated at their own expense outside the prison under specifically approved circumstances.

It should be noted that there is a small but promising offering of higher education programs in Polish prisons as well. Among these, one notable project was implemented between 2013 and 2016 by the Department of Social Psychological Prophylaxis of the Catholic University of Lublin on the basis of an agreement with the District Inspector of the Prison Service. The experimental program concerned a group of thirty-six incarcerated individuals who were tasked with going to a first-cycle[5] academic institution to study two majors: social work[6] and information technology.[7] During the first year of studies, the students were educated at penitentiary units, while over the next two years the education took the form of lectures carried out in a semi-open group at the university. Eighteen incarcerated students graduated from the university with a bachelor's degree. The remaining group of students declined to finish their studies, took a dean's leave, finished serving their imprisonment sentence, or continued their education using an individual study program. Though the researchers determined that higher education is an important intervention for students, further research was curtailed due to a lack of funding (Wróbel-Chmiel 2018, 289).

Another example of an effective higher educational initiative was the formation, under a 2011 agreement between the Radom University of Technology and the pretrial detention center in Radom, of the first full-time university program for incarcerated persons in Poland (Trela n.d.). These were bachelor-level engineering studies covering a three-and-a-half-year course of study in automotive industry logistics. As part of the recruitment procedure, twenty-nine incarcerated people were admitted as students, including two serving life sentences. During the admissions process, administrators took into consideration whether applicants possessed a secondary education certificate, as well as the length of the sentence remaining to be served. From the point of view of recruitment, an appropriate criminological and social risk assessment is also important (Juwa 2013, 127–30).

Distance learning arouses great interest among incarcerated students, many of whom, for various reasons, cannot pursue education outside prison. Looking forward, there is an increasing interest in e-learning, which was especially conspicuous during the Covid-19 pandemic. Needless to say, all forms of distance learning will continue to be explored as opportunities to create a more widely available academic education for incarcerated people in Poland (Szecówka 2011, 233, ff).

Work as Complementary Intervention

In addition to formal education, employment has been shown to be a particularly effective intervention in the reintegration of incarcerated people in Poland. The concept of employment is chiefly associated with the performance of a specific profession that offers remuneration, ideally ensuring satisfaction with the work undertaken and allowing the employed person to enjoy the fruits of their labor. It is also one of the oldest forms of offering incarcerated people the opportunity for self-rehabilitation.

Penal institutions and pretrial detention centers are total institutions that, apart from the actual deprivation of liberty, have severe effects on the psyche of the incarcerated. Work, on the other hand, allows the incarcerated person to break away from the everyday life of the prison cell and from the monotony of their environment, while at the same time teaching independence and responsibility. While performing work, people in prison spend their time productively and gain the opportunity to obtain monetary resources, which they often pass along to their family or use to pay off legal liabilities, including child support. Regardless of the nature of the work—paid or unpaid—it is important that it is productive and allows incarcerated people to increase their self-assessment and self-esteem.

Employment must adhere to several rules in order to fulfill the condition of the incarcerated person's social reintegration, and thus must have a positive impact on them. The rule of productive work consists in eliminating pointless tasks performed solely to "kill time." Such work does not have rehabilitative, social, or re-adaptive value and does nothing to increase the incarcerated person's sense of self-worth—and may even potentially accomplish the opposite. Instead, employment should be organized with the incarcerated person's future in mind, preparing them for life in society after leaving prison. In this process, it is important to enable the acquisition of skills useful for employment after release, allowing future employees to become financially independent. To this end, like education, the experience of work inside carceral institutions should be as similar as possible to that on the outside. In short, work should not be merely onerous; it should be edifying and protected and rewarding in the same way as work done in freedom. It should also ensure self-fulfillment for the worker (Pawela 2007, 192).

In prisons, work as a rehabilitative measure was originally only intended to *increase* punitive hardship and was thus intended to be as severe and onerous as possible (Pietrikowski 2004, 61). Indeed, it was often intentionally designed to be pointless and unproductive. Moreover, for many years, work was also largely subordinated to the economic motive, with its primary purpose to make as much profit as possible from the work done by incarcerated people. In consequence, this approach to work led to the total exploitation and objectification of incarcerated people, making reintegration a dubious goal at best.

In the twentieth century, the fundamental change in approach to the reintegrative function occurred with the ascendance of a more humanitarian view of the penitentiary system (Pietrikowski 2004, 61). It was at that moment, when the turn was made toward humanizing criminal law, that carceral employment began to play its fundamental role as an important rehabilitative measure. It was the first time that attention was paid to the incarcerated person's social improvement, taking into account the idea that the penalty should be executed in a way that would help prevent a person from committing a crime again. In the twenty-first century, in fact, it is the *educational* significance of employment that is most emphasized in the penal system. It is argued that the very fact of performing meaningful work has a positive effect on the experience of an incarcerated person (Pietrikowski 2004, 61).

There are many regulations on prison labor, concerning the legal basis of employment, the scope of rights and obligations of the incarcerated (including juveniles), the provision of workplaces, and the remuneration for work (Kalisz 2004, 193–215). Among the rights of incarcerated people in Poland, there is no mention of the right to employment, only the right—if employed—to receive the related remuneration and social insurance to the extent provided for in separate regulations, as well as assistance in obtaining disability benefits (ECL 1997, Art. 102, §4). Pursuant to the Constitution of the Republic of Poland, the obligation to work can be imposed only by legal act (Art. 65, para. 2). Therefore, an incarcerated person cannot demand to be employed, but may be required to be. The obligation to work is a form of legal order, failure to comply with which results in disciplinary action (ECL 1997, Art. 142, §1). Current regulations stipulate that an incarcerated person shall be enabled to perform work as far as possible (ECL 1997, Art. 121, §1), which in turn creates certain obligations on the part of the penitentiary unit's administration (Hołda et al. 2017, 165). One of the basic tasks of the Prison Service is to organize work conducive to the acquisition of professional qualifications—in short, work that educates.

Work will only be socially rehabilitative if it encourages the personal development of an incarcerated person (Machel 2003, 259). It is not only an element of punishment but also an important part of an incarcerated person's social reintegration. On the one hand, employment is a means of building up a person deprived of liberty; on the other, it is intended to prepare an incarcerated person for life after leaving prison precisely by enabling them to acquire professional qualifications so that they are more likely to find gainful employment after being released. It therefore aims at restoring the rights of the incarcerated person (Jaki 2017, 79).

In order to increase the effectiveness of reintegrating incarcerated people into society, incarcerated employees may perform work in different locations, depending on the system under which they are sentenced and the type of penal institution they are in. A person sentenced to life imprisonment, who serves their sentence in a closed-type prison, may only be employed on the premises of the prison (ECL 1997, Art. 121, §10), while someone in the same type of penal institution but serving a shorter sentence may also be employed outside the prison walls, provided that employment is carried out under constant supervision from correctional personnel (Art. 90, §2). Incarcerated people classified as security risks, as well as those convicted of a crime committed as part of an organized crime group, are placed in a closed prison and may only work within the ward in which they are serving their sentence (OBSIR 2016, §96, para. 4). Incarcerated people placed in semi-open penal institutions may perform their work with a reduced escort or without one, including single-person workplaces. On the other hand, incarcerated people who are placed in open-type facilities are mainly employed outside the prison's premises, without an escort, and perform work at single-person workplaces (Szymanowski 2017, 271).

The Polish legislature not only acknowledges the need to support incarcerated people in the process of their social reintegration while serving an imprisonment sentence; it has also created an institution tasked with financial support during the early stages outside of prison. The "iron cash" (ECL 1997, Art. 126) system aims to provide a person with basic financial resources after they have completed serving their sentence. It is specifically designed to help people cope with the nonprison environment and allow gradual adaptation. For example, these funds can help pay for the journey to a person's place of residence upon release, as well as for immediate living expenses. These funds are not subject to debt enforcement proceedings and, at the request of the incarcerated person, may be transferred to a selected bank account or savings deposit. The savings (ECL 1997, Art. 126, §2) are generated by withholding strictly defined fractions of remuneration until they reach the value of an average employee's remuneration.[8]

Unfortunately, not all incarcerated people have the opportunity to enjoy paid employment while serving their sentence. As a result, one effort designed to effectively reintroduce people to life upon release takes the form of basic financial assistance. As part of this program, anyone who does not possess sufficient personal funds and who has not yet secured employment outside the prison may be provided with financial assistance by the governor of the penal institution upon release. This assistance comes in the amount of up to one-third of the monthly salary of the average employed person in Poland, or its appropriate equivalent (ECL 1997, Art. 166, §3). This initiative further illustrates the commitment of the Polish penal system to rebuilding lives through education and employment.

Conclusion

Education in prison has been present in Poland for many years and is squarely rooted in the system of carceral rehabilitation. Nevertheless, it should be noted that while formal education and employment of incarcerated individuals each play an extremely important role in the reintegration process, other measures—including cultural, informal educational, and athletic activities—complement them and increase the effectiveness of these measures. Education and employment create conditions for an incarcerated person to spend free time actively and constructively. They also counteract periods of inactivity, eliminate the negative effects of long-term isolation, and are necessary for the proper development of human beings. It should be emphasized that cultural, educational, and physical activities are not an obligation but are considered a right for incarcerated persons (Szymanowski 2017, 315). Effective use of these activities helps in developing interests and teaches cooperation, which improves the atmosphere at a penal institution by alleviating conflicts and ultimately allowing for the productive use of time (Godyla 1998, 193).

Promoting social reintegration in Polish prisons is possible with the cooperation and involvement of both the incarcerated person and the prison administration. It would not be possible if the initiatives offered were the result of an obligation or top-down coercion of incarcerated students. From this point of view, it is also very important to individualize the way incarcerated people serve their prison sentences, which helps determine the selection and methods of measures used in social reintegration.

In the Polish prison system as it currently functions, as in others, complete reintegration will always face headwinds from the negative impact of criminal subculture in prison. And yet many positive initiatives, both educational and vocational, have been implemented. Especially in the case of young people, it is precisely vocational education that plays a special role because it performs an educational function while at the same time serving an economic, discipline-enhancing, and therapeutic purpose (Hołda and Postulski 2005, 290). Work helps develop prosocial attitudes and behaviors and builds productive habits as well as a sense of responsibility among juveniles. It also reduces the possibility of negative pressures such as isolation, inactivity, and the influence of the prison subculture (Soroko 1998, 7). Most importantly, education allows for better adjustment back into society, the goal of any effective system of incarceration.

Notes

1. In Poland, if a person is held in a pretrial detention center, it must be in a separate unit within the facility.

2. By comparison, in the United States, though there is no uniform standard, the American Correctional Association (ACA) recommends a minimum of a mere thirty-five square feet per person (ACA 2010, 3).

3. The inclusion of the regulation (Executive Criminal Law of 1997, art. 110, §2) stipulating the provision of a separate bed space for each incarcerated person is related to situations in the past, when their number was insufficient (Szymanowski and Świda 1998, 261).

4. In Poland, the only restriction put on participating in educational opportunities outside the prison is that this does not apply to those sentenced to life imprisonment.

5. Studies in Poland last five years, of which the first three years are for first-cycle studies, and the next two years are for second-cycle studies.

6. For social work, there is a specialty in "street-working," a form of social work aimed at helping people in solving problems and meeting needs in the environment of their daily functioning. It is also a mobile social work that consists in reaching people "where they are" and taking action to help. This social work specialty is offered at a pretrial detention center in Lublin.

7. Offered at a correctional facility in Opole Lubelskie.

8. The concept of the average remuneration is explained in the ECL (art. 242, §5), which describes it as the average monthly remuneration in the previous quarter, applicable from the first day of the following month after the president of Statistics Poland announces it in the Official Gazette of the Republic of Poland, *Monitor Polski*, for the purposes of pensions and annuities.

Works Cited

American Correctional Association. 2010. "Core Jail Standards." http://correction.org /wp-content/uploads/2014/09/Core-Jail-Standards-as-printed-June-2010.pdf/.

Civil Code (Poland) Act of April 23, 1964. *Journal of Laws* 16, item 93, as amended.

Constitution of the Republic of Poland. 1997, https://constituteproject.org/constitution /Poland_2009.pdf?lang=en.

Dąbkiewicz, Krzysztof. 2015. Kodeks karny wykonawczy. *Komentarz.*

Dawidziuk, Ewa. 2013. *Traktowanie osób pozbawionych wolności we współczesnej Polsce na tle standardów międzynarodowych*, Warszawa.

Executive Criminal Law (Poland) of June 6, 1997. *Journal of Laws* 90, item 557, as amended.

Godyla, Ryszard. 1998. "Podstawowe środki oddziaływania penitencjarnego kodeksie karnym wykonawczym z 1997 r." *NKPK* 3.

Hołda, Joanna, Zbigniew Hołda, Jerzy Migdał, and Beata Żórawska. 2017. *Prawo karne wykonawcze.* 5th ed. Warszawa.

Hołda, Zbigniew, and Kazimierz Postulski. 2005. *Kodeks karny wykonawczy: komentarz.* Gdańsk.

Jaki, Patryk. 2017. "Zatrudnienie skazanych Polsce na tle porównawczym— Zagadnienia wybrane." *PWP* 95.

Jaworska, Anetta. 2012. *Leksykon resocjalizacji.* Kraków.

Juwa, Marcin. 2013. *Kształcenie procesie resocjalizacji.* PWP 78.

Kalisz, Tomasz. 2004. *Zatrudnienie skazanych odbywających karę pozbawienia wolności, Zatrudnienie skazanych a efektywność wykonania kary pozbawienia wolności.* L. Bogunia (red.), Nowa Kodyfikacja Prawa karnego, Łódź.

Kuć, Małgorzata, 2007. *Indywidualizacja wykonywania kary pozbawienia wolności.* Lublin: Towarzystwo Naukowe KUL.

Kuć, Małgorzata. 2017. *Prawo karne wykonawcze.* Warszawa.

Landgeist. n.d. "Prison Population in Europe." https://landgeist.com/2022/01/06 /prison-population-in-europe/#:~:text=The%20European%20average%20is %20124,have%20a%20relatively%20low%20rate.

Machel, Henryk. 2003. *Więzienie jako instytucja karna i resocjalizacyjna.* Gdańsk.

Pawela, Stanisław. 2007. Prawo karne wykonawcze. *Zarys wykładu.* Warszawa.

Pietrikowski, Marek. 2004. "Teoretyczne podstawy resocjalizacji przez pracę trakcie wykonywania kary pozbawienia wolności." *PWP* 44–45.

Postulski, Kazimierz. 2017. "Kodeks karny wykonawczy." *Komentarz,* wyd. 4.

Prison Insider. n.d. "Poland." Accessed March 23, 2022. https://prison-insider.com /countryprofile/prisonspoland-2019#introduction-5d00f804351ce.

Regulation of the Minister of Justice of December 21, 2016. "On the Organizational Bylaws for Serving an Imprisonment Penalty." *Journal of Laws,* item 2231, as amended.

Rozporządzenie Ministra Sprawiedliwości z dnia 28 listopada 2016 r. w sprawie sposobu i trybu prowadzenia nauczania w zakładach karnych i aresztach śledczych Dz.U. 2016 poz. [Regulation of the Minister of Justice of November 28, 2016]. 2004. "On the Manner and Mode of Education in Penal Institutions and Pre-trial Detention Centers." *Journal of Laws,* item 2004, as amended.

Skrobotowicz, Grzegorz A. 2019. "Social and Living Conditions in Polish Prisons in the Context of International Legal Regulations—Selected Issues." *Review of European and Comparative Law* 39.

Soroko, Romuald. 1998. "Stan oraz kierunki rozwoju polskiej praktyki penitencjarnej (Wybrane problemy)." *Państwo i prawo* no. 7.

Szecówka, Alicja. 2011. "E-learning jako czynnik wspierający edukację osadzonych i ich readaptację społeczną." In *Kara pozbawienia wolności a readaptacja społeczna skazanych,* edited by A. Szerląg. Wrocław.

Szymanowski, Teodor. 2017. *Prawo karne wykonawcze z elementami polityki karnej i penitencjarnej.* Warszawa: Wolters Kluwer.

Szymanowski, Teodor, and Zofia Świda. 1998. "Kodeks karny wykonawczy." *Komentarz. Ustawy dodatkowe. Akty wykonawcze.*

Trela, Daria. n.d. "Studia wyższe więzieniu." *Służba Więzienna.* Accessed March 23, 2022. https://sw.gov.pl/aktualnosc/Studia-wyzsze-wiezieniu.

World Population Review. n.d. "Poland." Accessed March 23, 2022. https://world populationreview.com/countries/poland-population.

World Prison Brief. n.d. "Poland." Accessed March 23, 2022. https://prisonstudies.org /country/poland.

Wróbel-Chmiel, Agnieszka. 2018. *Edukacja zawodowa skazanych szansą na lepszą przyszłość dla kobiet i mężczyzn odbywających karę pozbawienia wolności.* Rzeszów.

PART III
Challenging the Silencing of Marginalized Voices

9 ||| AUTHORSHIP IN PRISON

STORIES OF IDENTITY, RESILIENCE, AND RENEWAL FROM EL SALVADOR

> "*Soy de mis 17 años porque me gusta andar en bicicleta*
> *Porque me siento alegre, como el amanecer.*"
> "I feel my seventeen years because I like to ride my bike,
> Because I feel content, like the dawn."
> —René,[1] seventeen years old

Introduction: The Lives of Authors

René was seventeen when we met. He was one of the young men serving time in one of the juvenile detention centers in El Salvador. He participated in our workshop "Soy Autor, Soy Autora" (in English, "I'm an Author"), a creative writing workshop in which participants write, share, and publish their life stories. René was an eager student, gang affiliated, cheerful, and intelligent. He was serving a sentence of thirteen years for drug dealing. René was killed inside the center that same year, a few short months after he published his memoir.

Santiago[2] was fifty-four when we met at an adult prison. He had served almost fifteen years when he participated in "Soy Autor, Soy Autora." Santiago was finally released a few weeks before the workshop ended, so, while he did not publish his story, he left two full notebooks with many of his memories: his upbringing, his teenage years as a *microbusero*[3] and a thief, the start and end of his career in the military, and his time as a "bodyguard." In his journal, he numbered the people he had killed and the countless times he had been beaten growing up. He also wrote about how much he liked the beach. After he was released, we kept in touch for some time. He worked as a cook at a beach hostel for a while and liked to spend time with his grandchildren. He also kept in touch with his "old friend,"

201

and, while he tried hard not to fall back into old patterns, out of money, friends, and motivation, eventually he stopped picking up the phone.

René was one of the hundreds of teenagers in juvenile detention centers, and Santiago was one of the thousands of men in the Salvadoran prison system. They could be the reflection of the "other": the vision of the passing time and the representation of the hope, complexity, paradox, and irony of our incarceration system—and our society. Prison is a prism through which to view Salvadoran society, a place to see how politics and history have discarded certain members. In their writings and those of the many authors who have published their stories through our program, we can weave together the history of El Salvador through the voices of the men and women who have lived it.

For example, José[4] wrote about the persecution that children suffered during the civil war by both the guerrillas and the military. In his story, he narrates that, as a child, he used to climb up a tree, tie himself to it, and try to fall asleep, hoping nobody would look up and find him. Santiago, who was in the military, wrote about his physical and mental training, and how after the peace agreement his "skills" were put to new use, since there were no opportunities for new beginnings elsewhere. Young men, on the other hand, tell us stories about abandonment, poverty, domestic violence, and gangs. Their stories give substance to the data academics and researchers present about human insecurity in El Salvador (Gellman 2022). Their narratives add the necessary texture to inform which policies will actually help strengthen democracy in the future.

Prison in El Salvador

Over the past twenty years, El Salvador has amassed the second-largest incarcerated population per capita in the world, after only the United States. It has increased its incarceration rate from 132 incarcerated persons per 100,000 inhabitants in 2000 to 617 in 2018 (Bergmann and Gude 2021). In 2018, El Salvador also topped the list of the most violent countries in the world, reaching 51 violent deaths per 100,000 inhabitants, and was classified by the Economic Commission for Latin America and the Caribbean (ECLAC) as the country with the highest rate of femicides in the Americas, registering 386 total violent deaths of women in 2018 alone (Agrupación Ciudadana por la Despenalización del Aborto et al. 2020). El Salvador's status as a highly violent country has not shifted under the Bukele administration, although its credibility as a democracy has (Gellman 2022, 4). After the 2022 murders of more than sixty-two people in one day by gang members, the government detained and incarcerated over eleven thousand men and women in a period of two weeks on charges of terrorism and gang affiliation, handing down sentences of up to fifteen to twenty years (Cué Barberena 2022). By April 2023, more than 64,000 people had been incarcerated under the State of Emergency, which was first declared in March 2022 (Gavarrete 2023).

Generally speaking, the problem of violence has mostly been attributed to gangs. To date, roughly half the prison population is gang affiliated (Bergmann and Gude 2021), and when violence increases, so does incarceration, and on and on. The way El Salvador has chosen to deal with crime is both archaic and dehumanizing. Not only does incarceration not solve the problem of violence, but it also disempowers communities from trying to heal and restore relationships.

When thinking about violence prevention and early ideas on reentry programs in El Salvador, much can be traced back to the late 1980s and early 1990s, when the United States began deporting a large number of men with criminal records who were involved with gangs. Hundreds of gang-affiliated men were "returned" to a precarious postwar country that, despite the recent peace agreement, had not been able to consolidate an inclusive social approach, much less to create a truthful reconciliation process that would acknowledge the collective grief and serve the individuals and communities that played a role during the conflict (Gellman 2022, 4–5). On the contrary, the "returned" citizens were as excluded in their homeland as they were in the United States. This time, however, they were able to strengthen the gang structure and expand their horizons. Violence then mutated to gang violence, responding mostly to the social need for protection and a sense of belonging rather than a political ideal.

Early interventionists such as Salvador Hernández, director of Asociación Movimiento de Jóvenes Encuentristas (The Movement for Youth Gathering), witnessed the expansion of gangs in the 1980s and 1990s and spoke about the power of community to build sustainable and long-term transformation, leading youth to desist from violence both on an individual and a collective level. However, such efforts were completely shattered by the implementation of security strategies such as *mano dura*.[5] These

harsh security strategies have applied technical solutions to adaptive challenges, but the problem of violence takes more than a quick fix. The vision
of peace requires trust, a radical imagination, and permanent dialogue.

For about a decade now, I have worked for ConTextos, a transnational
civil society organization made up of passionate community leaders, formerly incarcerated people, artists, and educators. Led by women, it has a
mission deeply rooted in fostering reconciliation, peace, critical thinking,
radical imagination, and civic participation so that the voices and the stories of any children, youth, men, and women are not left unheard.

ConTextos as Education in Prison

While many contributors to this volume discuss access to college for incarcerated people in other countries, El Salvador's educational challenges take
place long before that—in the K-12 system. College is still a relative luxury
for even nonincarcerated Salvadorans. The challenges that exist now are
less about access and more about quality of education: something beyond,
or perhaps in addition to, academic performance, excellence, and innovation. Quality of education means relevance, inclusion, critical thinking,
and emotional development to learn about the past; it means having the
potential to heal and restore, to make sense of who we are now as individuals and as a country. These absences in the educational system are not
by coincidence—quite the opposite. After decades of oppression, racism,
and inequality, critical thinking is still perceived as a weapon, writing and
expression as missiles.

As a civil society organization attempting to navigate a political transition, ConTextos recognizes that not only is El Salvador a young and
fragile democracy, but that it also has a painful and unresolved history
that persists in piercing the social fabric. ConTextos started working in
El Salvador in 2011 with teachers in mostly rural public schools holding
professional development spaces and coaching sessions based on literacy
practices. Before we got involved, teachers at these schools relied mostly
on dictation and rote copying to teach their students. Whether it was a
social studies or math class, teachers would fill the chalkboard with cold
and meaningless words based on the content assigned for the day. That
was the way they, like most of us, were taught in school. The classroom was
not a place to make sense of the world; it was a place to mute ourselves,

to write the words and repeat the ideas of others. To change this, teachers had to become students again and experience what it felt like to write what they feel and say what they think.

Little by little, school began to make sense for teachers—and, as a result, for students. I remember a time when Señorita Rosa,[6] the preschool teacher, told me of how she had no idea what to do when the woman who sold fruit outside the school gate was killed right before class one day. She and her students were already inside the building, but they were able to hear the gunshot and remained quietly inside. Everybody was nervous, and some of the children started to cry. Rosa remembered, "I started singing to them so they would calm down. After a little while, they all went home. A few days later, we did a 'read aloud' with one of the children's books we have in the library, to talk about what had happened and how we felt."

Teachers like Rosa have decided to confront the problem of history closely and engage their students in dialogue to express their anger, hope, and fear. They reflect on the complexity of violence, as well as the complexity of peace and restoration. It is certainly not an easy quest. That conversation goes beyond the dichotomy of good and bad, right and wrong. It is about recognizing that the same people we all grew up with in the same neighborhood, who we played soccer with and hung out with in the alley, are the same ones who wear the blue uniform of cops or sport the tattoos of gangs. These men and women, these simultaneous victims and perpetrators, are not colonizers of distant lands nor incomprehensible strangers; there is much more that we share than what separates us. The classroom, then, has the potential to host conversations across boundaries, to denormalize violence, and to let students grow in empathy and humanity to rebuild our social fabric. Deployed to that end, education is not just about academics: it is about citizenship, dignity, and community.

Eventually, teachers at these schools started asking their students powerful and bold questions: What do you think about Rodrigo not wanting to come to school? What would you do if you were as angry as Sofía? What would you tell Red and Blue to help them get over their differences? How do you think Laura felt when her mom abandoned her? Why do you think her mom left? How did she feel? What did you feel when you heard the news about the bus on fire? More importantly, they learned to listen to the stories that students had to tell.

Siempre he querido contar esta historia o escribirla, pero no es hasta ahora que he podido desahogar todo lo que llevo dentro. Una tarde, yo jugaba con mis hermanas, mamá se ocupaba del trabajo de la casa y papá trabajaba en el campo. Ese día, papá prendía fuego a la tierra donde más tarde sembraría maíz y frijoles. Yo estaba bajo un árbol de mamón cuando oí que alguien gritaba: "¡Irma, Irma!" Mi mamá subió corriendo por el camino y encontró a mi papá con las vestiduras desgarradas. Mi papá podía caminar y hablar, mi mamá lo tomó de las manos lo ayudaba a llegar a la casa. Mi mamá nerviosa le preguntaba: "¿Nelson, qué pasó?" pero mi padre no respondía, y recuerdo que yo solo daba vueltas alrededor del árbol de mamón y en mi mente pensaba, "Sara, es un sueño, esto no ha pasado"; cerraba y abría los ojos, los cerraba de nuevo y miraba a mi papá, las llamas lo habían lastimado, pero él no había perdido el conocimiento.

I have always wanted to tell this story or to write it, but it is not until now that I have been able to vent everything that I carry inside. One afternoon, I was playing with my sisters; Mom did the housework and Dad worked in the fields. That day, Dad set fire to the land where he would later grow corn and beans. I was under a *mamón* tree when I heard someone yell, "Irma, Irma!" My mom ran up the road and found my dad with his clothes torn. My dad could walk and talk, and my mom took him by the hands and helped him get home. My mother asked nervously, "Nelson, what happened?" but my father did not answer. I remember that I just walked in circles around the *mamón* tree, and in my mind I thought, "Sara, this is a dream, this has not happened!" I closed and opened my eyes and closed them again and looked at my dad: the flames had hurt him, but he hadn't lost consciousness. (Sara,[7] thirteen years old)

That was the beginning of the story of the death of Sara's papá. Many other students were also sharing their stories of trauma, with nobody else to listen to them but their teachers and classmates. Most of these students spoke about the longing of being the one who stays: the one who sees loved ones depart on a journey of migration, the one who waits for their loved one to come back from prison, the one who stays behind while their parents disappear. Their stories were full of questions about the ones who left. But what about the ones in prison? The ones on a journey of migration? The ones who disappeared? What is the other side of the story?

Students' stories took us to all these places as we tried to find the missing pieces of the puzzle and then give them back to those who were trying to make sense of their lives and dealing with the mystery of the absence of their loved ones. While working with "returned" citizens and teaching inside the prison, we realized that people returning from far away or living behind bars had for a long time crafted these missing stories over and over again, waiting for the opportunity to tell them. At the same time, they were also trying to make sense of their own lives absent of hope.

Working inside the prison was a big transition for ConTextos. Violence is not foreign to any of us; we had all, by that time, been mugged, followed, robbed, threatened, or had lost family members to violence. The idea of working in prison meant being with those who had mugged, followed, robbed, and threatened us. Working in prison carries a stigma of its own, as if working there poisons you; you become "one of them," or you might not last long. In fact, we kept our work secret for over a year, telling no one about "Soy Autor, Soy Autora": not on our social media, not even our friends and supporters. I even waited for over two years to tell my mother I was working in prison. In the individual and collective imagination, prison was—and still is—the symbol of everything that could hurt you or had hurt you before.

Before starting this work, I had never in my life talked about the men who had hurt me or my family and had not referred to them beyond their acts—not with my family, much less in my school. They were all "different," lost in their own criminal world, one-dimensional, and enigmatic. This distance that we create deepens the misunderstanding of a problem that affects us all, and what we do not understand we push away, isolate, and lock up in the hope that it will disappear on its own. The truth is that it is only when you get closer, as close as you can, that you are able to see through the fog and listen to the voices speaking their truth. And, when you do, it is not hard to understand why someone would take the life of others or why someone would stab you to get your phone. But to truly understand and forgive, I believe, takes more than reasoning.

In 2012, we started working at a mixed gang-member-affiliated prison. We had twenty-four incarcerated authors: twelve men and twelve women (as well as two children who accompanied their mothers to class). At the time, prisons in El Salvador were operating at 300 percent capacity and lacked even basic sanitary services. The smell of wet mud, rotten food, heavy air, and sweat filled the entire place. The prison school, though, was a breath of fresh air within the facility: murals, classroom routines, plants. The school itself was not so different from the ones outside in terms of infrastructure and atmosphere. Sadly, teacher practice was also very similar to what we see on the outside: rote memorization and dictation to every class.

Statistics about schools were (and still are) very discouraging too. Data from the Directorate General of Prisons show that, as of 2020, 36 percent of the incarcerated population had attained only primary education, 37 percent had attained only secondary education, and 19 percent had attained only high school. Fewer than 2 percent of people have any college education, and less than half a percent have received some technical education. There are a few private universities that offer college education in prison for "civilians," but all of these are small and rely on private funding and grants, or are short-term projects. In addition, educational opportunities in carceral settings typically exclude gang-affiliated men and women, who have limited, if not zero, access to any sort of educational opportunity.

When we began our work inside, we visited four or five men's and women's prisons to learn about the system and its rules and to decide where to launch the program. The staff showed us around the classrooms, let us intrude into people's cells, and even encouraged us to check to see that the beds had been made. In the courtyards and halls, thousands of men sat in desks writing out the alphabet in their notebooks or full words in English, working out in the makeshift gym, or simply hanging out. The prison we were showed last was an 18th Street Gang prison. It smelled the worst out of all of them. As we walked in, the gang leader came to greet us, and the first thing he asked was if we were going to run the children's educational program that they had been promised for some time. "Creative writing," we said. He was very intrigued, and while he did not become an author in our program, his wife did, writing a beautiful memoir about the birth of their son, who was born in prison not too long before.

In the civilian prisons, the program "Yo Cambio" (I Change) had the most people, as well as the best behaved; they were busy learning to crochet and speak English, making shoes, baking, hairdressing—all in addition to their formal education. The mission of the program was in fact to keep everybody as busy as possible so they would not think about "doing bad things." In truth, it was difficult to think about anything else at all, although through occupational and cognitive behavior therapy officials seemed confident that they could keep people engaged for the entire length of their sentence. For this reason, we chose to work in the gang-affiliated prison.

When we finally came to the wing we would be operating in and introduced ourselves, we found ourselves talking about ConTextos to a room full of shirtless men. As we talked about creative writing, books, and sharing stories, they welcomed us. The workshop was not about grades or academics; it was about identity, exploration, dialogue, and about learning from one another. That day, twenty-four people signed up to be part of the "Soy Autor, Soy Autora" workshop, and the next day they came to class. Both teachers and students were full of curiosity and uncertainty about the other, but by the end of the class we were all transformed, and we left the room with an excitement that was simply overwhelming. Since then, we have worked with a number of prisons and juvenile detention centers in El Salvador, as well as the Cook County Jail in Chicago, where some ConTextos staff are based.

The Ones Who Love the Most

With the opening of a new 40,000-bed prison in 2023 to address overcrowding from arrests during the 2022–23 State of Emergency, there are twenty-four prisons, four juvenile detention centers, and one intermediate center for youth over eighteen years old in El Salvador. In 2020, there were 37,570 incarcerated adults in El Salvador: 92.4 percent men and 7.6 percent women (Bergmann and Gude 2021). In 2023, though the number of incarcerated women is roughly the same, the number of men has nearly doubled to more than 65,000, and there have been 7,900 documented complaints of human rights violations for those detained, at least 90 deaths in custody, and extensive detention of minors (Hurtado 2023).

Prisons in all parts of the world are warehouses for those the state has deemed undesirable, so resources granted to prisons are *very* scant. When one considers the resources allotted to the Salvadoran prison system for food—three US dollars per person per day—the question of how to effectively rehabilitate overpopulated and underfunded prisons in any real way is daunting. While the general conditions of prisons in El Salvador (such as poor water, electricity, and bedding, among others) have improved in recent years, prisons are still overcrowded and offer limited rehabilitative services, healthcare attention, and educational opportunities, particularly for gang-affiliated prisons or sectors. This is not to say that more resources necessarily means a better system. As a matter of fact, the authors I met in Cook County Jail were often in shock when hearing about the conditions of prison in El Salvador. And, while they were getting their laundry done and would never run out of water, it did not take them long to realize that the same system of punishment and dehumanization was holding them.

Mónica teaches at the school in one of the juvenile detention centers in El Salvador. She participated in "Soy Autor, Soy Autora" too, and wrote her story alongside the young authors from the center. About her first years working at the juvenile detention center, she recalled, "I remember us playing soccer with the young people and seeing them having fun as children do." She also remembered that, at one time, gang members used to have much more visible tattoos: "Their faces were green!" she commented in her book, as she remembered how things used to be more than fifteen years ago. Mónica has worked in the system for over fifteen years, alongside five other teachers.

The rest of the staff at the center have had similar experiences. The psychological team consists of a psychologist, one or two social workers, and a lawyer. There are also *orientadores* (counselors), who, in practice, are in charge of opening and closing the doors, taking headcounts, and placing handcuffs. Most of us who have worked on the inside can paint a picture of the staff at traditional and highly punitive correctional facilities: officers coming to work unmotivated and tired, stressed, and without much hope about the "rehabilitation" process of the incarcerated population. We can also see the men and the women who, despite it all, come to work with a smile and a willingness to do a good job. We observe the advice they give to incarcerated men and women from time to time, hoping they will finally "listen" and "change." Talking about the staff also comes with some complexity, as I believe the staff love these incarcerated youth the most. Seeing children incarcerated pushes us, whether consciously or subconsciously, to question a system that has devised caging young people as a solution to society's ills.

On the day that René was murdered inside the juvenile detention center, staff had had a wonderful day with the young people. It was Children's Day, and they had prepared a full slate of games, music, and food. There was a soccer tournament, and the staff even stayed past their shift to finish the last game. At the end, the teachers and technical staff left feeling like they had had such a good day, knowing that the bonding they had experienced was beneficial for the youth and for them as well. Hours later, however, the director of the center received a call. He was informed that a teenage boy had been murdered and torn apart. The director had to come down in the middle of the night. A few others came along. They could not touch the body at all; they had to wait for the police to come. They stayed for a while without doing much. It was one of the saddest days of their lives. The next day, they had to show up like normal. They declared an emergency state, so the youth were isolated for a week or so. The staff talked about the loss of René among themselves, and after a while they went back to the old routine, though this time much less open to providing opportunities to those boys who had just betrayed one of their own—and them. This is just one example of the typical dynamic of the centers, but aggression inside and outside the center marks the experience of incarcerated people and the way they will build rapport or not.

Having motivated, informed, and professional staff at prisons is an urgent need within carceral spaces. Most of the staff who currently work at facilities in El Salvador did not choose to be part of the carceral system; they were placed there as a result of misconduct or negligence in their previous job. Without specialized training, self-care routines, a constant dialogue about reentry, as well as decent salaries and working conditions, the ability of the staff to connect, engage, and be creative in such a punitive context is limited. To add to all that, what happens when there is only one psychologist for the entire population? To this day, the juvenile detention center that I referred to before has only had a single psychologist for a population of anywhere between approximately one hundred and three hundred youth. Staffing challenges at adult prisons are even worse, with two psychologists for a population of three thousand or more. However, is the solution to hire an army of psychologists and social workers? In the absence of or as a complement to psychological services, writing not only fills the staffing void but also creates a community of authors who explore and create new identities, using their stories to make sense of the world. Writing might not be therapy, exactly, but it does have therapeutic impact.

The Dynamics of Collective Writing

Authors in the "Soy Autor, Soy Autora" circle eventually get used to being called authors; they have certainly been called many things throughout their lives, but almost never authors. They initially get very excited about the possibility of writing their own version of their story. I remember my first class in the prison. As soon as the class ended, the students all stood up and gathered around me in a circle just to tell me what they were going to write about. Many were talking over each other, while others were leafing through the books we brought for the class to read. The power of writing—of authorship—is the power to choose what story to tell, or, better yet, the power to tell the story we are *ready* to tell.

Authors write about all sorts of topics: a memorable birthday they had, the birth of their child, a journey of migration, cooking lasagna, getting married, wanting to have children. But they also write about joining a gang when they were eight years old, the civil war, experiences of domestic or sexual violence, or about having gang-derived wealth but never really feeling like they belong anywhere. Being an author means having the power to choose the words, the punctuation, even the silences to express oneself. While there are many methods and styles of writing, I believe that writing solo is overrated. Collective writing is process-oriented and allows much more room for dialogue, exchanges, and construction of meaning. This collective approach becomes a relief for authors because their educational experience has mostly been prescriptive, rigid, and unaccompanied. Writing is hard, and it is much more so when it is about ourselves. But it gets easier when we write as a collective.

We have had groups of anywhere from twelve to thirty authors, and in an overcrowded prison setting, numbers make a big difference. I also make sure they know that even though I am the facilitator, they are just as responsible for the class as I am. That means showing up on time, preparing the space, bringing supplies, and taking care of the materials. Being responsible for the class also means holding each other accountable for our actions in the classroom, as well as throughout the writing process. Writing together this way takes on a completely different dynamic when we are going through drafts together. We accompany each other every step of the way as we are appropriating new literary and dialogue tools to tell stories about our lives. Holding each other accountable throughout this process is much more profound, as we need to probe each other's stories and make sure we are writing with perspective, authenticity, and vulnerability.

The community of authors is strengthened by this particular support. We get to know each other so well as writers and thinkers that we know we can trust one another and that there is profound mutual respect, admiration, and love. Being responsible for each other also entails providing emotional support when needed: giving words of encouragement, passing a tissue or a glass of water when the person who is sharing starts crying, giving hugs or otherwise demonstrating connection, and holding each other up when someone else is down. Since I will also write and share my own story, I tell them that I will need those things too.

In a context where the teacher is typically a symbol of authority and expertise, this idea of universal vulnerability comes as a novelty. In 2018, a colleague and I ran the "Soy Autor, Soy Autora" workshop at the prison where I met Santiago. We had close to thirty students. We all got to know each other a little bit as the class started. We cocreated the classroom routines and talked about holding the space together, as we will need each other in the process of writing our stories. We talked about brainstorming, drafting, revising, and editing as part of the writing process, and started the class by doing some brainstorming writing exercises. We played with different stories we might want to share, and, to provide some modeling, I shared mine.

At the time, my dad had been diagnosed with cancer. I had just moved back to my parents' house to take care of him. Being a caretaker for my dad has been one of the most painful and tender experiences I have ever had. I told the class that I wanted to write about it. I recalled how my weekends were spent at the hospital, and I talked about the conversations I had with my mom about death. I told them that my dad was a fantastic teacher, and that without even realizing it I had learned a lot from him about being a teacher. Midway through my story, I was already crying and had to sit down. But I did not stop. I told them the whole story. A few months later, my father died, and I shared with my siblings what I wrote as a result of that day.

At the time, however, Raul was next to me, his hand on my shoulder as I was telling my story. He said he was sorry to hear about my dad and that he hoped he would get better soon. Santiago also said that he knew how I felt: he had not seen his dad for decades, so, in a way, it was as if he had lost a dad too. Many more words of encouragement later, the authors were ready to choose their stories and broke off to write their first drafts. Modeling is not just about providing scaffolding to help students learn writing techniques or a literary resource; it is also about modeling how to share emotions, talk about difficult things, cry, and speak our truth.

After authors work at putting their stories down on paper, they eventually feel ready to share. When this happens, they come to the "authors' chair." Everyone sits in a circle, and an author volunteers to read their story aloud; the rest of us listen, respond, ask questions, and provide feedback afterward. Reading our own story aloud becomes a different experience from simply writing it: we get to say the words, we listen to our story for a second time, and, more importantly, we get the responses of an audience.

Josue was an author at a juvenile detention center. His story was about himself and his family. They grew up in Honduras, and when he was very young, his mom decided to migrate to El Salvador to work. When he read his first draft, it was full of anger and hatred toward his mom; in fact, he wrote about being abandoned by his mom and blamed her for his ending up in prison. After he finished, it was time for the audience to respond: "Why do you think your mom left? Did she keep in touch while she was in El Salvador? Did she visit you and your brothers?" These questions brought Josue some perspective, so he talked about how precarious the situation was in Honduras and the way his mom used to send money for them to eat and go to school. He also mentioned that she would visit them every fifteen days and take them to the river to have some time together. He also remembered that she was the only person with him at his hearing. "How do you think your mom felt when she left?" This question made him realize that his mom left not because she did not love him, but because she *did*. A few drafts later, his memoir had changed drastically, from a story of resentment to one of understanding, empathy, and love.

One time, a woman who worked at another nonprofit organization told me that writing was a cliché because authors were not telling the stories the way they "really" happened, but the way they wanted them to happen. I told her that if I wanted to know what "really" happened, I would go to the newspaper or to their records and read it there, but that I was not interested in that. I wanted to know how they and the people who were involved *lived* their stories, because writing from that perspective had the potential to become a pivot point in their lives, from where growth could happen.

As we continue writing and sharing, authors become a community in which they can trust, share, and be vulnerable. It is a community that creates new group dynamics corresponding to their new identities as authors. Authors share, think critically, and support one another; they actively listen to each other, express disagreement in a respectful manner, cry if they want to, and learn how to speak up and say just the right thing when someone is having a hard time writing or sharing their story. As we open up more and more, we need to know that we will be taken care of in the process. These classroom dynamics also break established norms and behaviors that we have all internalized over the years—particularly for gangs, who have their own code in which violence is part of the norm.

Writing and Dialogue for Connection

How does an author's identity break through their gang identity? This is a very important question, as roughly half the people in Salvadoran prisons are gang members, who also happen to serve longer sentences (Bergmann and Gude 2021). The "Soy Autor, Soy Autora" space is an opportunity to challenge our own paradigms, reassess our values, reflect on the past, confront the present, and envision the future. While it is certainly not easy to do that, it becomes even more difficult to speak about and share findings and discoveries about yourself, knowing that your "new self" might challenge the gang culture that you are still part of.

In spite of this, most of the stories that gang members write are narratives of redemption centered around self-awareness and regret. The following two examples illustrate this particularly well.

> *En el año 1995 fue cuando una vida tranquila como el cielo se convirtió en una oscura tormenta que ni siquiera vi venir.*
> *Yo tenía apenas 14 años, tenía una buena familia, económicamente estable.*
> *No tenía necesidad de nada.*
> *Fue entonces que conocí muchachos que más tarde serían mis amigos.*
> *La calle es oscura y fría como la noche. Puede convertir a los jóvenes en otras personas.*
> *Años más tarde, me encontraba recluido en una cárcel donde vivir es tan difícil, es como caminar sobre el filo de una navaja.*
>
> *Pero en un día como los otros dentro de la prisión, desperté en mi celda y estando recostado, vi a mi alrededor.*
> *Vi a mis compañeros de celda, algunos aún dormidos y otros con la mirada perdida.*
> *Fue entonces que pensé: ¿Así quiero vivir toda mi vida?*
> *Sentí un dolor tan inmenso que no podría explicarlo, me dolía el alma y gritaba "ya no sigas así."*
> *Sentí que la tristeza cubría mi mente y mi alma con una oscuridad interminable.*

Sentí ganas de llorar, de gritar, de salir corriendo.
Pero sabía que nada iba a conseguir con eso.
Fue entonces que tomé la mejor decisión: "hacer de mi vida, una
    nueva vida."
No fue fácil desprenderme de toda esa manera de vivir.
Más cuando te encuentras entre tanta gente, que ni siquiera se
    le pasa por la mente la palabra cambiar.

The year 1995 was when a life as calm as the sky turned into a dark
    storm that I didn't even see coming.
I was just fourteen years old, had a good family, and was financially
    stable.
I had no need for anything.
It was then that I met some boys who would later become my friends.
The street is as dark and cold as the night. It can turn the youth into
    other people.
Years later, I found myself locked up in a prison where living is so
    difficult, it's like walking on a razor's edge.

But on a day like any other day in prison, I woke up in my cell and,
    while I was lying down, I looked around me.
I saw my cellmates, some still asleep and others staring blankly.
It was then that I thought: *Is this how I want to live my whole life?*
I felt such immense pain that I could not explain it. My soul ached
    and I cried out, "Don't go on like this."
I felt sadness cover my mind and soul with an endless darkness.
I felt like crying, screaming, running away.
But I knew that nothing would come of it.
It was then that I made the best decision: "to make my life a new life."
It was not easy to let go of all that way of living.
Even more so when you find yourself among so many people who
    don't even think of the word "change." (Armando, age unknown)

En esos segundos mi vida dio un gran cambio. Para mí, ha sido la
    decisión más difícil. Saber que he tirado tantas rocas al río sin
    darme cuenta de las circunstancias o el mal que he ocasionado.
    ¡Cosas que jamás podré enmendar!

In those seconds my life took a big change. For me, it has been
the most difficult decision. To know that I have thrown so many
rocks into the river without realizing the circumstances or the
evil I have caused, things I will never be able to make amends for!
(P. A. Hernández, age unknown)

When, after a few months of intense writing and sharing, we are finally
ready to publish, we set a date and start preparing for the big event. The
publishing event is the day where we present our *Illustrated Memoir* to
an audience. We usually invite authors' families, prison staff, correctional
officers, teachers, fellow authors, organization leaders, politicians, judges,
and community members. Prior to the event, we come together as a class
again to plan and design the agenda and the decorations, talk about body
language, and discuss what we are going to wear. We also go over some
of the questions the audience might ask and practice our answers. But,
more importantly, we reflect on our time together and everything we have
learned as a group, the things we are now able to do. We tell them that, at the
publishing event, we are going to meet people who did not go through the
same writing experience we did, but that we want them to also come with
their own stories. We stress that the most important thing is to listen, ask
them questions about their lives, and try to find each other in the stories.

We do not have time to prep audiences as well, but we do give them
ideas of questions they might ask regarding the heart of the story, the
author's intention, and the meaning of words or phrases used in the story.
Prior to the event, we send them the "safety protocol," which is mostly
about being respectful of the rules of the prison so as not to get the authors
or themselves in trouble and making sure that audience members only ask
questions that they themselves are ready to answer.

We start the event by welcoming everybody and providing some introduction. An author stands up and talks about the writing process and what
being an author means to the group. In one iteration of the workshop, Raul
was chosen by the other authors to give the "words." He came up front to
talk about being vulnerable and sharing his story for the first time. His
daughter and wife could not make it to the event, but he talked about
dedicating his memoir to his daughter as a promise of seeing each other
again and watching her grow. His voice was shaking, his eyes watering,
but he kept going, and waves of snaps filled the air to show connection,
empathy, and support.

Authors then go to their stations, and the guests all spread around the room to mingle with them. We read the books and ask questions to learn more about authors' lives. Raul wrote about being a "kangaroo parent" when his daughter was born, so we asked about his daughter, who at that time was probably between five and six. Many authors talk about the day they were apprehended and use metaphors to talk about their mistakes. They also talk about the future, their goals, and their desire to help others who are or have been in their shoes.

Audience members also share their stories and find moments of connection, similarities, and differences. We laugh, hug, shake hands, and give words of encouragement to each other. During the event, the question "Why are you here?" stops being very important. Both Armando and P. A. Hernández, quoted previously, were active gang members when they wrote and published their stories. Their voices are unique in our social context, and they demonstrate that every story, even theirs, has room for tenderness, innocence, and redemption. We know enough about the other side— the pain, violence, and fear that we have experienced firsthand and that are also in the headlines of newspapers, political campaigns, and security strategies. Little do we know, though, about the other side of the stories.

Jimmy, for example, spoke about years of violent abuse from his stepfather. He described different ways in which his stepfather would humiliate, repress, and beat him for no apparent reason. He even stated that sometimes he was made to find and choose the branch with which his stepfather was to beat him. Jimmy also talked about going to school and the way his favorite teacher would show him kindness, like she knew something was going on at home. He wrote about joining the gang and the sense of protection and belonging he received from his friends. At the end of the story, he went on to express gratitude and forgiveness toward his family, since he hoped that one day he would be able to come home and meet them again. He did see them again a few months later, when he was finally released after ten years of incarceration. After he was released, he got in touch with us, and we went to the beach with him and his five-year-old daughter. He had moved back home with his parents and was willing to do it all right this time.

I do not want this to be read as absolving the "criminal." Rather, I simply show that stories like Jimmy's complicate narratives around victims and victimizers. And I propose writing as a way to heal the deep wounds of history that hold us back from real reconciliation.

Conclusion

The "Soy Autor, Soy Autora" writing process is part of a long tradition in Latin American literature referred to as *testimonio*. This tradition was forged under authoritarian regimes in the region and was a popular form of resistance-through-writing that spoke truth to power (Beverley 1989). Testimonio was a response to the intense state-led violence throughout the region and was seen as a literary vehicle for recording the voices of those most oppressed. The stories that authors have shared also record the history of El Salvador. José was part of the "Soy Autor, Soy Autora" class of 2018, and he started out his story by painting a beautiful image of children playing in a field. Imagination took them to all parts of the country, until their game was finally ended by the "guys in olive." The military was recruiting mostly children to be part of the armed forces; on the other side, guerrillas were recruiting children as well. His story is about escaping, climbing up trees to hide, moving from town to town just to stay alive. He talks about losing so many friends and family members, the ones who did not make it through those difficult times.

> *Esa era solo trajo dolor, muerte, destrucción y familias dolidas.*
> *Nos robaron el sueño y la ilusión y sus secuelas aún resuenan en*
> *   mi diario vivir.*

> That era brought only pain, death, destruction, and wounded
>   families.
> We were robbed of our dreams and illusions and its aftermath
>   still echoes in my daily life. (José, age unknown)

José did not write about being incarcerated, but he was then serving a sentence of thirty years. While writing, José realized that his story is not just about him, but that it is really *our story*, our history. His lived experiences light the way to show how violence has mutated over time, to realize that breaking down barriers means switching the perspective of who is able to provide testimonio of what has happened in this country. José's story is also a story of the failure of the state and the brutality of Salvadoran history. And yet, if more people can learn to write their stories, El Salvador may begin to rewrite its own as well.

Notes

1. René is a pseudonym to protect the identity of the author.

2. Santiago is a pseudonym.

3. The person who collects money from bus passengers and gives change back.

4. José is a pseudonym.

5. In general, *mano dura* is a byword for authoritarian and populist approaches to law and order, to refer to authoritarian and populist approaches to maintaining public order, as well as the excessive use of military and police force to deal with crime (Igarapé Institute 2018).

6. Rosa is a pseudonym.

7. Sara is a pseudonym.

Works Cited

Agrupación Ciudadana por la Despenalización del Aborto, Asociación Tiempos Nuevos Teatro, Azul Originario, Cristosa, Fundación de Estudios para la Aplicación del Derecho, Fundación para el Debido Proceso, Los Siempre Sospechosos de Todo, and Servicio Social Pasionista. 2020. "El Salvador: Régimen y Condiciones de las Personas Privadas de Libertad, Impactos y Efectos en sus Derechos Humanos: Informe presentado por organizaciones de la sociedad civil en el 178 período de sesiones de la comisión interamericana de derechos humanos." December 3, 2020. https://en.calameo.com/read/005879919dc3427d3f1fo.

Bergmann, Adrian, and Rafael Gude. 2021. "Set Up to Fail: The Politics, Mechanisms, and Effects of Mass Incarceration." *Latin American Law Review* 7: 43–59.

Beverley, John. 1989. "The Margin at the Center: On '*testimonio*' (testimonial narrative)." *Modern Fiction Studies* 35 (1): 11–28.

Cué Barberena, Ramiro. 2022. "Dos semanas de guerra contra pandillas en El Salvador: detenciones masivas y violaciones de derechos." Accessed April 15, 2022. https://france24.com/es/am%C3%A9rica-latina/20220414-guerra-pandillas-el-salvador-bukele-detenciones.

Dirección General de Centros Penales (DGCP). 2020. "Estadística Penitenciaria." https://transparencia.gob.sv/institutions/dgcp/documents/407851/download.

Gavarrete, Julia. 2023. "A Family with Nothing to Hide Flees from the State of Exception." *El Faro*. https://elfaro.net/en/202303/el_salvador/26776/A-Family-with-Nothing-to-Hide-Flees-from-the-State-of-Exception.htm.

Gellman, Mneesha. 2022. "The Democracy Crisis in El Salvador: An Overview (2019–2022)." Columbia University's Center for Mexico and Central America's Regional Expert Paper Series No. 4. https://drive.google.com/file/d/1y9F6SeYjZUkoF-T4VaDBOXMzQIjQa8WW/view.

Hurtado, Marta. 2023. "El Salvador State of Emergency." Press briefing, Office of the High Commissioner for Human Rights. https://ohchr.org/en/press-briefing-notes/2023/03/el-salvador-state-emergency.

Igarapé Institute. 2018. "La Mano Dura." https://igarape.org.br/en/la-mano-dura/.

MARIA GARRO, MASSIMILIANO SCHIRINZI,
GIOACCHINO LAVANCO, AND MICHELANGELO CAPITANO

10 ||| RETHINKING EDUCATION AND MEDIATION FOR INCARCERATED IMMIGRANTS IN ITALY

As recently as the 1950s, prison authorities in Italy sought to provide only a basic level of literacy for Italians who were incarcerated. Over the years, however, authorities have faced increasing calls not only to integrate courses on Italian language and culture for those from outside Italy, but also to extend its mandate to provide education at all levels. Indeed, today, the educational curriculum available in Italian prisons, at least on paper, starts from elementary school and continues all the way to university, with the intention of granting the greatest possible choice of education. To this end, Article 19 of Law 354 of 1975 (Norms on Prison Regulations and Measures to Implement the Deprivation of Liberty)[1] establishes that those teaching the state school curriculum in prisons must offer the same characteristics as schools in the outside community when it comes to programs and teaching methods.

Before 1975, the prison system in Italy had been conceived as an impermeable structure isolated from society. In the ensuing years, cultural and organizational changes have taken place—especially since the passage of Law 354/1975—that have redefined the roles and functions of prison staff, placing special emphasis on legal compliance and on support for the individual in prison. Though prison, by its very nature, is isolated from the outside community, the Italian penal system advocates for the education of people who are incarcerated with an eye to their social reintegration.

The 1975 law introduced a model of rehabilitative justice based on the inherent dignity of the person and the gradual social reintegration of those who have been incarcerated. In this new formulation, punishment cannot consist of treatment contrary to a sense of human dignity and must work toward the education and reintegration of the convicted person. While this system is dedicated to facilitating personal change, the law includes the imperative that, above all, an individual's identity must not be confused with one's situation of being incarcerated.

To this end, people incarcerated in Italian prisons typically have access to recreational, cultural, and training activities aimed largely at facilitating their social reintegration. Of particular note are education courses at the school and university level organized within Italian prisons, where the programs and teaching methods have the same characteristics as external schools and universities (Art. 19 of Law 354/1975 and Art. 44 decree June 30, 2000, n. 230). Paradoxically, however, educational needs do not seem to be a priority, either for people who are incarcerated or for prison officials. For the latter, education is often not seen as important for integration into the world of work. For incarcerated people themselves, short-term economic needs often drive them to put work skills before education.

There are also some particularly problematic aspects of Law 354, at least in its implementation. One key challenge is represented by the increased educational needs of incarcerated people who do not speak Italian, for whom access to education courses is practically impossible. Immigrants are some of the most marginalized people incarcerated in Italy and face additional identity-based challenges to accessing the rights of incarcerated people. In the ensuing chapter, this challenge and some solutions—including the organization of education courses in Italian prisons—will be explained in detail.

Education within Italian Prisons

To the consternation of some educators, work is still the favored activity in attempting reintegration and resocialization, implying that having a job upon release is preferential to gaining an education while incarcerated. Therefore, it is not surprising that the preference for work over education plays out in participation rates. Between 2019 and 2020, the dropout rate for educational programs in Italian prisons in general was 88 percent, a high level compared with external institutions, largely due to the early departures from jail, relocation to other institutions, or access to work (*Associazione Antigone* 2021).

Unfortunately, educational programs in prison risk being poor imitations of external schools because the educational programs offered do not meet the perceived needs of this specific group of adult students. Hence, adult students are highly selective, and they subject themselves to a broad

Table 10.1.

Incarcerated people in Italy enrolled vs. completed within educational courses for adults, divided into levels and teaching periods (2020–21). *Source:* Head of General Secretariat Department: Statistical section.

Teaching time	No. of courses	Enrolled		Completed		% Completed
		Total	Non-citizens	Total	Non-citizens	
FIRST LEVEL						
Alphabetization and learning Italian language	407	3,326	2,996	1,385	1,212	41.6
First teaching time	292	2,392	1,444	942	594	39.4
Second teaching time	213	1,971	639	786	312	39.9
Total first level	912	7,689	5,079	3,113	2,118	40.5
SECOND LEVEL						
First teaching time	329	4,199	1,081	2,105	384	50.1
Second teaching time	248	2,266	482	1,380	238	60.9
Third teaching time	166	1,070	238	747	153	69.8
Total second level	743	7,535	1,801	4,232	775	56.2
TOTAL	1,655	15,224	6,880	7,345	2,893	48.2

and general study, as do young people (Paterniti Martello 2021). According to the law, the issue is linked with strict educational paths aimed at allowing students to obtain a qualification (at least at the most basic level). In order to build a model educational program that is both flexible and tailored, it is necessary to start from students' actual needs (La Regina 2018). Nevertheless, because education is a personal and socially rehabilitative element that aims to humanize a person while they fulfill their sentence, education is strongly promoted for incarcerated women and men regardless of the qualification sought (see UNODC 2011).[2]

In this regard, educational programming in Italian prisons is divided into two levels. The first level, elementary school and literacy training, is provided by provincial centers for adult education (*centri provinciali istruzione adulti*, CPIA) and is open to most people who are incarcerated, including people from outside Italy. The second level includes technical, professional, and artistic education (Ministry of Justice, February 19, 2020). People who are incarcerated participate widely in the first type of education, even those in pretrial detention or serving a short sentence, as can be seen in table 10.1. Many educational programs suffered during the Covid-19 pandemic, mainly in those correction facilities where remote teaching was prohibited. Moreover, many incarcerated people were excluded from any group activities due to the need to keep safe distances in the classroom.

From the outset, it is crucial to point out that general literacy courses are automatically recommended to non-Italian-speakers because they offer an important tool to navigate many aspects of life inside prison, such as writing to legal representatives, communicating with prison officials, and keeping in touch with loved ones. To be successful, however, teachers in the prison setting must be able to assess the educational level of the student as well as their motivation to study. Accordingly, lessons should consider different contextual factors as well as students' difficulties learning and concentrating, which are often due to both a lack of Italian language skills and to cultural differences. To this end, the intervention of mediators and interpreters who can welcome and carry out this first stage of educational assessment and planning with incarcerated individuals should be encouraged.

University-Level Education in Italian Prisons

Beyond the first category of basic education, there is a small but growing population of incarcerated students in Italy who enroll in university coursework. This group traces its roots back to the 1970s, when a small but notable portion of the incarcerated population in Italy were already university students who attended schools around the country. Over the years, the number of incarcerated students increased, especially among those with medium or long prison sentences, and universities began paying the prison system more attention. As a result, prison university centers were created to meet this growing need. Nevertheless, access to a university education is still not available to everyone. Availability varies by prison and depends on the ability of an incarcerated person's loved ones to advocate with the administration and with institutions of higher education, as well as on the interest and availability of instructors. For this reason, many geographical areas (entire regions, in fact) and many penitentiary institutions do not offer this opportunity—at least at the moment—despite the signed protocols. Internally, it has created another source of inequity between the north and south of Italy. This was the case, at least, up until 2021, when the country recorded an increase in the number of universities (40 out of 96) operating in more than 82 prison institutions across Italy (Corrado 2021).

Structurally, educational programs at the postsecondary level are established by Italian universities and created through agreements with the Department of Penitentiary Administration and the regional superintendency, with the stated aim of providing a university education to all incarcerated people. University prison extensions have already been established in many Italian regions, and the forty Italian universities involved (such as the Universities of Milan, Palermo, Cagliari, and Turin) sponsor educational programs and coordinate with the penitentiary institutions to provide a university education inside Italian prisons. All this works to make the right to education uniformly available for all those who wish to exercise it.

The University of Milan: A Case Study

Since 2015, the public University of Milan, through open enrollment days, has introduced some of its undergraduate courses to people interested in becoming students while in prison. This educational program promotes an inside-out model, combining incarcerated and traditional students in the classroom. This program was made possible thanks to an agreement with the regional superintendent for prison administration (*provveditorato regionale amministrazione penitenziaria*).

The modules and workshops included in these courses last twenty hours and offer three transferable credits. These courses—on philosophy, law, literature, drama and art, writing and narration, and image theory—involve multiple professors offering a single or entire cycle of lessons. For incarcerated students who cannot attend external lessons, these educational activities are a significant opportunity for study. Moreover, these courses can represent a powerful experience for traditional students who wish to learn more about realities and contexts different from their own.

In addition, the University of Milan, thanks to its students, has created a network of dozens of tutors dedicated to launching and fostering the university careers of incarcerated students. Hence, at the beginning of the academic year, each newly admitted student in detention is accompanied by a tutor who meets with the student twice a month. Moreover, degree programs recognize tutorial service as an educational activity. Tutors provide support by helping incarcerated students choose subjects and write a study plan, learn methods, request and deliver library books, and communicate with teachers before exams (University of Milan 2021).

On February 25, 2021, a protocol agreement was signed between the Universities of Palermo, Catania, Messina, and Enna, the Region of Sicily, the regional superintendent for prison administration, and the guarantor of prisoners' rights (*garante diritti dei detenuti*) to further promote the right to university education within penitentiary faculties (University of Palermo 2021). Still, more is needed. These university courses, in fact, are accessible only to a small number of incarcerated students, as prison university centers are still active in fewer than half of Italian prisons (82 out of 190) (Regione Sicilia 2021).

However, it is also true that students taking courses at the university level in prison rarely drop out and typically manage to graduate with excellent results. In addition to tax breaks, these students are also granted opportunities for private study space, library admissions, and meetings with university tutors. Where possible, incarcerated students are assigned educational spaces suitable for carrying out their studies, and students can be authorized to keep books, school supplies, and all other course materials in their rooms and study areas. In addition, select classrooms may be equipped with network-connected computers, desks, a blackboard, and a projection screen. Without a doubt, this is a sure model for success, if only it could be achieved on a wider scale and for all people who are incarcerated.

Unfortunately, one of the most substantial obstacles is that too few incarcerated students have achieved the secondary education qualification required to access university courses. Despite this, in Italy during the academic year 2020–21, there were 1,034 incarcerated students enrolled at the university level (970 men and 64 women), representing an increase of 29.9 percent compared to 2018–19 (796 total students, of which only 28 were women) (Corrado 2021). Of the 1,034 total incarcerated students in 2021, 925 were attending classes across 82 different prisons, while 109 were serving their term of incarceration externally. Moreover, besides this last group of 109 (10.5 percent) students subject to community criminal enforcement, 549 (53.1 percent) were serving a prison sentence in medium security settings, 355 (34.3 percent) were in high security, and 21 (2.1 percent) in the 41-bis regime (Caiffa 2021).[3]

As for degree pursuit, in 2021, a total of 896 students were enrolled in bachelor's degree programs (87 percent of the total number of students in detention), while 137 attended master's degree programs (13 percent). The subject most studied by incarcerated students was the social sciences (25.4 percent), followed by fine arts and literature (18.6 percent), law (15.1 percent), sciences (13.7 percent), education (7.4 percent), history and philosophy (7.3 percent), economics (6.5 percent), and other areas (6 percent). In 2020, 23 incarcerated students earned their degree in the three-year bachelor's program, while six earned a master's degree (Corrado 2021).

Finally, as for the general demographic composition of prisons in Italy, educational classes and university courses are heterogeneously composed: international and local students are enrolled together, which, while beneficial for cultural acclimation, means that multiple levels of linguistic skills and previous education among students could make it challenging to find a standard teaching approach.

Incarcerated Migrants in Italy

In the broad and multifaceted context of immigration, there are many obstacles that make life difficult for people coming to a new country. For example, there are myriad occasions when a migrant can easily break the law in the host country without intending to. Here, we highlight that one of the reasons is cultural, since migrants are often unaware of nuanced social structures and behavioral norms in the country of arrival, and these are sometimes different from their own cultural norms. Another reason, perhaps the most common and definitely the most pernicious, is the vulnerability of migrants without residence documents. Their irregular status makes them vulnerable to informal employment arrangements and paints them as attractive targets for criminal organizations that may seek to absorb them for use in drug trafficking, sexual exploitation, and other criminal enterprises they might otherwise shun. The reality is that this mainly happens when linguistic and cultural mediation services are ineffective or nonexistent in prisons as well as in Italy's permanent centers for repatriation (*centri di permanenza per il rimpatrio*, CPRs), where they are essential to ensuring safety and well-being (Polidoro 2021).

At an international level, public authorities are required to take adequate measures to ensure there is sufficient information given to a person regarding their penal status, such as the reasons for restrictive measures and the possible appeal or reexamination of one's trial. In this way, the noncitizen is at a significant disadvantage compared to the local detainee because the action that a mediator is called to perform goes beyond simple interpretation. Ultimately, mediators are relied upon to decode the language of the noncitizen for the official and that of the official for the noncitizen, putting two different cultures in contact, facilitating the reception process, and improving the quality of official interaction (Caputo and Di Mase 2013). Unfortunately, in practice, it is actually quite common for the intercultural mediator to misrepresent what a migrant reports when applying for asylum or during a trial. On many occasions the results are unsuccessful due to mistranslations, sloppy summaries, and inaccuracy of the words reported by the mediator (Edwards, Temple, and Alexander 2005; Ngalwa 2007).

As of January 2022, the Department of Penitentiary Administration, Statistics Section reported that the detained population in Italy was 54,372, of which 17,103 were noncitizens (Ministry of Justice 2022). The number of foreign-born people incarcerated in Italy has greatly increased in recent years due to a significant uptick in migration flows (Paoletti 2014). Statistically speaking, Italy is the main European destination for migrants from outside Europe, many of whom arrive seeking to escape conditions in their places of origin rather than because of any particular attraction to the destination (Istituto Nazionale di Statistica 2021). Indeed, the flow of migrants entering Italy are increasingly motivated by the search for international protection and not by any motivation that is structured or planned around Italy itself (Garro et al. 2022). The challenge this produces, therefore, is that many incarcerated migrants do not intend to stay in Italy but intend to settle in other countries upon release.

Partly due to its geographical position, Italy experiences the particularly acute phenomenon of having an inconsistent pattern within itself. The center-north boasts the presence of "older" migrant communities (e.g., Eastern Europe) of people who arrive by land, while the South, particularly the regions of Sicily, Calabria, and Puglia, faces almost daily landings of "new" migrants by both land and sea (Istituto Nazionale di Statistica 2021). Thus, on one end of the country, there is the management of an advanced stage of integration characterized by a large number of long-term residence permits, family reunifications, and increasing acquisition of citizenship. On the other end, there is a wildly different context with high levels of marginalization and prejudice toward new arrivals.

The integration of immigrants is defined as "a multidimensional process aimed at peaceful coexistence, within a given historical and social situation, between culturally and/or ethnically different individuals and groups, based on mutual respect for ethno-cultural diversity" (Cesareo 2009, 23). However, this idyllic process is often hindered by anti-immigrant sentiment on the part of locals, a prejudice caused by the perceived threat of the presence of the "other." In this regard, Isabella Merzagora (2017), taking up Theodor Adorno and colleagues (1950), does not hesitate to underline how prejudice is closely related to the phenomena of insecurity and social unrest, taking root more among disadvantaged host country nationals who feed on the idea that outsiders steal their work. To some, the "other" is frightening, or at least fundamentally different; there is a clear "us versus them" mentality linked to the psychological value of belonging. There is also a spontaneous tendency to turn any type of difference into the complete rejection of the "other" (Allport 1954; Tajfel 1972, 1981; Tajfel and Turner 1979; Turner and Oakes 1986; Turner et al. 1987). Generally speaking, because the prevailing reaction to uncertainty is to close ranks, the "other" in this case comes to be seen as an enemy, a non-Italian, a threat to be protected against (Salvatore et al. 2019).

Accordingly, there is a "criminalization of immigrants" that turns them into a "symbol and target of all social anxieties" (Wacquant 1999, 219), leading to a perception of them as outsiders more in need of social control than of aid and subject to harsher punishment. Therefore, even today there is often a pervasive bias in favor of light-skinned Europeans—even on the part of prison workers, which implies the obviously spurious claim of belonging to a superior ethnic group. This is an issue left unresolved by colonialism, which nurtures various forms of domination, dependency, and cultural hegemony (Fylkesnes 2018).

Within this framework, the ways in which migrants approach the host country also play an important role. This involves a focus on adaptability skills and patterns of assimilation (through which an individual sees themself as belonging exclusively) and acculturation (through which an individual identifies with both ethnic minority and majority groups). These factors significantly impact mental health as well as physical and emotional well-being (Gurieva, Kõiv, and Tararukhina 2020). In addition, in Italy, there are repressive dynamics and complicated procedures of entry and stay regarding immigration, mostly aimed at control or a possible withdrawal of citizenship for "public safety reasons" (Law n. 132/2018, the Substitution of Security Decree n.113/2018, art. 14; and 2019). These laws only increase a culture of suspicion and intolerance among locals and risk harming migrants' human rights (UNCHR Italia, 2021–22). It also further highlights parallels between the treatment of migrants and that of incarcerated people, both of whom are treated as "others" and framed as threats to public safety.

Along with the education system, the labor market is a main vehicle for immigrant integration. Despite government rhetoric, the exploitation of migrants in the workplace often sees them excluded and marginalized. Of course, this becomes exacerbated in a context like that of Italy, where the labor market is characterized by a large amount of illicit employment on the gray market and other irregular practices (Cecchi 2011). One consequence is an increase in levels of detention of migrants, who make up a large portion of the informal labor economy. The sheer magnitude of the phenomenon poses the pressing question of whether Italy is committed to the protection and safeguarding of immigrants, a particularly vulnerable group of people.

As previously implied, there is a commonly held but unsupported perception that connects immigration and crime, even though the prison population does not have a balanced proportion of immigrants and host nationals.[4] Moreover, a prison sentence is not a reliable indicator to help understand the relationship between a discrete group of people and the law (i.e., the ethnicization of crime), since it is the result of a complex and fraught process influenced by layers of bias. Other factors include the social and cultural status of a defendant, the social alarm caused by the crimes committed, the extensiveness of social and family networks, and the understanding of the laws of the host country (Colombo 2013). However, detention is one accepted indicator to assess the degree of integration—or criminalization—of immigrants in a national context (Cecchi 2011).

Again, people, when forced to migrate, are at great risk of breaking the law upon arriving in a host country. This happens in Italy as in other places, not only for bureaucratic reasons (e.g., lack of immigration status, difficulty of obtaining residence permits) but also because of the great lack of cultural and linguistic mediation in immigrant processing centers and all along the path that should facilitate integration. Administrative or criminal detention is therefore made even more difficult because migrants often carry with them pre- and post-migration trauma, as well as the effects of exclusion that began long before they entered prison (e.g., prejudice, stereotyping, out-grouping). Trauma also occurs because of the limited space made available for merely existing, as the minuscule size of some Italian prison cells violates the international standard of three square meters per person, adding to an already inhumane situation (European Convention on Human Rights [ECHR], art. 3).[5]

The accusations raised over time against national policy regarding migration and the state of migrant detention—which, as will be shown in the following section, involve serious violations of human rights—call for the promulgation of guidelines as to how to manage the crisis humanely, including regulations aimed at protecting the welfare of all incarcerated people, as well as ensuring access to education.

Administrative Detention

In Italy, the detention facilities for irregular migrants, created in 1998 through the Turco-Napolitano Law (Consolidation Act on Immigration), have changed their structure and name over time. Started as centers for temporary stay and assistance (*centri di permanenza temporanea e assistenza*, CPTAs), they were subsequently defined as identification and expulsion centers (*centri di identificazione ed espulsione*, CIEs), and, in 2017, finally assumed the name of permanent centers for repatriation (*centri di permanenza per il rimpatrio*, CPRs) (Italian Parliament, Chamber of Deputies 2021).

As part of our research, we look at what these centers actually comprise and why education is an important element of their mission. To begin, if a citizen of a foreign country is subject to an expulsion or deportation order that cannot be implemented immediately for reasons related to migration policies, they are detained at a repatriation center for a maximum of ninety days, during which their personal freedom is restricted (Lamorgese Decree n.130/2020). In reality, such detention periods are often greatly exceeded, reaching upward of two years in some cases. This is allowed by a loophole contained in Article 5 of the European Convention on Human Rights (ECHR), which states: "Everyone has the right to liberty and security. No one shall be deprived of his liberty *except in the following cases (i.e., expulsion and deportation)* and in the manner provided for by law" (emphasis added).

An immigrant may therefore be detained for offenses as minor as not renewing their residence permit, an administrative detention that has no criminal sanction, since the detained foreigner has not committed any crime. Nevertheless, in practice, it limits the personal freedom of noncitizens, even though it was designed to be used only as a last resort. In 2017, for example, around forty-five thousand people underwent some form of migration-related detention. Of these, around four thousand were in one of Italy's long-term detention centers, and around forty thousand entered through "hotspots."

For these reasons, in 2014, the Ministry of the Interior approved a decree (July 25, 1998, 286 and subsequent amendments) to attempt to ensure uniform levels of reception and rules for the organization of centers and the provision of services within them, including education. Still, education is often placed lower on the list of priorities in such a broken system. As mentioned, language barriers and low educational attainment are the main causes for entry into these centers.

Migrant Imprisonment in Penal Institutions: Causes and Conditions

Data from the Council of Europe highlight that no country in Europe has more immigrant detainees than Italy. Furthermore, among the countries in the European Union, the percentage of noncitizens in the total population in Italy is among the highest, with only Greece and Austria having higher percentages (Council of Europe, SPACE I 2011). It is worth mentioning that as of January 2022 the population in Italian prisons was 54,372, of which 31.4 percent were not citizens of Italy. In terms of country of origin, data from January 2022 show that 19.8 percent of all migrants incarcerated in Italy were from Morocco, 11.9 percent were from Romania, 10.7 percent were from Albania, and 10.2 percent were from Tunisia (Ministry of Justice 2022).

International standards state that detention should not be the "rule" in immigration control, but rather a measure to be adopted as a last resort. However, poor or incomplete cultural mediation and education at the time of reception, the presence of which facilitates integration into the host country, can cause foreigners to adopt behaviors that constitute a crime in the country of arrival and result in them being reported or detained. For example, in Italy, a woman was reported for wearing a burqa, considered an obstacle to the recognition of a person, while a man was charged because he was in possession of a kirpan, the ritual knife of the Sikh religion, which is considered a weapon in Italy (Merzagora 2017).

In addition, some crimes with cultural implications—such as violence in the family, genital mutilation, child slavery, crimes against sexual freedom, and others—have also been causes for arrest, while still other crimes relate to the use of substances commonly used in the culture of origin or the failure of parents to comply with their children's schooling obligations. All these crimes are widely reported in literature pertaining to immigration detention and Italian immigration laws (Abeya, Afework, and Yalew 2012; Ali, Yassin, and Omer 2014; Cardillo 1997; Chiu 2006; Frick 2014; Kim and Sung 2000; Lee and Lawy 2001; Leye et al. 2007; Mestre i Mestre and Johnsdotter 2019; Rimonte 1991; Sorenson 2006; Van Broeck 2001; Yick 2007). Thus, one speaks of a "culturally motivated offense" when someone from a minority cultural group carries out behavior deemed a crime by the majority cultural group, even without the minority group's knowledge of the illegality of that action in their new legal and cultural context (Beger and Hein 2001; Durst 2000; Gallin 1994; Gordon 2001; Kim 1997; Van Broeck 2001).

Nevertheless, because immigrants belong to many different cultures and have a wide range of core values and customs, Italy as the host society needs to reassess and understand its own set of values on a fundamental level. Undoubtedly, the host community has a certain measure of responsibility toward new arrivals, especially in terms of basic education. Migrants in Italy must instead deal with a foreign legal system, often for reasons they do not fully understand and in a language that is often unfamiliar. Simple, nontechnical language is seldom used, making the information difficult to understand and thus difficult for the migrant to appeal to a court should they wish to challenge the legal grounds for any decision.

On an international level, public authorities are required to take appropriate measures to ensure migrant detainees are given sufficient information—in a known language—regarding the type and grounds for any measure limiting a person's liberty, as well as the procedure for challenging or reviewing the decision to detain. A person detained for any reason, including immigration control purposes, has the right to be informed promptly of the reasons for the adoption of the measure to deprive him of his liberty (ECHR, Art. 5.2). Yet international and European courts, like judicial institutions in general, are unwilling to force countries to bear the costs of safeguarding diversity. Apart from narrow exceptions or national political compromise, the authorities in control typically only support the assimilation of majority culture and language (Paz 2014).

This is an impediment that makes the moment of entry into prison highly problematic, whether it involves understanding the rules of the facility, submitting to the required medical examination, interviewing with a psychologist, or interacting with prison staff. However, the current status quo lacks any suitable form of communication that takes into account the migrant's level of education as well as the legal assistance necessary for a better understanding of the factors that led to detention, including available remedies (Gibb and Good 2014; Henderson, Moffatt, and Pickup 2012; Kishindo 2001; Lubb 2009). Moreover, once in prison, an incarcerated noncitizen encounters difficulties linked to social and cultural marginalization, which come in addition to a sense of exclusion that began before imprisonment, due to prejudice. Inevitably, as mentioned previously, the prison context is affected by a process of ethnicization of crime, that is, when certain patterns of criminal behavior are associated with nationality, ethnicity, and/or illegal status (Brown and Douglas Wilson 2007; Faloppa 2011). Thus, for example, some country's nationals end up being perniciously associated with theft, others with drug dealing, and so on, to the detriment of all.

In addition, loneliness and isolation risk reaching unbearable levels as well because of the absence of family, friends, and other social networks, the lack of which automatically excludes them from many prison conversations or even telephone contact. Moreover, even though Law 354 of 1975 states that prison regulations must be applied equally to all incarcerated people, migrants often do not enjoy the same alternative forms of detention as incarcerated Italians,[6] as they are typically subjected to increased measures that force them to stay in prison pending sentencing. This is also due to the tendency of Italian judges to rule out the option of house arrest for migrants because they often lack a residence permit or stable address.

Education in Prison for Migrants Too?

As seen throughout this volume, education has many applications in the prison context. Not only is it an essential tool for fostering a critical assessment of one's actions, but it also helps activate the processes of reintegration into community life. Education courses within the Italian penitentiary context are provided at the level of compulsory schooling (primary), upper secondary courses, and university studies; the latter, as has been seen, are conducted through agreements with local academic authorities (Regulations of Execution 2000, Art. 41–44). The provincial centers for adult education (*centri provinciali di istruzione per adulti*, CPIAs) are involved in the implementation of educational measures aimed at the recovery, integration, and support of minors and adults, even after they leave the detention system.

Despite the great demand for various levels of education expressed by people in prison, the responses provided by the Italian education system have not always been successful. The reasons for this failure are to be found in an educational model that struggles to meet the needs of both newly arrived migrants and those of the society into which they will hopefully someday be fully integrated. Finally, as is the case in many other countries, the physical space for school in prison is often minimal and not very compatible with the needs of students. Overcrowding in the sections or cells hampers study and prohibits students from living and working apart from nonstudents.

Nevertheless, there is some cause for optimism. For example, a new curriculum provides for the development of literacy and Italian language courses in prisons, aimed at overcoming the many difficulties presented by the language barrier. At its most basic level, this includes activities within the prison that are carried out only in Italian, but there is also a need to offer opportunities to gain proficiency in Italian to promote social and cultural integration. Without a doubt, it is necessary to allow foreign incarcerated people to take advantage of the same educational and socializing opportunities enjoyed by Italians who are incarcerated. This was especially true for the approximately 17,000 foreign citizens present in Italian prisons in December 2021, the most recent date for which there are data: only 152 had a college degree, almost always obtained in their country of origin, while a full 11,193 people had obtained no educational qualifications.

In addition, opportunities for job training are often available in prison, including graphic art and painting, crafts, cooking, construction, electrics, plumbing, and other practical subjects. These vocational courses promote skills functional outside the prison facilities and would ideally ensure minimum wage to incarcerated people who work in them. Over the years, the number of people enrolled in the provided courses diminished, prompting an increase in educational investment after funding for training activities dried up and professional training at the national level lagged. As a result, the market for classroom education in Italian prisons is again growing (Allegri 2020).

Training for Prison Staff

One additional area of education firmly embedded in Italian prisons that bears mentioning here is that of staff development. Indeed, there is continuous training and retraining of penitentiary staff and administration, helping to create a culture of education within Italian prisons from the top down. The courses offered aim to provide the essential tools for working with incarcerated people and of prison conditions and to encourage the development of working models oriented toward integration and professional cooperation. A central point in this first phase is the creation of a common "cultural and operational language" among the various professionals (within and outside the institution as well as from outside the administration of justice) entrusted with the well-being of incarcerated people.[7]

Periodically, all staff (e.g., educators, police officers, legal officials, social workers, prison administrators) are required to attend professional refresher courses both on-site and at the training school. These courses are specialized, multidisciplinary, and designed to address one or more specific knowledge areas (in particular, those that have recently reported legal or scientific innovations) and are always aimed at improving the quality of service. Staff training is also provided through agreements with some universities that give special permission for prison staff to attend academic courses or pursue a master's degree, also making use of "study permits" (paid up to a maximum of a hundred fifty hours per year). And yet, despite all this training, prison staff often still fail to provide foreign incarcerated people adequate instruction to understand basic prison regulations and penal processes.

Migrant Minor Detainees in Penal Juvenile Institutions

What has been written so far concerning challenges facing migrants within the Italian detention system is also valid for those faced by noncitizen minors passing through the Italian juvenile justice system.[8] Jurisdiction over minors is ascribed to judicial bodies, usually with shared, collegial responsibilities, which makes the system qualitatively different from the one designed for adults. The tendency to establish specialized judicial bodies for juveniles, shaped by the progressive development of human sciences, points to greater attention to the phenomena of distress and maladjustment of young people, so that young people can be adequately supported during their personality development when deviant pressures intervene to disturb positive growth (Capitano and La Bua 2021).

The Italian juvenile justice system, therefore, is based less on the prevalence of restrictive measures and more on institutions that allow the application of corrective measures that do not interrupt the opportunities offered by the environment for the development of the young person's personality. This is also the reason why only a small number of young people are subjected to detention, though within this group too there are a disproportionately high number of noncitizens. On May 15, 2020, of the 280 juveniles present in penal institutions for minors, 133—almost half—were noncitizens (Dipartimento Giustizia minorile e di comunità 2020). Once again, education plays a particularly important role here: over time, educational courses, as well as vocational activities, can keep young people away from further crime. When possible, young detainees are allowed to attend educational and vocational training courses outside the facility. This can occur with the agreement of the relevant penal institutions, employers, and cooperatives or associations, when it is believed that external attendance facilitates their educational career and contributes to the enhancement of individual potential for social reintegration.

The management of young migrants within this group who have just arrived in Italy, however, appears to be of particular complexity. This is due to several factors. For one, a lack of knowledge of the language is a critical obstacle. While there may be some familiarity with the basics of Italian, proficiency is typically nonexistent. Instead, very often these young people know English or French and revert to interacting in those languages instead. Alternatively, other young people do their best to act as interpreters for their companions who struggle with Italian, but such mediation understandably cannot extend to educational or judicial situations, where informal translators are not allowed (Snow and Powell 2004).

A second obstacle is a lack of familiarity or comfort with Italian customs, as many young people who arrive here have a partial or distorted knowledge of Italy borrowed from television programs. On the one hand, it is a world that attracts them, while, on the other, it represents distance from their culture of origin. This disparity causes many to seek integration as best they can, but it often falls far short, fueling a sense of frustration and nonacceptance. A final difficulty lies in finding targeted resources in the prison space: access to literacy courses (the timetables are often difficult to meet), to professional or vocational courses (remuneration is often only offered at the end of the course, i.e., after six or twelve months), and also to public health care (Ministry of the Interior, Prefecture–Territorial Office of the Government of Rome 2016). All this creates a sense of subjugation that is sometimes transformed into a longer stay in juvenile penal institutions and a failure to set up successful plans on the outside.

Disappointed and disoriented noncitizen minors entering the penal system often lack important context about the severity of their situations. They tend to externalize responsibility and initially do not express any demand for psychological or educational help (Sortino and Ragusa 2021). The transformation of "accountability" into "opportunity" is therefore only possible if young people are adequately supported and informed. The daily life context of the incarcerated young person must be structured as a learning community able to contribute to their reintegration, supporting a process of self-improvement that makes it possible to find a way to regain ability and insight.

In this light, the presence of educational facilitators such as cultural mediators in prisons, as well as staff who can offer psychosocial intervention opportunities for incarcerated people, becomes fundamental. They are not mere language translators but professionals who have to bring together two worlds unknown to each other or, harder still, that know each other unfavorably because of the worst things each group is known to express about the other. At best, these facilitators represent a useful support for an effective path toward social inclusion that can reduce the risk of crime, promote respect for diversity, and secure the values of civil coexistence (Garro and Schirinzi 2018).

The peculiarities of the incarceration of young noncitizens in Italy highlight the critical need for linguistic-cultural mediation in prison settings. At the very least, this mediation can represent a significant step toward adequately addressing the psychological distress of foreign detainees and thereby make it possible to guarantee equal treatment in the pursuit of social integration, regardless of age.

Conclusion

An imbalance of power and lack of reciprocity can result in invasive, conditioning, and dehumanizing practices. It is also well known that abuses of power can, over time, weaken individual agency and create vulnerability. Educational access can assist incarcerated people from many backgrounds in ways that will facilitate the protection of human rights in Italy. The evidence presented in this chapter indicates how difficult it can be to reconcile the educational needs of incarcerated people in Italy with the conditions available for education in Italian prisons. Instead of quiet lounges, students study in overcrowded cells; instead of a campus environment, incarcerated students are the vast minority in their penitentiary communities. There is no access to personal computers, wireless internet, or technological support, which are staples of modern college education. These challenges are, moreover, compounded for migrants.

When it comes to the education of migrants in Italian prisons, there might arise the temptation to separate them from the general population to avoid difficulties between the two populations as they interact. Instead, authorities should utilize the powerful tool of cultural mediators to enhance cultural integration and open new avenues of learning for this particularly vulnerable population. This is especially true considering that incarcerated migrants need to acquire a command of the Italian language to navigate both the penal and legal systems as well as society upon release. Education in prison—from literacy to university—is necessary to guarantee social and cultural integration. It is clear that even the most basic education can be a critical intervention for any incarcerated person, but especially for those most on the margins, such as noncitizens. Resources should be provided and regulations should be made more flexible when a person first enters prison so that incarcerated noncitizens can maintain dignity and autonomy and have greater control over their fate. A lack of understanding of various cultures of origin, Italian language and cultural barriers, and the internal dynamics of ethnic communities, as well as the vagaries of state bureaucracy, are all sources of risk for the migrant.

In Italy, conditions of distress and isolation, especially in cases of detention, are amplified by the absence of a comprehensive system of not only basic but also higher education courses within the prison. These would offer more opportunities for inclusion and integration after detention, which at the moment are entrusted merely to the individual and their own often limited resources. The system of detention affects interpersonal relations, placing the incarcerated noncitizen in a series of subordinate relationships. This is especially true when it comes to social reintegration, which, in the case of non-Italian-speaking people held in Italian prisons, is often twofold: rebuilding identity both as individuals who have had to atone for their mistakes and as European Community citizens welcomed into a society other than their own. This discussion reveals that a guilty verdict does not limit the right to university studies, nor should a sentence deny it. With this in mind, the pressing issue here is not necessarily more research but better organization, since it is undeniable that detention may represent an insuperable obstacle to realizing the right to education and a life with dignity more broadly.

Notes

1. (Italian) *Norme sull'ordinamento penitenziario e sulla esecuzione delle misure privative e limitative della libertà.*

2. The General Assembly invites member states to take into consideration the specific needs and realities of incarcerated girls and women when developing relevant legislation, procedures, policies, and action plans, drawing on the Bangkok Rules as appropriate. For example:

> Rule 32: Female prison staff shall receive equal access to training as male staff, and all staff involved in the management of women's prisons shall receive training on gender sensitivity and prohibition of discrimination and sexual harassment. . . . Rule 37: Juvenile female prisoners shall have equal access to education and vocational training that are available to juvenile male prisoners. (United Nation Office on Drugs and Crime [UNODC] 2011)

3. The amendment of Articles 4-bis and 41-bis of the Law n. 354 of July 26, 1975: a specific prison regime—"hard prison"—aimed at harsh offenders (e.g., organized gangs, terrorism, mafia). In November 2021, people incarcerated under Art. 41-bis totaled 749 (among them 13 women) residing in twelve specific penal facilities (Belli 2021). In 2003, Amnesty International claimed that 41-bis was "cruel [and] inhuman" (Amnesty International 2003).

4. By December 2021, noncitizens detained in Italian prisons comprised 31 percent of all incarcerated people (Ministero della Giustizia 2021). Usually, crimes committed by immigrants have a low offensiveness index (i.e., culturally motivated). Still, because of economic, linguistic, and technical differences and scarce resources, alternative adopted measures make them more visible than local incarceration (Pavone 2005). In this sense, the general trend of opinion is to consider a foreign-born incarcerated person as a discrete and comprehensive demographic box, socially undifferentiated, subject to prejudice in itself. Over time, the idea of becoming an integral part of Italian society should reduce the number of incarcerated people belonging to each ethnic community.

5. In 2013, Italy was convicted of violating the right to freedom from cruel, inhumane, or degrading treatment (Garro and Pace 2017).

6. In order to encourage contact with society, alternative measures to detention are provided for, such as being put on probation to the social services (with a possibility of facing a probationary period outside the penitentiary institution, and successful compliance deletes the sentence); semi-freedom (the possibility of spending part of the day outside the prison to participate in activities to help social reintegration); premium release (lasting no more than fifteen days, issued to allow the cultivation of emotional, cultural, and work interests); conditional release (the possibility of completing the sentence outside the prison under a regime of probation); home detention (the sentence is served in one's own home or in a state-provided place of care, assistance, or hospitality); and early release (reduction in sentence) (Law 354/75).

7. For the penitentiary police (civilian police department), there is additional education typical of the police force (e.g., formal training, use of weapons).

8. The juvenile services in Italy deal with young people between fourteen and eighteen years of age and young adults up to age twenty-five, by order of the Juvenile Court.

Works Cited

Abeya, Sileshi G., Mesganaw F. Afework, and Alemayehu W. Yalew. 2012. "Intimate Partner Violence against Women in West Ethiopia: A Qualitative Study on Attitudes, Woman's Response, and Suggested Measures as Perceived by Community Members." *Reproductive Health* 9: 14.

Adorno, Theodor, Else Frenkel-Brunswik, Daniel Levinson, and Nevitt Sanford. 1950. *The Authoritarian Personality*. New York: Harper & Brothers.

Ali, AbdelAziem A., Khalid Yassin, and Rawia Omer. 2014. "Domestic Violence against Women in Eastern Sudan." *BMC Public Health* 14: 1136. https://doi.org/10.1186/1471-2458-14-1136.

Allegri, Perla Arianna. 2020. *Dalla parte dei lavoratori. Il lavoro e la formazione in carcere*. Retrieved from https://rapportoantigone.it/.

Allport, Gordon. 1954. *The Nature of Prejudice*. Cambridge, MA: Addison-Wesley.

Amnesty International. 2003. "Report: Italy." https://refworld.org/docid/3edb47d8c.html.

Associazione Antigone. 2021. "La scuola in carcere: diritto o privilegio?" Retrieved from https://rapportoantigone.it/.

Beger, Randall R., and Jeremy Hein. 2001. "Immigrants, Culture, and American Courts: A Typology of Legal Strategies and Issues in Cases Involving Vietnamese and among Litigants." *Criminal Justice Review* 26 (1): 38–61.

Belli, Marco. 2021. *Carceri, 10 mila i detenuti in Alta sicurezza: 749 al 41-bis*. https://gnewsonline.it/carceri-10-mila-i-detenuti-in-alta-sicurezza-749-al-41-bis/.

Brown, David, and Ian Douglas Wilson. 2007. "Ethnicized Violence in Indonesia: Where Criminals and Fanatics Meet." *Nationalism and Ethnic Politics* 13 (3): 367–403.

Caiffa, Patrizia. 2021. *Carcere: oltre 1.000 gli studenti detenuti iscritti all'università. +29,9% in 3 anni*. Retrieved from https://agensir.it/.

Capitano, Michelangelo, and L. La Bua. 2021. *I Servizi a tutela del minore e della comunità. Il Sistema di Giustizia Minorile.* In *Psicodinamica delle reti territoriali e dei servizi socio-sanitari. Famiglie, contesti e metodologie di intervento,* edited by Maria Garro and Sonia Tinti Barraja, 197–218. Palermo: Palermo University Press.

Caputo, Gabriella, and Daniela Di Mase. 2013. "Il carcere degli stranieri: problematiche e aspetti gestionali nella pratica operativa della polizia penitenziaria. Essere stranieri in carcere: profili di gestione e linee di intervento." *Dispense ISSP,* 2. http://ristretti.it/commenti/2013/ottobre/pdf2/issp_dispensa2.pdf.

Cardillo, Cathy C. 1997. "Violence against Chinese Women: Defining the Cultural Role." *Women's Rights Law Reporter* 19: 85.

Cecchi, Sergio. 2011. "The Criminalization of Immigration in Italy: Extent of the Phenomenon and Possible Interpretations." *Italian Sociological Review* 1 (1): 34–42.

Cesareo, Vincenzo. 2009. "Quale integrazione?" In *Indici di integrazione. Un'indagine empirica sulla realtà migratoria italiana,* edited by Vincenzo Cesareo and Gian Carlo Blangiardo, 11–28. Milano: FrancoAngeli–Fondazione ISMU.

Chiu, Elaine M. 2006. "Culture as Justification, Not Excuse." *American Criminal Law Review* 43: 1317.

Colombo, Asher. 2013. "Foreigners and Immigrants in Italy's Penal and Administrative Detention Systems." *European Journal of Criminology* 10 (6): 746–59.

Corrado, Maria Vittoria. "Carceri, cresce il numero di detenuti iscritti all'Università." May 8, 2021. Retrieved from https://gnewsonline.it/.

Dipartimento Giustizia minorile e di comunità. 2020. *Minorenni e giovani adulti in carico ai Servizi minorili Analisi statistica dei dati 15 maggio 2020.* https://giustizia.it/resources/cms/documents/Analisi_Servizi_minorili_15.05.2020-uso_esterno.pdf/.

Durst, Ilene. 2000. "Lost in the Translation: Why Due Process Demands Deference to the Refugee's Narrative. *Rutgers Law Review* 53: 127–65.

Edwards, Rosalind, Bogusia Temple, and Claire Alexander. 2005. "Users' Experiences of Interpreters: The Critical Role of Trust." *Interpreting* 7 (1): 77–95.

European Court of Human Rights (ECHR), Council of Europe. 1950. *European Convention on Human Rights.* 67075 Strasbourg cedex, France. Retrieved from https://echr.coe.int/.

Faloppa, Federico. 2011. *Razzisti a parole (per tacere dei fatti).* Bari: Laterza.

Frick, Marie-Luisa. 2014. "The Cultural Defense and Women's Human Rights: An Inquiry into the Rationales for Unveiling Justitia's Eyes to 'Culture.' " *Philosophy & Social Criticism* 40 (6): 555–76.

Fylkesnes, Sandra. 2018. "Whiteness in Teacher Education Research Discourses: A Review of the Use and Meaning Making of the Term 'Cultural Diversity.' " *Teaching and Teacher Education* 71: 24–33. https://doi.org/10.1016/j.tate.2017.12.005.

Gallin, Alice J. 1994. "The Cultural Defense: Undermining the Policies against Domestic Violence." *Boston College Law Review* 35: 722–45.

Gao, Fengping. 2006. "Language Is Culture: On Intercultural Communication." *Journal of Language and Linguistics* 5 (1): 58–67.

Garro, Maria, and Francesco Pace, eds. 2017. *Sorveglianza dinamica e regime aperto: Cambiamenti normativi, organizzativi e psicosociali.* Milano: FrancoAngeli.

Garro, Maria, and Massimiliano Schirinzi. 2018. "Reversing the Trend: A Psychosocial Intervention on Young Immigrants in Sicily." *Journal of International Migration and Integration* 19 (4): 883–89.

Garro, Maria, Massimiliano Schirinzi, C. Novara, and Alonso E. Ayllon. 2022. "Immigrant Prisoners in Italy. Cultural Mediation to Reduce Social Isolation and Increase Migrant Prisoner Well-Being?" *International Journal of Prison Health.*

Gibb, Robert, and Anthony Good. 2014. "Interpretation, Translation, and Intercultural Communication in Refugee Status Determination Procedures in the UK and France." *Language and Intercultural Communication* 14 (3): 385–99.

Gordon, Neal A. 2001. "The Implications of Memetics for the Cultural Defense." *Duke Law Journal* 50 (6): 1809–34.

Gurieva, Svetlana, Kristi Kõiv, and Olga Tararukhina. 2020. "Migration and Adaptation as Indicators of Social Mobility Migrants." Behavioral Sciences 10 (1): 30.

Henderson, Mark, Rowena Moffatt, and Alison Pickup. 2012. *Best Practice Guide to Asylum and Human Rights Appeals.* Retrieved from http://ein.org.uk/bpg /contents.

Istituto Nazionale di Statistica. 2021. *Cittadini non comunitari in Italia. Anni 2020– 2021.* https://istat.it/it/files/2021/10/Cittadini-non-comunitari_2020_2021.pdf/.

Iversen, Valentina C., Wenche L. Mangerud, Trine Tetlie Eik-Nes, and Ellen Kjelsberg. 2013. "Communication Problems and Language Barriers Between Foreign Inmates and Prison Officers." *Journal of Immigrant & Refugee Studies* 11 (1): 65–77.

IWIM—Institutional Working Party on Intercultural Mediation. 2009. *Linee di indirizzo per il riconoscimento della figura professionale del Mediatore Interculturale.* Rome: Italian Ministry of the Interior.

Kim, Jae Yop, and Kyu-taik Sung. 2000. "Conjugal Violence in Korean American Families: A Residue of Cultural Tradition." *Journal of Family Violence* 15 (4): 31–45.

Kishindo, Pascal. 2001. "Language and the Law in Malawi: A Case for the Use of Indigenous Languages in the Legal System." *Language Matters* 32 (1): 1–27.

La Regina, Katia. 2018. "Istruzione e formazione professionale in carcere." *Interventi e relazioni* Retrieved from http://lalegislazionepenale.eu.

Lavanco, Gioacchino, and Cinzia Novara. 2017. "Comunità chiuse, comunità aperte: rimanere chiusi "fuori" dal carcere." In *Sorveglianza dinamica e regime aperto: Cambiamenti normativi, organizzativi e sociali,* edited by Maria Garro and Francesco Pace, 155–74. Milano: Franco Angeli.

Lee, Mo Yee, and Phyllis F. M. Lawy. 2001. "Perceptions of Sexual Violence against Women in Asian American Communities." *Journal of Ethnic and Cultural Diversity in Social Work* 10 (2): 3–25.

Leye, Els, Jessika Deblonde, José García-Añón, Sara Johnsdotter, Adwoa Kwateng-Kluvitse, Linda Weil-Curiel, and Marleen Temmerman. 2007. "An Analysis of the Implementation of Laws with Regard to Female Genital Mutilation in Europe." *Crime, Law, and Social Change* 47 (1): 1–31.

Lubbe, J. 2009. *The Right to Language in Court: A Language Right or a Communication Right?* https://dialnet.unirioja.es/descarga/articulo/3199505.pdf/.

Merzagora, Isabella. 2017. *Lo straniero a giudizio. Tra psicopatologia e diritto.* Milano: Cortina.

Mestre i Mestre, Ruth M., and Sara Johnsdotter. 2019. "Court Cases, Cultural Expertise, and 'Female Genital Mutilation' in Europe." *Studies in Law Politics and Society* 78: 95–113.

Ministero della Giustizia. 2020. "Ufficio Del Capo Del Dipartimento Segreteria Generale." Attività scolastiche. https://giustizia.it/giustizia/it/mg_2_5_6_1.page.

Ministero della Giustizia. 2021. "Detenuti italiani e stranieri presenti e capienze per istituto—aggiornamento al 31 dicembre 2021." https://giustizia.it/giustizia/it/mg_1_14_1.page?facetNode_1=0_2&facetNode_2=0_2_10&facetNode_3=0_2_10_3&contentId=SST360932&previsiousPage=mg_1_14.

Ministero della Giustizia. 2022. "Detenuti presenti—aggiornamento al 31 gennaio 2022." https://giustizia.it/giustizia/it/mg_1_14_1.page?facetNode_1=0_2&contentId=SST365654&previsiousPage=mg_1_14.

Ministero dell'Interno, Prefettura—Ufficio Territoriale del Governo di Roma. 2016. "Assistenza Sanitaria per Cittadini Stranieri." http://prefettura.it/roma/contenuti/Assistenza_sanitaria_per_cittadini_stranieri-4940.htm.

Ngalwa, Sibusiso. 2007. "Language Policy in Courts in the Dock." *Daily News*, June 13, 2007.

Paoletti, Emanuela. 2014. "The Arab Spring and the Italian Response to Migration in 2011." *Comparative Migration Studies* 2: 127–50.

Parlamento Italiano, Camera dei Deputati. 2021. *I Centri di permanenza per i rimpatri.* https://temi.camera.it/leg18/post/cpr.html.

Paterniti Martello, Claudio. 2021. "Lo scrittore. Insegnare in carcere. Dialogo con Edoardo Albinati." *Controluce*, April 25, 2021. https://controluce.it/notizie/lo-scrittore-insegnare-in-carcere-dialogo-con-edoardo-albinati/.

Pavone, Mario. 2005. "Le misure alternative alla detenzione sono applicabili anche ai clandestini." *Ristretti.* http://ristretti.it/areestudio/stranieri/ricerche/pavone13.htm.

Paz, Moria. 2014. "The Tower of Babel: Human Rights and the Paradox of Language." *The European Journal of International Law* 25 (2): 473–96.

Polidoro, Riccardo. 2021. "Carcere, ormai non è più tempo di commissioni." *Il riformista*, October 20, 2021. https://ilriformista.it/carcere-ormai-non-e-piu-tempo-di-commissioni-255720/.

Rimonte, Nilda. 1991. "A Question of Culture: Cultural Approval of Violence against Women in the Pacific-Asian Community and the Cultural Defense." *Stanford Law Review* 43 (6): 1311–26.

Regione Sicilia. 2021. *Poli penitenziari: Regione Siciliana*. https://regione.sicilia.it/sites
/default/files/2021-03/Poli%20penitenziari%20definitivo.pdf/.

Salvatore, Sergio, Terri Mannarini, Evrinomi Avdi, Fiorella Battaglia, Marco
Cremaschi, Viviana Fini, Guglielmo Forges Davanzati, et al. 2019. "Globalization,
Demand of Sense and Enemization of the Other: A Psychocultural Analysis of
European Societies' Sociopolitical Crisis." *Culture & Psychology* 25 (3): 345–74.

Snow, Pamela C., and Martine B. Powell. 2004. "Interviewing Juvenile Offenders:
The Importance of Oral Language Competence." *Current Issues in Criminal Justice*
16: 220–25.

Sorenson, Susan B. 2006. "Judgments about Intimate Partner Violence: A Statewide
Survey about Immigrants." *Public Health Reports* 121 (4): 445–52.

Sortino, Loredana, and Adriana Ragusa. 2021. "Il lavoro nei Servizi della Giustizia
Minorile: percorsi psicologici ed educativi dall'IPM alle misure in Area Penale
Esterna." In *Psicodinamica delle reti territoriali e dei servizi socio-sanitari: Famiglie,
contesti e metodologie di intervento*, edited by Maria Garro and Sonia Tinti
Barraja, 233–54. Palermo: Palermo University Press.

Tajfel, Henri. 1972. "Social Categorization. (English manuscript of La categorization
sociale.)" In *Introduction a la psychologie sociale, Vol. 1*, edited by Serge Moscovici,
272–302. Paris: Larousse.

Tajfel, Henri. 1981. *Human Groups and Social Categories: Studies in Social Psychology*.
Cambridge: Cambridge University Press.

Tajfel, Henri, and John C. Turner. 1979. "An Integrative Theory of Intergroup
Conflict." In *The Social Psychology of Intergroup Relations*, edited by William G.
Austin and Stephen Worchel, 33–47. Monterey, CA: Brooks/Cole.

Turner, John C., and Penelope J. Oakes. 1986. "The Significance of the Social Identity
Concept for Social Psychology with Reference to Individualism, Interactionism
and Social Influence." *British Journal of Social Psychology* 25: 237–52.

Turner, John C., Michael A. Hogg, Penelope J. Oakes, Stephen D. Reicher, and
Margaret S. Wetherell. 1987. *Rediscovering the Social Group: A Self-Categorization
Theory*. Oxford: Blackwell.

UNCHR Italia. 2021–22. *Il diritto d'asilo*. https://unhcr.org/it/cosa-facciamo
/protezione/diritto-asilo/#.

University of Milan. 2021. *Studiare in carcere*. https://unimi.it/it/corsi/studiare-carcere.

University of Palermo. 2021. *Istituito il Polo Penitenziario Universitario. Rettore
Micari: "UniPa sempre più inclusive."* https://unipa.it/Istituito-il-Polo
-Penitenziario-Universitario.-Rettore-Micari-UniPa-sempre-pi-inclusiva/.

UNODC. 1955. *Standard Minimum Rules for the Treatment of Prisoners*. https://unodc
.org/pdf/criminal_justice/UN_Standard_Minimum_Rules_for_the_Treatment_of
_Prisoners.pdf/.

UNODC. 2011. *The Bangkok Rules: United Nations Rules for the Treatment of
Women Prisoners and Non-custodial Measures for Women Offenders with Their
Commentary*. https://unodc.org/documents/justice-and-prison-reform/Bangkok
_Rules_ENG_22032015.pdf/.

Van Broeck, Jeroen. 2001. "Cultural Defence and Culturally Motivated Crimes (Cultural Offences)." *European Journal of Crime, Criminal Law and Criminal Justice* 9 (1): 1–32.

Wacquant, Loïc. 1999. "Suitable Enemies: Foreigners and Immigrants in the Prisons of Europe." *Punishment & Society* 1 (2): 215–22.

Yick, Alice G. 2007. "Role of Culture and Context: Ethical Issues in Research with Asian Americans and Immigrants in Intimate Violence." *Journal of Family Violence* 22: 277.

DORIEN BROSENS,
SILKE MARYNISSEN, AND
LIESBETH DE DONDER

11 ||| EFFECTIVENESS OF PEER LEARNING AND PEER SUPPORT IN PRISON

A REALIST-INSPIRED REVIEW OF OUTCOMES, MECHANISMS, AND CONTEXTUAL FACTORS

Introduction

Within prisons and in recent research surrounding them, a noteworthy shift is that more and more attention is being paid to opportunities for active citizenship by incarcerated people, instead of viewing them as mere subjects of systems. This shift implies that there is a greater recognition of the ability of incarcerated people to participate in and contribute to everyday life while in prison. For many incarcerated people, education is a critical gateway to opportunity. It serves as a place of hope within a challenging prison environment, offering chances for personal growth and self-improvement where skills and knowledge can be developed. While many educators in prison dedicate themselves to working with incarcerated people who need support and want to learn, they are not able to provide the full range of help needed.

To be able to provide more support and increased learning opportunities for incarcerated people, peer learning and peer support programs have been introduced in several prisons globally. In these programs, incarcerated people are trained to educate, tutor, or otherwise support their fellow incarcerated persons. Such programs are often strong informal learning practices that provide opportunities for both peer workers and peer recipients to learn and contribute to the greater goal of education. This kind of mutually beneficial interaction provides further evidence that criminal legal systems acknowledge that prisons should offer incarcerated people opportunities to achieve some form of meaning and purpose during their time of incarceration (Perrin, Frost, and Ware 2018).

One notable systematic review, published in 2015, revealed that incarcerated people prefer peer programs over professional programs. This preference is largely attributed to the fact that peer workers share similar lived experiences with incarcerated persons who make use of them. Also important is the sense that peer workers are nonjudgmental, trusted, easier to talk to, more accessible, and that they have more available time compared to professionals (Bagnall et al. 2015). Although peer programs are an established part of the prison system in several countries like the United Kingdom or the United States, their existence in other countries such as Belgium is a relatively recent phenomenon.

For the continued development of such policies and programs, a deeper understanding of how peer-based approaches in prison work is of utmost importance. The current chapter addresses this gap and aims to provide the reader a better understanding of the two most common types of peer-based approaches in prison: peer learning and peer support. More specifically, it starts from the perspective of realist methodology to review the literature on these types of programs. An analysis of twenty-nine international empirical articles and reports will aim to provide insight into the effectiveness of such programs for individual peer workers, peer recipients, and prisons. As a fundamental understanding of how, why, for whom, and under which circumstances peer programs lead to such outcomes remains an untapped vein for exploration, this chapter also focuses on the underlying mechanisms and contextual factors that give rise to these outcomes. This chapter showcases examples of peer programs in various countries such as Belgium, Canada, France, Switzerland, the United Kingdom, and the United States. While previous studies on peer programs have been conducted all over the world, most of them report only on programs that exist in the United Kingdom and the United States.

The chapter begins with an overview of the most common peer-based approaches that exist in prisons and categorizes them by whether they are peer-learning or peer support programs. It then ventures into the literature to unveil the outcomes of peer programs for all stakeholders involved: peer workers, peer recipients, and the prison institutions. Furthermore, we delve into the mechanisms and contextual factors that either facilitate or hinder the realization of these outcomes. Ultimately, the chapter offers insights into what works in which context, by intertwining the elements of context, mechanisms, and outcomes. Our aim is not only to inform but rather to inspire practitioners, further research, and ongoing evaluation of peer-based approaches within the complex world of prisons.

Peer-Based Approaches in Prison

Peer-based programs are still a largely new phenomenon in the prison setting globally, but some patterns can already be detected. Figure 11.1 presents an overview of two types of peer-based approaches that are most commonly described in the literature: peer learning and peer support. It is not our intention to provide a full overview of peer-based approaches that exist within prison settings around the world today, but rather to give a glimpse of current trends in order to stimulate discussion and innovation. It is important to note at the outset that not all forms of peer learning or peer support are formally organized. While these interactions may also happen spontaneously and naturally between incarcerated persons, figure 11.1 gives an overview of those programs that are formally organized.

After having conducted their systematic review, Anne-Marie Bagnall and colleagues (2015) critiqued the fact that almost none of the studies they included defined the term "peers." For this reason, it is important to start by defining peer work in this chapter: peer work consists of "any interactions that are carried out by prisoners that involve the act of working with a person of the same status" (Nixon 2019, 44). Importantly, we focus on peer interactions within prisons and do not look at peer programs that take place outside prison walls with people who have been previously incarcerated.

Peer learning, generally, can best be described as "the acquisition of knowledge and skills through active helping and supporting among status equals or matched companions. It involves people from similar social groupings who are not professional teachers helping each other to learn and learning themselves by so doing" (Topping 2005, 632). From this definition, within the literature on peer learning in prisons, a further division is made between peer education and peer tutoring.

The first type of peer learning, *peer education*, often focuses on health awareness in prison, such as the prevention of HIV and risk reduction (Bagnall et al. 2015). One example of a peer education program is the Community Based Health and First Aid (CBHFA) program in Ireland, operated by the Irish Red Cross, Irish Prison Service, and the Education and

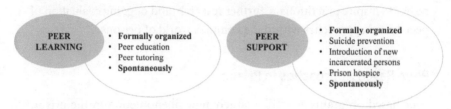

Figure 11.1.
Most common peer-based approaches in prison.

Training Board. The CBHFA program was piloted in Wheatfield prison in 2009 and by the end of 2014 was operating in all fourteen prisons in Ireland (Betts-Symonds 2016). Before participating, the incarcerated peer workers must first undergo a training, a course with seven modules. Afterward, they become peer educators who promote health, hygiene, and first aid among their fellow incarcerated persons. This has, for instance, led to the wider dissemination of important health messages surrounding topics such as tuberculosis awareness and swine flu prevention, translation of health promotion information into understandable materials in different languages, and advocacy for a voluntary HIV testing campaign (Mehay and Meek 2016).

In the second type of peer learning, *peer tutoring*, tutees receive training from a tutor in a more formal educational setting. There is a high focus on curriculum content, and clear procedures for interactions between tutor and tutee must be followed (Topping 2015). One example of this is the Toe-by-Toe program of the Shannon Trust that exists in prisons in England. Incarcerated high-level readers act as tutors to assist the less literate, with the aim of improving the literacy skills of the latter (Perrin 2017; South, Bagnall, and Woodall 2017). Beyond this, incarcerated people can also support teachers during classes. Different prisons in England assign peer mentors who are present during group lessons to support both teachers and learners. In this program, peer workers help with paperwork and encourage learners to finish the course or encourage them to take up other courses (Brosens and De Donder 2016).

Besides formally organized peer learning programs, research reveals that peer learning can also happen spontaneously. For instance, the Belgian Foreigners' Involvement and Participation in Prison (FIP2) research project demonstrates that incarcerated people from different countries can learn each other's languages in informal and unprogrammed ways.

For instance, one of the respondents went to the prison library to borrow books that could help him create English exercises for his cellmate. Even after changing cells, he kept making and correcting exercises for when they still saw each other on the yard (Croux et al. 2023).

Another common type of peer program in prison, distinct from peer learning, is *peer support*. Commonly understood, peer support is "a system of giving and receiving help founded on key principles of respect, shared responsibility, and mutual agreement of what is helpful" (Mead, Hilton, and Curtis 2001, 135). In several countries, such support is formally organized in the form of peer support programs. Most of this support is delivered on a one-on-one basis, and only a minority involves group work (South, Bagnall, and Woodall 2017). There is a wide variety of formally supported peer support programs in prison, such as suicide prevention programs, orientation programs for newly incarcerated persons, and prison hospice programs.

The first, suicide prevention programs, can be found in several countries such as Canada, France, England, and Wales. They have been of particular importance as suicide rates in prison are at least three times higher than in the general population (Fazel, Ramesh, and Hawton 2017). In France, for example, there is a suicide prevention program delivered in partnership with the Red Cross called Codétenus de Soutien (Supporting Other Incarcerated Persons). To support incarcerated people at risk of suicide, peer workers are trained in CPR and first aid, in the identification of suicidal crises, and in how to listen to people in need of help (Auzoult and Abdellaoui 2013).

In addition, the Listener program is widely adapted in prisons in England and Wales (South, Bagnall, and Woodall 2017). Here, incarcerated peer workers provide face-to-face confidential and emotional support to other incarcerated people who request help (Perrin et al. 2018). After completing training, peer workers can start their role as a Listener. To provide twenty-four-hour service to everyone who needs help, the team of peer workers establishes a rotation system (Perrin 2017). Beyond these types of suicide prevention programs, there are also various programs whereby peers watch others who are at risk of suicide but do not take up an active supporting role (South, Bagnall, and Woodall 2017).

The second type of peer support programs are orientation programs for newly incarcerated persons. Incarcerated people provide reassurance, information, and practical assistance to new arrivals with the aim of reducing stress and anxiety related to being in prison for the first time (Perrin 2017; South, Bagnall, and Woodall 2017). Throughout the literature, different terms are used for this phenomenon: insider scheme, peer-led introduction, support for new incarcerated persons, induction programs, and buddy working, among others. One notable example is the Belgian variation of the buddy project. A few years ago, this program was introduced as a pilot project in a pretrial detention center in Belgium. The prisoner council[1] had emphasized the need for newly arrived persons to get practical information about life in prison soon after their arrival. After following the training program for peer workers by the Ligo Center for Basic Education, buddies have individual conversations with newly arrived persons. Because the pilot project was seen to be effective, several other prisons decided to introduce the peer program as well.

Third, research has shown that incarcerated people experience poorer health and are more likely to require palliative care at a younger age compared to the broader population (McParland and Johnston 2019, 2021). The need for appropriate medical care for incarcerated people has become a growing field of interest around the world, perhaps most notably in Canada, Switzerland, the United Kingdom, and the United States (Depner et al. 2018). Prison hospice programs can be a way to meet this humane need. Such programs are based on the concept of "compassionate prison," that is, a place where the dignity of individuals is recognized and where individuals are treated with respect (Wright and Bronstein 2007). In the United States, some prisons have implemented peer care in these programs, in which peer workers provide extensive end-of-life care (Depner et al. 2018). Peer workers develop a caregiver relationship with an ill incarcerated person and provide hospice patient care, companionship, and psychosocial and spiritual support (Cloyes et al. 2017).

In a prison context, support also frequently occurs naturally both within and outside of these programs. For instance, from interviews conducted with incarcerated people in prisons across Belgium, one study found that incarcerated people play a vital role in providing information and support to each other about the ins and outs of prison life. This often happens during walks, in prison workplaces, or in cells. Getting this support from peers is seen as very important for new arrivals (Brosens 2019). In addition, many foreign nationals incarcerated in Belgium experience the dissemination of information by peers as essential, whether about activities being organized, changes in visiting hours, or other vital topics.

Frequently, speakers of non-native languages experience difficulties in understanding information that is spread via the official communication channels. To get the necessary information, people who speak the same language or who have been in prison for a longer period play a key role in announcing prison activities and translating important information, as demonstrated in the following quote: "When I came here [in prison], there was someone in my cell [who informed me about the yard], and that's the system here. From the moment you come into the system, everything [information] goes automatically through other people [who are staying in prison] (foreign-speaking, non-European, male)" (Croux et al. 2023, 47).

Next to informational support, stories abound of incarcerated people providing instrumental literacy support to their peers, such as reading letters, flyers, or brochures for peers who cannot read and write, offering help with writing report notes, and signing peers up for certain activities (e.g., the gym, religious services) (Croux et al. 2023). In addition, examples of situations in which emotional support is given are also numerous, such as when peers are confronted with the loss of a family member or with relationship problems.

Peer programs are often strong informal learning practices and can supplement more traditional types of education in prison, such as language courses, reading and writing courses, vocational training programs, and higher education. While many staff dedicate themselves to working with incarcerated people who want to learn and need support, they are not able to provide all the help necessary. For that reason, the role that peer programs play in the learning of incarcerated persons should not be underestimated.

Outcomes, Mechanisms, and Contextual Factors Realized by Peer Programs in Prison

In the following section, the focus remains on peer programs in prison that are formally organized rather than the spontaneous types of peer learning and peer support, important as they are. To this end, an analysis of twenty-nine international empirical articles and reports provides insight into contextual factors, mechanisms, and outcomes of peer programs (see table 11.1).

An important distinction should be made between categories of outcomes for peer workers, peer recipients, and prisons. In the following sub-

Table 11.1.

Overview of contextual factors, mechanisms, and outcomes (CMOs) of peer programs in prison.

CONTEXTUAL FACTORS	MECHANISMS	OUTCOMES
Micro-level (peer worker)	Supporting peer workers	For peer workers
• Recruitment requirements • Motivation	• Staff involved in the peer program • Correctional staff • Fellow peer workers • Self-care • Family and friends outside prison	• Identify desistance • Relational desistance • Improved knowledge and skills • Improved/deteriorated mental health • More meaningful time in prison • Changes in life circumstances after imprisonment
Exo-level (prison)		
• Institutional profile • Training and hands-on experiences of peer workers • Institutional buy-in		
	Developing human relationships	
Macro-level (national)	• Trust • Equality	
• Government support • Resources		For peer recipients
	Functioning as role models	• Identity desistance • Improved mental health • Increased knowledge
	Adopting a non-judgmental and empathetic attitude	For prisons
		• Fewer institutional infractions • Improved atmosphere • Eased pressure on professional staff • Security threats

sections, we first describe which outcomes are identified throughout the literature for peer workers, then touch on the outcomes for peer recipients and, finally, the outcomes for prisons.

Outcomes for Peer Workers

For peer workers, six categories of individual outcomes are identified, as can be seen in figure 11.2. Then, we describe how these categories are described in the corresponding literature.

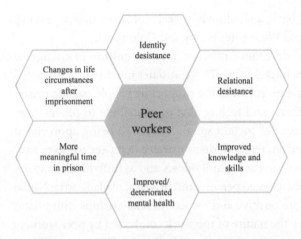

Figure 11.2.
Categories of
outcomes of peer
programs for peer
workers.

Notably, previous studies mainly support the conclusion that peer learning and peer support can contribute to identity desistance, which refers to the internalization of a nonoffending identity as an effect of taking up the role as peer worker during incarceration (Nugent and Schinkel 2016). Evidence suggests that many peer workers strive toward a changed self, a changed identity. Peer programs serve as an impetus for change and are considered a transformational experience (Cloyes et al. 2017; Edgar, Jacobson, and Biggar 2011; Nixon 2019; Stewart 2018; Thornton et al. 2018). They contribute to transformed personal identities, changes in cognitive thinking, changes in attitudes, or intentions to change behavior (Bagnall et al. 2015; Cloyes et al. 2014; Perry et al. 2021; Thornton et al. 2018). Peer workers take responsibility for their behavior, become mindful of their own conduct, develop and enact a new, noncriminal self, and feel like different kinds of people on the path of reform (Collica 2010; Jaffe 2012; Nixon 2019; O'Sullivan, Hart, and Healy 2020). Ultimately, they develop a prosocial identity (Jaffe 2012; Nixon 2019; O'Sullivan, Hart, and Healy 2020). Peer programs also boost a sense of self, contribute to enhanced sense of self-worth among peer workers, improve self-identity, change self-efficacy, and influence a positive shift in self-image (Cloyes et al. 2014; Edgar, Jacobson, and Biggar 2011; Griffiths and Bailey 2015; O'Sullivan, Hart, and Healy 2020; Thornton et al. 2018; Walby and Cole 2019). Peer workers gain self-esteem, build confidence, and discover or express the true self (Cloyes et al. 2014; Edgar, Jacobson, and Biggar 2011; O'Sullivan, Hart, and Healy 2020; Thornton et al. 2018; Walby and Cole 2019). They dissociate with labels such as "prisoner," "criminal," or "sex offender" by doing good or giving back, and, ultimately, feel more human (Cloyes et al. 2014; Perrin, Frost, and Ware 2018; Walby and Cole 2019).

Second, relational desistance refers to the recognition of change by others (Nugent and Schinkel 2016). This translates into being appreciated by other people in prison, enjoying the support by people outside prison such as family members, and feeling able to contribute to others' lives and to the development of social capital. Related to being appreciated by other people in prison, research demonstrates that peer workers have the feeling of being seen as caring individuals and as individuals who are respected by other incarcerated persons and prison staff (Jaffe 2012; Nixon 2019). They enjoy more positive and respectful relationships with prison staff as they recognize the nature of the work conducted by peer workers (Jaffe 2012). Fellow incarcerated people and prison staff see peer workers as human beings, rather than as incarcerated persons (Edgar, Jacobson, and Biggar 2011).

Concerning feeling supported by people outside prison, such as family members, research shows that peer workers frequently have the feeling that relationships with their family members have been improved by being a peer worker and that their positive attitudes and changes are recognized by family members (O'Sullivan, Hart, and Healy 2020). Peer workers experience enhanced relationships with family due to their improved communication skills and better understanding of problems from other individuals' perspectives (Jaffe 2012). Some feel able to make up for past wrongs toward family and God or feel chosen by God to offer end-of-life care to fellow incarcerated persons (Cloyes et al. 2014). Peer workers feel appreciated by family members of peer recipients when these family members thank the peer workers for their support (Edgar, Jacobson, and Biggar 2011).

Related to the feeling of being able to contribute to the lives of others, research demonstrates that incarcerated persons who function as peer educators teach other persons within their sphere of influence (e.g., fellow incarcerated people, family, and friends outside the prison walls). They share, for instance, information about HIV or infectious disease transmission outside classrooms (Thornton et al. 2018). Last, research reveals that functioning as a peer worker contributes to the development of social capital (Nixon 2019). Peer workers develop a desire to serve others, discover a newfound ability to support other incarcerated persons, and feel more able to demonstrate empathy and to understand problems from another individual's perspective (Edgar, Jacobson, and Biggar 2011; Jaffe 2012; Thornton et al. 2018). They experience feelings of joy when being able to help or even contribute to saving a life, improve communication skills, learn to function as a team member, and express their feelings (Edgar, Jacobson, and Biggar 2011; Jaffe 2012; Perry et al. 2021; Walby and Cole 2019).

Serving as a peer worker also leads to improved knowledge and skills. In addition to the development of social capital (see relational desistance), peer workers also improve other types of skills, such as presentation, leadership, planning and organization, problem-solving, and conflict resolution; counseling and mentoring; marketable job skills; and self-reflection (Collica 2010; Collica-Cox 2016; Perrin et al. 2018; Thornton et al. 2018). Which skills are targeted depends on the specifics of the training that is offered during the peer program. An increase of knowledge is mainly experienced among incarcerated people who are trained as peer educators in the following areas: health issues such as HIV, the hepatitis C virus and harm reduction strategies, and sexually transmitted infections (Ross et al. 2006; Sifunda et al. 2008; Thornton et al. 2018).

In addition, several studies also hint at the potential impact of peer programs on mental health outcomes for peer workers. On the one hand, these programs can improve mental health, as research demonstrates that conducting peer work allows peer workers to channel their energy and emotions as well as alleviate loneliness (Bagnall et al. 2015; Cloyes et al. 2014; Walby and Cole 2019; Woodall et al. 2015a). Increased levels of confidence, self-esteem, and self-worth (Woodall et al. 2015a), which also contribute to identity desistance, are related to this as well. Participation in a peer program as a worker offers a chance for incarcerated people to take off the mask and show their emotional and spiritual sides (Cloyes et al. 2014).

On the other hand, it should be noted that being a peer worker can also deteriorate mental health. It can be demanding work, which may lead to burnout, causing stress, which can be mentally taxing (Edgar, Jacobson, and Biggar 2011; Walby and Cole 2019). This is especially true in programs in which peer workers offer emotional support to fellow incarcerated persons who self-harm or are at risk of suicide. Accompanying self-harming people can be a distressing experience, causing negative emotions such as feeling frustrated by not being able to do more for someone, feeling sad when someone tries to take their own life, or having the feeling of not having done enough, which can cause anxiety (Jaffe 2012; Walby and Cole 2019).

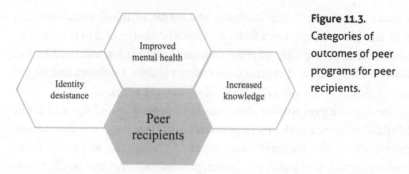

Figure 11.3.
Categories of outcomes of peer programs for peer recipients.

A fifth outcome sees peer roles contributing to a more meaningful time in prison. Peer workers can get the feeling of doing something constructive with their time in prison, give meaning to time in prison, or get a sense of purpose from it (Collica 2010; Edgar, Jacobson, and Biggar 2011; Jaffe 2012; Perrin 2022).

Last, outcomes related to changes in life circumstances after imprisonment were researched. Support for this latter outcome is rather limited, however, as not many studies examine the long-term outcomes of peer work after release. The few studies available on long-term outcomes demonstrate that taking up the role of peer worker during incarceration contributes to lower rates of recidivism (Collica 2010). Many peer workers work for community-based organizations providing social services on, for instance, HIV, mental health, or substance abuse after release. In general, their experiences of working with at-risk populations are valued (Collica-Cox 2016).

Outcomes for Peer Recipients

Although evidence is stronger to support the notion that participation in peer programs benefits peer workers more than peer recipients (Bagnall et al. 2015), the literature also reveals three key categories of outcomes for the users of these services (see figure 11.3). These outcomes are mainly described in studies on peer support programs aimed at preventing self-harm or suicide.

A first category shows that being able to call on the support of peer workers can provide identity desistance for peer recipients as well. This implies a greater sense of mastery and autonomy in coping with problems. Talking to peer workers functions as a form of communication with themselves, increasing their potential to trigger a new phase in their adjustment process, to move forward in a positive way, and to cope with the current situation (Jaffe 2012).

Second, peer programs have the ability to stimulate improved mental health outcomes (South, Bagnall, and Woodall 2017; Woodall et al. 2015a). Participating in peer programs reduces self-harming behavior and lowers end-of-life symptom prevalence and severity. It can lead to an adaptation of healthy behaviors and reduce risky behavior, stress, and anxiety (Bagnall et al. 2015; Cloyes et al. 2017; Perry et al. 2021; Perrin, Frost, and Ware 2018; South, Bagnall, and Woodall 2017; Thornton et al. 2018; Walby and Cole 2019). It can also relieve individual tensions, making it easier for participants to get things off their chests, release pressures, lift their mood, and avoid bottling things up and exploding (Jaffe 2012; Walby and Cole 2019). Peer recipients experience a sense of comfort sharing their problems and feel understood and heard, which makes them feel acknowledged (Jaffe 2012; Walby and Cole 2019).

Finally, peer education programs can also increase the knowledge of recipients, for instance, regarding HIV, hepatitis C, or building healthy habits in addition to other health-related issues (Ross et al. 2006; Thornton et al. 2018).

Outcomes for Prisons

In addition to benefits for peer workers and peer recipients, peer programs can also generate outcomes for the functioning of prisons themselves (Bagnall et al. 2015). Like the outcomes for peer recipients, these outcomes, too, are less commonly described in the literature compared to the outcomes for peer workers. Figure 11.4 reveals how three categories of positive outcomes for prisons and one negative category are mentioned in the literature.

The first positive category is fewer institutional infractions, as peer workers demonstrate better institutional conduct, so fewer institutional or disciplinary infractions need to be given (Collica 2010; Collica-Cox 2014). The literature describes that peer workers achieve higher rates of institutional success as there are fewer disciplinary problems, less violence and disruption, and a better social order within the prison (Collica 2010; Edgar, Jacobson, and Biggar 2011; Woodall et al. 2015a).

Second, linked with the first outcome, there is also an improved atmosphere within the prison (Nixon 2019). This refers to a more caring, humane culture through increased positive relationships between staff and

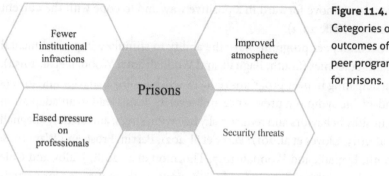

Figure 11.4. Categories of outcomes of peer programs for prisons.

incarcerated persons as rapport is built between these groups (Jaffe 2012; Nixon 2019; O'Sullivan, Hart, and Healy 2020; South et al. 2016; Stewart 2018; Thornton et al. 2018; Woodall et al. 2015a).

Third, peer programs can cause an eased pressure on prison staff and health counseling professionals (Devilly et al. 2005; Jaffe 2012; Magee and Foster 2011; Perry et al. 2021), as peer workers relieve some of the load of the work of these professionals. This occurs, for instance, when peer workers provide support to fellow incarcerated persons who are in emotional and psychological distress, provide information or practical support to newly arrived incarcerated persons, or direct individuals to services available inside prison (Magee and Foster 2011; Woodall et al. 2015a).

Last, the only negative category of outcomes is that of security threats, referring to the fact that some peer workers abuse their power, responsibilities, or trust by distributing contraband such as drugs or mobile phones (Edgar, Jacobson, and Biggar 2011; Magee and Foster 2011; Woodall et al. 2015a). Greater freedom of movement makes them ideal "runners" for drugs and other substances (Woodall et al. 2015a).

Mechanisms That Contribute to These Outcomes

Beyond the outcomes themselves, it is important to evaluate the mechanisms that contribute to the realization of the outcomes described in the previous sections. These mechanisms contribute to the formal and informal learning processes behind peer programs. As mentioned previously, a great deal of learning can happen during educating, tutoring, or supporting fellow incarcerated persons. Based on the studies included in the review, a total of four categories of mechanisms have been found:

supporting peer workers, developing human relationships, functioning as role models, and adopting nonjudgmental and empathetic attitudes.

First, studies have identified the support of peer workers as an important mechanism leading to the previously discussed outcomes. This support can be provided by staff involved in the peer program, correctional staff, fellow peer workers, family and friends outside prison, or through self-care. Related to the support provided by staff involved in the peer program (e.g., healthcare professionals, medical staff, psychologists, staff from external organizations, the voluntary sector), research indicates that these staff have an important role in making peer workers more skilled and knowledgeable (Cloyes et al. 2017). This occurs by organizing regular meetings with staff members (e.g., individual sessions or weekly meetings in groups with other peer workers) (Devilly et al. 2005; Edgar, Jacobson, and Biggar 2011) and the provision of supervision and support during which peer workers can confidentially discuss difficult issues. This contributes to ensuring motivation and commitment of peer workers (Devilly et al. 2005). Correctional staff also play a role in making peer workers more skilled and knowledgeable (Cloyes et al. 2017). They can encourage the formation and maintenance of prosocial identities among peer workers and stimulate incarcerated people to secure positive roles like becoming a peer worker (Nixon 2019; Perrin 2020).

Fellow peer workers are also important in providing support. On the one hand, there are formal mentorship structures to make peer workers more skilled and knowledgeable (Cloyes et al. 2017; Thornton et al. 2018). These formal structures allow participants to learn from each other, share successful strategies, and pair newer peer workers with more experienced ones to build skills and confidence (Cloyes et al. 2017; Thornton et al. 2018). This creates a safe space where incarcerated peer workers can explore new roles without being judged on their past behavior (Collica 2010).

On the other hand, informal mentorship structures arise based on the creation of supportive groups and camaraderie among peer workers (Collica 2010; Collica-Cox 2016). For instance, when feeling upset, peer workers often go to their fellow peer workers to offload feelings, process emotions, or debrief to reduce feelings of burden (Cloyes et al. 2017; Jaffe 2012). Older or more experienced peer workers often serve as mentors for younger peer workers (Collica-Cox 2016; Stewart 2018). Moreover, this support frequently moves beyond peer roles (e.g., peer workers supporting each other when a family member dies or when someone does not get a visit), often serving as an extended family (Cloyes et al. 2014; Collica 2010; Collica-Cox 2014, 2016). Mentorship can also provide a safe space that is protected from cultural pressures around masculinity (Cloyes et al. 2014). Another important element is self-care, such as religious activity, going to the gym, or creating artwork (Walby and Cole 2019). The literature also reveals that family and friends outside prison have an important supporting role. Peer workers feel that the support of this network is crucial to being able to take on this challenging work, even if they do not directly discuss events in prison with their families and friends (Walby and Cole 2019).

Second, developing human relationships is also seen as an important mechanism. These human relationships are characterized by trust (e.g., between peer workers and staff involved in the peer program, between peer workers and correctional staff, and between peer workers and peer recipients) and equality between peer workers and peer recipients. The literature describes trust between peer workers and staff involved in the peer program. This trust can be built when trainers treat peer workers like human beings, with dignity and respect (Collica 2010; Edgar, Jacobson, and Biggar 2011). Trainers who are committed to their work make an impact on how seriously peer workers take their work (Collica 2010). Trust can also be built between peer workers and correctional staff; being treated like a human being and not like a number is important (Collica 2010). Peer workers want to gain recognition of their potential and be treated as of equal moral worth, with dignity and respect by correctional staff (Collica 2010; Jaffe 2012; Magee and Foster 2011; Nixon 2019; O'Sullivan, Hart, and Healy 2020).

Trust can also be created between peer workers and peer recipients. Building this trust requires patience and is a time-consuming process (Walby and Cole 2019). Peer workers need to be seen as credible and trustworthy by other incarcerated persons (Woodall et al. 2015b). Peer recipients can talk to people who have been in the same place and have felt the same range of emotions before (Walby and Cole 2019). Confidentiality is important in this regard because in some peer programs anything a peer recipient shares with a peer worker needs to remain confidential and cannot be reported to correctional staff (Devilly et al. 2005; Jaffe 2012; Perrin 2022; Walby and Cole 2019; Woodall et al. 2015b); peer workers need to reassure peer recipients that their stories are kept confidential. Sometimes, however, it happens that correctional staff attempt to compromise confidentiality and ask peer workers about what has been discussed with the incarcerated person who asks for help (Jaffe 2012; Perrin 2022). In some programs (e.g., the Listener program), breaking the code of confidentiality is likely to lead to the end of the peer role for that person (Perrin 2022).

Related to equality between peer workers and peer recipients, the literature emphasizes that it is important to recognize that incarcerated people are not staff, and this opens doors in their work (Walby and Cole 2019). Peer workers and peer recipients often have shared experiences and similar backgrounds, and can offer personal expertise through that experience (Griffiths, Bailey, and Slade 2020; Walby and Cole 2019; Woodall et al. 2015b). It is described that peer workers can function as "wounded healers," where they experience their offending history as an asset, giving them authenticity, empathy, and relatability (O'Sullivan, Hart, and Healy 2020; Stewart 2018). Without a doubt, respect from peer recipients toward peer workers is of utmost importance (Collica 2010; Nixon 2019; Thornton et al. 2018).

A third category of mechanisms indicates that peer workers are often seen as role models by other incarcerated people and by correctional staff (Collica-Cox 2014; Nixon 2019; Thornton et al. 2008). They are seen as people who can positively influence other incarcerated people (Nixon 2019). Peer workers think that correctional staff and incarcerated people perceive them as more dependable, more educated, more respected, more trustworthy, more knowledgeable, or more supportive than other incarcerated people (Collica-Cox 2014). Peer workers place high expectations on their fellow peer workers and a desire to meet these expectations (Collica-Cox 2016); if someone does not demonstrate the expected qualities of a role model (e.g., by trafficking drugs), this negatively reflects on the whole group of peer workers (Jaffe 2012).

Last, being able to adopt a nonjudgmental and empathetic attitude as a peer worker is considered an important fourth category of mechanisms. Learning to demonstrate a nonjudgmental attitude takes specialized training, in which peer workers learn to keep their own emotions under control, reserve their opinions, and be there for those who need help (Griffiths, Bailey, and Slade 2019; Jaffe 2012; Walby and Cole 2019). It is important to care for others without discrimination and judgment (Cloyes et al. 2014). This can be difficult when supporting someone imprisoned for a crime they themselves detest (e.g., sexual offenders) (Edgar, Jacobson, and Biggar 2011; Jaffe 2012; Magee and Foster 2011; Walby and Cole 2019). To be able to demonstrate an empathetic attitude, it is important that peer

Figure 11.5.
Overview of contextual levels of influences on peer programs in prison.

workers consider the feelings of the ones they are helping, understand their perspective, and empathize with them (Jaffe 2012; Stewart 2018). It is recognized throughout the literature that peer workers can demonstrate a greater level of empathy compared to staff through their expertise by experience (Jaffe 2012; Nixon 2019).

Contextual Factors That Influence the Realization of Mechanisms and Outcomes

Although peer programs have the potential to improve outcomes for individual peer workers, peer recipients, and prisons, the realization of this constellation of outcomes depends on the surrounding context (O'Sullivan, Hart, and Healy 2020). Accordingly, figure 11.5 presents an overview of contextual factors on the micro, exo, and macro levels. We explain how these factors are described in the literature.

The micro level refers to characteristics of individual peer workers. On this level, both the recruitment requirements and the motivation to become a peer worker play a role. Concerning the recruitment requirements, the literature makes clear that these vary widely between different programs based, for example, on the literacy level of the peer workers. For some programs, it is not necessary to be able to read and write, as the training is adapted to the prison population, of which many have literacy levels ranging from low to having obtained the eighth-grade literacy level

(Edgar, Jacobson, and Biggar 2011; Jaffe 2012; Thornton et al. 2018). Other recruitment criteria include the remaining time left on one's sentence (e.g., at least one year left), one's communication skills, a risk assessment, or exclusion of those who are a security risk due, for instance, to distribution of contraband (Edgar, Jacobson, and Biggar 2011; Jaffe 2012; South et al. 2016; Thornton et al. 2018; Walby and Cole 2019).

Several peer programs described in the literature strive for a representation of different subcultures present in the prison or for diversity in age and ethnicity (Devilly et al. 2005; Thornton et al. 2018). Nevertheless, some dispute remains about the involvement of people who have committed sexual offenses. The risk exists that other peer workers are not happy to be trained together with them or that incarcerated people do not want to rely on peer workers with that type of offense (Magee and Foster 2011).

Related to the motivation of incarcerated persons to become a peer worker, the literature describes that having the "right" motivation from the beginning is essential. This encompasses other-centered motivations, having prosocial or altruistic concerns for others, really caring, providing help and comfort to those who need it most, and wanting to give something back to the community (Cloyes et al. 2014; Jaffe 2012; Stewart 2018). It is also about the human nature of peer work, expressing the true nature and capacity to care, feeling like God has called them to do this work, or providing end-of-life care that they want for themselves or their family (Cloyes et al. 2014; Perrin 2022). Examples of "wrong" reasons or questionable motives are wanting to gain privileges, a greater freedom of movement around the prison, enhanced respect of staff, or positive recognition or approval from others (Cloyes et al. 2014; Jaffe 2012; Perrin 2022).

The exo level refers to impacts at the level of the prison. It is on this level that the institutional profile of the prison, the training and hands-on experiences of peer workers, and the institutional buy-in are located. Related to the institutional profile of the prison, the delivery model of the peer program is important. Active management or coordination of peer programs is necessary to enable smooth delivery (South et al. 2016), and the delivery model should be adapted to the particular type of facility (e.g., pretrial detention center, training prison). For example, pretrial detention centers are confronted with high turnover in populations and challenges in the training and retention of peer workers (Devilly et al. 2005; Woodall et al. 2015b). Consequently, the duration of a person's remaining sentence can become a critical recruitment criterion, as lengthy training programs are more feasible in longer-stay prisons (Woodall et al. 2015b). If training is based on similar peer programs in other countries, it should be adapted to the local situation (Sifunda et al. 2008).

Another aspect related to the institutional profile of the prison is whether the prison is a therapeutic environment. In general, incarcerated people prioritize peer programs over professional programs (Auzoult and Abdellaoui 2013; Bagnall et al. 2015). There is one exception, however: professional programs are preferred in prison sites that operate as therapeutic communities where relationships of trust between professionals and incarcerated people are built (Griffiths, Bailey, and Slade 2019).

In regard to offering training and hands-on experiences to peer workers, it is important to note that training regimes for peer workers vary in content, duration, frequency, and intensity (South et al. 2016). When trainings are used that are also given to a nonprison population, it is important to adapt them to a prison context (Cloyes et al. 2017). In addition, ongoing training opportunities are necessary, as existing peer workers will continue to need refresher courses (Devilly et al. 2005; Sifunda et al. 2008). An important factor in realizing training and hands-on experiences for peer workers is the training content. Peer workers need to be trained to ensure that they effectively and efficiently fulfill their tasks. All training programs should address core skills, such as listening, communication, problem-solving, and empathy (Devilly et al. 2005). Additionally, it is important to include topics relevant for the specific peer program, such as teaching strategies, knowledge on specific diseases to become able to educate fellow incarcerated people, first aid, or identification of suicidal crisis (Auzoult and Abdellaoui 2013; Thornton et al. 2018).

Additionally, the teaching approach plays a role, as there must be qualified trainers who are able to develop training materials, recruit potential peer workers, supervise peer workers, and engage with prison management (Devilly et al. 2005). The research shows that it is also important to include role-playing and discussions in the training, starting from a strengths-based approach (Devilly et al. 2005; Jaffe 2012; Nixon 2019; O'Sullivan, Hart, and Healy 2020). In addition, the importance of including a gendered approach in female prisons is paramount. For instance, when training women who provide support to women in custody who self-harm, it is important to train peer workers to understand the triggers for self-harm that relate to difficulties with men, displacement of their mothering role, and the needs of attachment in prison (Griffiths, Bailey, and Slade 2020).

It is also important to offer experiential learning opportunities (Devilly et al. 2005). Peer workers place higher value on hands-on experiences compared to classroom learning and structured training where theory can be put into practice (Cloyes et al. 2017). For example, on-the-job learning and training, ongoing learning opportunities, and shadowing opportunities are all valued (Cloyes et al. 2017; Edgar, Jacobson, and Biggar 2011; Jaffe 2012). It is important to have active experiences and to observe others who have gained experience as well. Afterward, peer workers can reflect on those experiences, draw understanding and conclusions from them, and attempt them again (Devilly et al. 2005).

Another key aspect in addition to the institutional profile of the prison and the training and hands-on experiences of peer workers is institutional buy-in. This implies that broad support is essential, including senior-level support (i.e., prison administrators) as well as that of security staff (Edgar, Jacobson, and Biggar 2011; Woodall et al. 2015b). Raising awareness about the peer program, helping prison staff understand its rationale and value, having dedicated staff who oversee the program (e.g., unlocking and escorting incarcerated people, managing the logistics), co-constructing the peer program with staff at all levels, having prison staff as front-line workers, and having peer programs that are part of the regime all increase the likelihood of success (Edgar, Jacobson, and Biggar 2011; Woodall et al. 2015b). It is also essential to begin with a manageable scale. This includes starting with a small number of participants (i.e., chiefly those who are considered the most reliable) and broadening to more challenging profiles of peer workers after gaining sufficient experience (Edgar, Jacobson, and Biggar 2011). Among the challenges to achieving institutional buy-in are staff resistance and security concerns (e.g., abuse of position of trust by peer workers through distributing contraband such as tobacco or mobile phones) (Edgar, Jacobson, and Biggar 2011; South et al. 2016; Woodall et al. 2015b).

Last, on the macro or national level, the amount of government support and the resources available for peer programs both influence the realization of the outcomes and mechanisms. Concerning the amount of government support, for instance, the United Kingdom has a unified national policy regarding peer programs in prison. There are formal instructions about "prisoners assisting other prisoners" (see, for example, National Offender Management Service 2020; Stewart 2018). Notably, the literature does not mention national government support in any other country. Related to the resources, the literature indicates that dedicated resources are necessary, including staff time to support the program (Woodall et al. 2015a). Lack of funding is a barrier for expansion and replication, and shrinking staffing budgets might lead to the perception among prison officers that incarcerated persons can replace prison staff (Thornton et al. 2018; Woodall et al. 2015a).

What Works in Which Context? Bringing Together Context, Mechanisms, and Outcomes

The previous sections separately identify the outcomes, mechanisms, and contextual factors of peer programs in prison, without explaining how these aspects are interrelated. Although the literature does not frequently describe these interconnections, it does give an occasional glimpse into them.

First, there are some links found between mechanisms and outcomes. For example, the literature highlights that support for those who take up a role as peer worker during their time of incarceration (the mechanism) is crucial to teaching them how to cope with negative mental health outcomes, such as dealing with stress and high-pressure situations, emotional regulation, and preventing burnout (Cloyes et al. 2017; Collica-Cox 2014, 2016; Perrin, Frost, and Ware 2018; Walby and Cole 2019; Woodall et al. 2015a). This applies to support that is provided by staff involved in the peer program, fellow peer workers, and self-care (Cloyes et al. 2017; Collica-Cox 2016; Walby and Cole 2019; Woodall et al. 2015a). Getting the support of fellow peer workers is also explicitly linked to the realization of identity desistance or adoption of a prosocial identity (Collica-Cox 2016). An important association is also described between the mechanism regarding serving as a role model and the outcome of lower institutional infractions. As peer workers learn, they become more mindful of their conduct at all times, which impacts their own personal decision-making, since they do not want to jeopardize their position by engaging in unlawful or deviant behaviors; this in turn leads to lower rates of institutional infractions (Collica 2010; Collica-Cox 2014).

Second, several explicit connections are made between contextual factors and outcomes. For instance, in prisons where correctional staff exhibit institutional buy-in for the peer program, the general atmosphere improves, resulting in more positive and respectful relationships between peer workers and correctional staff (Jaffe 2012). Also, peer training is linked with a greater willingness among correctional staff to collaborate with peer workers (Stewart 2018). The training also contributes to improvements in knowledge and skills among peer workers. For instance, training teaches peer workers to better understand the impact of body language or the tone of their voice, resulting in improved communication skills, teaching skills, or even knowledge about topics such as hepatitis C or sexually transmitted infections (Jaffe 2012; Thornton et al. 2018). This all contributes to their learning process.

Conclusion

Based on an analysis of twenty-nine empirical articles and reports on peer programs in prison, this chapter demonstrates that outcomes for peer workers are more extensively described than outcomes for peer recipients and prisons. In our opinion, this should not be interpreted as suggesting that these programs are less effective for peer recipients and prisons, but rather that those outcomes on the level of peer workers are often the most studied.

In addition, this chapter exemplifies that, to realize outcomes through peer programs, it is also crucial to gain insight into the learning processes behind peer programs and to provide reasons for why some programs are more effective or successful than others. By having these insights, professionals in prisons all over the world can try to improve the learning that can be realized through existing peer programs, both for peer workers and peer recipients, or develop new programs that work in a more evidence-based way. Critically important is that the programs are adapted to the specific context in which they occur, such as in different types of prisons, where sentences have different functions and where the implementation of the peer program and the training of the peer workers have significant consequences.

To conclude, as demonstrated by a host of international literature, peer programs are often strong learning practices, both formal and informal. They can supplement other, more classical, educational programs that are offered in prisons such as language courses, reading and writing courses, second-chance education, vocational training programs, or higher education. Training to become a peer worker, as well as hands-on learning experience, empowers students to educate, tutor, and support their fellow incarcerated persons. When implemented under the right contextual factors from prison to prison, and by attending to the mechanisms underlying peer programs, these programs can have benefits for peer workers, peer receivers, and prisons. Mainly, when peer programs target peer learning, the instructional chances for both peer workers and peer recipients appear to be great. Moreover, in peer support programs, everyone involved learns. Accordingly, learning opportunities or courses that lead to diplomas or certificates are important, but they are not the only important instruments. A great deal of meaningful learning also happens during interactions with other people, specifically during interactions in which peer workers educate, tutor, or support fellow incarcerated persons.

Notes

This book chapter has been written with support of the Flemish Research Foundation (FWO; grant number: 12B9222N).

1. Other terms that can be used for prisoner councils are "prisoner forums," "inmate committees," "representative councils," and "consultative committees." A prisoner council is an example of democratic participation in prison. Incarcerated persons who have been elected by their peers discuss matters relating to the general conditions of imprisonment.

Works Cited

Auzoult, Laurent, and Sid Abdellaoui. 2013. "Perceptions of a Peer Suicide Prevention Program by Inmates and Professionals Working in Prisons: Underestimation of Risk, the Modification of the Field, and the Role of Self-consciousness." *Crisis* 34 (4): 289–92.

Bagnall, Anne-Marie, Jane South, Claire Hulme, James Woodall, Karen Vinall-Collier, Gary Raine, Karina Kinsella, et al. 2015. "A Systematic Review of the Effectiveness and Cost-Effectiveness of Peer Education and Peer Support in Prisons." *BMC Public Health* 15 (290).

Betts-Symonds, Graham. 2016. *An Evaluation of the Process of the Community Based Health & First Aid in Prisons Programme (2009–2014): A Collaborative Study Using a "Realist Approach."* Ontario: Western University.

Brosens, Dorien. 2019. "Prisoners' Participation and Involvement in Prison Life: Examining the Possibilities and Barriers." *European Journal of Criminology* 16 (4): 466–85.

Brosens, Dorien, and Liesbeth De Donder. 2016. *Educational Participation of European Citizens Detained in a Foreign European Country*. Brussels: Vrije Universiteit Brussel.

Cloyes, Kristin G., Susan J. Rozenkranz, Dawn Wold, Patricia Berry, and Katherine P. Supiano. 2014. "To Be Truly Alive: Motivation among Prison Inmate Hospice Volunteers and the Transformative Process of End-of-life Peer Care Service." *American Journal of Hospice & Palliative Medicine* 31 (7): 735–48.

Cloyes, Kristin G., Susan J. Rosenkranz, Katherine P. Supiano, Patricia Berry, Meghan Routt, Sarah M. Llanque, and Kathleen Shannon-Dorcy. 2017. "Caring to Learn, Learning to Care: Inmate Hospice Volunteers and the Delivery of Prison End-of-Life Care." *Journal of Correctional Health Care* 23 (1): 43–55.

Collica, Kimberly. 2010. "Surviving Incarceration: Two Prison-Based Peer Programs Build Communities of Support for Female Offenders." *Deviant Behavior* 31 (4): 314–47.

Collica-Cox, Kimberly. 2014. "Counting Down: HIV Prison-Based Peer Education Programs and Their Connection to Reduced Disciplinary Infractions." *International Journal of Offender Therapy and Comparative Criminology* 58 (8): 931–52.

Collica-Cox, Kimberly. 2016. "All Aboard the Desistance Line: First Stop, Producing Prosocial Prison Attachments within an HIV Prison-Based Peer Program." *Journal of Prison Education and Reentry* 3 (2): 67–91.

Croux, Flore, Liesbeth De Donder, Bart Claes, Stijn Vandevelde, and Dorien Brosens. 2023. "Peer Support as a Bridge for Participation in Prison Activities and Services: A Qualitative Study with Foreign National Prisoners." *Criminology & Criminal Justice* 23 (1): 39–59. https://doi.org/10.1177/17488958211031347.

Depner, Rachel M., Pei C. Grant, David J. Byrwa, Jennifer M. Breier, Jennifer Lodi-Smith, Debra L. Luczkiewicz, and Christopher Kerr. 2018. "'People Don't Understand What Goes on in Here': A Consensual Qualitative Research Analysis of Inmate-Caregiver Perspectives on Prison-Based End-of-Life Care." *Palliative Medicine* 32 (5): 969–79.

Devilly, Grant J., Laura Sorbello, Lynne Eccleston, and Tony Ward. 2005. "Prison-Based Peer-Education Schemes." *Aggression and Violent Behavior* 10 (2): 219–40.

Edgar, Kimmett, Jessica Jacobson, and Kathy Biggar. 2011. *Time Well Spent: A Practical Guide to Active Citizenship and Volunteering in Prison.* Prison Reform Trust.

Fazel, Seena, Taanvi Ramesh, and Keith Hawton. 2017. "Suicide in Prisons: An International Study of Prevalence and Contributory Factors." *The Lancet Psychiatry* 4 (12): 946–52.

Griffiths, Louise, and Di Bailey. 2015. "Learning from Peer Support Schemes: Can Prison Listeners Support Offenders Who Self-Injure in Custody?" *International Journal of Prisoner Health* 11 (3): 157–68.

Griffiths, Louise, Di Bailey, and Karen Slade. 2019. "Professional and Peer Support Preferences for Women Who Self-Harm in Custody." *Journal of Criminal Psychology* 9 (3): 109–21.

Griffiths, Louise, Di Bailey, and Karen Slade. 2020. "Exploring the Listener Scheme in a Women's Prison: The Importance of a Gendered Approach to Peer Support for Women Who Self-Harm in Custody." *Journal of Mental Health Training, Education and Practice* 15 (6): 347–60.

Jaffe, Michelle. 2012. "Peer Support and Seeking Help in Prison. A Study of the Listener Scheme in Four Prisons in England." PhD diss., Keele University.

Magee, Helen, and John Foster. 2011. *Peer Support in Prison Health Care. An Investigation into the Listening Scheme in One Adult Male Prison*. London: University of Greenwich.

McParland, Chris, and Bridget Johnston. 2019. "Palliative and End of Life Care in Prisons: A Mixed-Methods Rapid Review of the Literature from 2014–2018." *BMJ Open* 9 (e033905). https://doi.org/10.1136/bmjopen-2019-033905.

McParland, Chris, and Bridget Johnston. 2021. "Caring, Sharing, Preparing and Declaring: How Do Hospices Support Prisons to Provide Palliative and End of Life Care? A Qualitative Descriptive Study Using Telephone Interviews." *Palliative Medicine* 35 (3): 563–73.

Mead, Shery, David Hilton, and Laurie Curtis. 2001. "Peer Support: A Theoretical Perspective." *Psychiatric Rehabilitation Journal* 25 (2): 134–41.

Mehay, Anita, and Rosie Meek. 2016. "The Development of a Peer-Based Approach for Promoting Prisoner Health in an English Male Young Offender Institution." In *The Voluntary Sector in Prisons. Encouraging Personal and Institutional Change*, edited by Laura S. Abrams, Emma Hughes, Michelle Inderbitzin, and Rosie Meek, 143–70. New York: Palgrave Studies.

National Offender Management Service. 2020. "Prisoners Assisting Other Prisoners —PSI 17/2015." https://assets.publishing.service.gov.uk/government/uploads /system/uploads/attachment_data/file/905564/psi-17-2015-prisoners-assisting -other-prisoners.pdf/.

Nixon, Sarah. 2019. "'I Just Want to Give Something Back': Peer Work in Prison." *Prison Service Journal* 245: 44–53.

Nugent, Briege, and Marguerite Schinkel. 2016. "The Pains of Desistance." *Criminology & Criminal Justice* 16 (5): 568–84.

O'Sullivan, Róisín, Wayne Hart, and Deirdre Healy. 2020. "Transformative Rehabilitation: Exploring Prisoners' Experiences of the Community Based Health and First Aid Programme in Ireland." *European Journal on Criminal Policy and Research* 26 (1): 63–81.

Perrin, Christian. 2017. "The Untapped Utility of Peer-Support Programs in Prisons and Implications for Theory, Policy, and Practice." PhD diss., Nottingham Trent University.

Perrin, Christian. 2022. "Maximizing the Utility of Peer Support in Carceral Settings: A Few Stumbling Blocks to Consider." *European Journal of Criminology* 19(4): 730–45. https://doi.org/10.1177/1477370820919717.

Perrin, Christian, Andrew Frost, and Jayson Barry Ware. 2018. "The Utility of Peer-Support in Enhancing the Treatment of Incarcerated Sexual Offenders." *International Journal of Therapeutic Communities* 39 (1): 35–49.

Perrin, Christian, Nicholas Blagden, Belinda Winder, and Gayle Dillon. 2018. "'It's Sort of Reaffirmed to Me That I'm Not a Monster, I'm Not a Terrible Person': Sex Offenders' Movements Toward Desistance via Peer-Support Roles in Prison." *Sexual Abuse* 30 (7): 759–80.

Perry, Amanda E., Mitch G. Waterman, Veronica Dale, Keeley Moore, and Allan House. 2021. "The Effect of a Peer-Led Problem-Support Mentor Intervention on Self-Harm and Violence in Prison: An Interrupted Time Series Analysis Using Routinely Collected Prison Data." *eClinicalMedicine* 32. https://doi.org/10.1016/j.eclinm.2020.100702.

Ross, Michael, Amy Jo Harzke, Deborah P. Scott, Kelly McCann, and Michael Kelley. 2006. "Outcomes of Project Wall Talk: An HIV/AIDS Peer Education Program Implemented within the Texas State Prison System." *AIDS Education and Prevention* 18 (6): 504–17.

Sifunda, Sibusiso, Priscilla S. Reddy, Ronald Braithwaite, Torrence Stephens, Sibusisiwe Bhengu, Rob A. C. Ruiter, and Bart van den Borne. 2008. "The Effectiveness of a Peer-Led HIV/AIDS and STI Health Education Intervention for Prison Inmates in South Africa." *Health Education & Behavior* 35 (4): 494–508.

South, Jane, Anne-Marie Bagnall, and James Woodall. 2017. "Developing a Typology for Peer Education and Peer Support Delivered by Prisoners." *Journal of Correctional Health Care* 23 (2): 214–29.

South, Jane, James Woodall, Karina Kinsella, and Anne-Marie Bagnall. 2016. "A Qualitative Synthesis of the Positive and Negative Impacts Related to Delivery of Peer-Based Health Interventions in Prison Settings." *BMC Health Services Research* 16 (1): 525.

Stewart, Warren. 2018. "What Does the Implementation of Peer Care Training in a U.K. Prison Reveal About Prisoner Engagement in Peer Caregiving?" *Journal of Forensic Nursing* 14 (1): 18–26.

Thornton, Karla, Miranda L. Sedillo, Summers Kalishman, Kimberly Page, and Sanjeev Arora. 2018. "The New Mexico Peer Education Project: Filling a Critical Gap in HCV Prison Education." *Journal of Health Care for the Poor and Underserved* 29 (4): 1544–57.

Topping, Keith. 2005. "Trends in Peer Learning." *Educational Psychology* 25 (6): 631–45.

Topping, Keith. 2015. "Peer Tutoring: Old Method, New Developments." *Infancia y Aprendizaje: Journal for the Study of Education and Development* 38 (1): 1–29.

Walby, Kevin, and Dwayne Cole. 2019. "Beyond Emotional Labour: Emotions and Peer Support in a Canadian Prison." *Emotion, Space and Society* 33: 100631. https://doi.org/10.1016/j.emospa.2019.100631.

Woodall, James, Jane South, Rachael Dixey, Nick de Viggiani, and William Penson. 2015a. "Expert Views of Peer-Based Interventions for Prisoner Health." *International Journal of Prisoner Health* 11 (2): 87–97.

Woodall, James, Jane South, Rachael Dixey, Nick de Viggiani, and William Penson. 2015b. "Factors That Determine the Effectiveness of Peer Interventions in Prisons in England and Wales." *Prison Service Journal* 219: 30–37.

Wright, Kevin N., and Laura Bronstein. 2007. "Creating Decent Prisons." *Journal of Offender Rehabilitation* 44 (4): 1–16.

JUSTIN MCDEVITT AND MNEESHA GELLMAN

CONCLUSION

DRAWING LESSONS FROM COMPARATIVE

EDUCATION IN PRISON

This volume has brought together scholars and educators from ten different countries across the United States, Latin America, and Europe in order to highlight key principles from the work of education in prisons in a variety of contexts. Our hope is that this volume helps stakeholders learn from each other and furthers the critical mission of increasing educational access in carceral spaces. Throughout the book, the contributors have collectively expressed several key themes: education is a fundamental right for incarcerated people; education is crucial to helping people reintegrate into society after release; education must be part of a larger, more integrated set of interventions that include work experience; and more must be done to ensure that education will thrive in correctional systems as long as human confinement practices continue to exist.

First and foremost, education is a fundamental right of all people, and people who are currently incarcerated are certainly no exception. As Article 26 of the United Nations Universal Declaration of Human Rights makes clear, access to basic education should be free and universally provided in prison, while vocational training and higher education ought to be accessible as well (United Nations 1948). While some may argue that basic rights such as these should be suspended when someone is convicted of breaking the social contract by violating laws, we push back to say that a genuine vision of public safety must include access to the tools of transformation and self-actualization. In fact, if anything, the rights of people who are incarcerated must be safeguarded as carefully as those of the general population, given their vulnerable status in society. And to truly make safer societies, we must interrupt ongoing structural injustices that exclude some people from access to living dignified lives. Educational access is one such intervention to this end.

How this right to education is expressed shows considerable variation across the case studies included here. Several authors in this volume representing various EU countries quickly draw attention to the EU's recognition of education as a protected right, too, with Article 14 of the EU Charter of Fundamental Rights stating, "Everyone has the right to education and to have access to vocational and continuing training" (2000). Some countries have taken the additional step to integrate this right to education into their national laws as well, as is seen in Grzegorz A. Skrobotowicz's chapter on Poland. Even when not initially recognized by a governmental body, some universities take steps to affirm their commitment to education as a fundamental right, as Natasha Bidault Mniszek outlines in the section of her chapter on the development of PESCER in Mexico City.

In the United States, unfortunately, such a commitment to educational access regardless of circumstance is less clearly espoused. The legacy of discrimination in education is long and ugly, as Maria K. McKenna describes forcefully in her chapter. Like many systems of privilege, education has often been co-opted to serve the needs of the powerful majority at the brutal expense of marginalized communities. Moreover, when it comes to education in prison in particular, the federal and state commitment to providing the means for such education—in terms of access, institutional support, and resources—has been spotty at best, subject to political headwinds, and a frequent casualty of opportunistic grandstanding by insincere politicians. Max Kenner's US case study demonstrates how an entire educational infrastructure that took years to build can be destroyed in an instant. The immense devastation wrought by the removal of Pell funding in 1994 will not be easily rebuilt even as that funding is restored. Generational impact from lack of educational access takes time to overcome. The EU's approach to mainstreaming education as a fundamental right surely offers lessons for stakeholders in the United States and elsewhere.

Second, another key takeaway from this volume is that education is a crucial part of helping people reintegrate into society upon release from prison. In fact, as Chester Lee argues in his chapter on the Netherlands, reintegration must be the starting point from which we approach educational efforts in the first place. Importantly, Lee does not refer to education as a paternalistic tool of control that seeks to "reeducate" citizens who have lost their way. Instead, he points to the power of education to provide the qualifications and critical skills needed for successful participation in society upon release. Indeed, education helps incarcerated people enter a workforce that may have previously been closed to them, as Walter Hammerschick presents in his chapter on the Austrian education system in prison, and this sentiment is echoed in other chapters.

This is especially true considering that incarcerated people are not only a vulnerable population themselves; they often come from already marginalized populations as well. As several authors point out across multiple chapters, including urgently in the case of Norway, the education level of those in prison is often much lower than that of the total population (see chapter 6). These authors emphasize that, more than being simply a right on paper, offering education to those in prison goes a long way toward meeting a need that society beyond the wall has failed to address.

From this lens, educating those behind bars is not just an afterthought or a technicality, but is instead affirmatively addressing the need for education where it is most urgent. In the case of particularly vulnerable populations in prisons, such as juveniles (e.g., Poland), women (e.g., Slovakia), victims of violence (e.g., El Salvador), racial minorities (e.g., United States), and immigrants (e.g., Italy, Austria, and Norway), the need is especially acute where these populations face layers of challenges and discrimination. As Jennifer Coreas points out in her chapter on El Salvador, education can help vulnerable populations find their voices where all else has failed. In this case, a space for learning and self-expression is a life raft that incarcerated people can use to keep themselves from sinking into invisibility and despair.

Third, though education is a crucial part of the reintegration process, another key takeaway from this volume is that education is most effective when combined with work experience and vocational training. As several authors point out, only a holistic approach will be effective in preparing people for reentry into society. This is a critical pivot point, since it should serve as a warning that even the most conscientious educators with the most abundant resources may be fighting an uphill battle without a greater consideration of how to integrate the education they provide into a larger system of practical engagement with the mechanisms of employment—whether that is through hands-on work experience and training, or with more dedicated support for career development and placement upon graduation and release. Likewise, the chapters from both the Netherlands and Poland stress the central role of practical experience and workforce training and qualification.

Fourth, the chapters here show that education alone is not enough to guarantee success by any measure. The work of education in prison does not exist in a universe of its own; it must operate in communication with partners and with an eye toward opportunities for employment after release. More broadly, education in prison will be most effective when it is seen as part of a new approach to public safety, one that dismantles previous barriers to upward socioeconomic mobility such as institutional racism, classism, gang profiling, and educational tracking systems. Educational access is part of centering the holistic well-being of people who are incarcerated, and it includes a hard look at systemic reasons why people may not have been able to have that access prior to incarceration. In short, recidivism reduction is a significant reason, but only one of the many reasons that educational access in carceral settings is so important. The long view requires confronting many structural injustices including institutional racism, and, in places like the United States, may entail the work of many lifetimes. But the degree of difficulty facing stakeholders in the field of education in prison is not justification for turning away. Rather, it highlights the need to come together and learn from each other across states, countries, and continents.

Finally, one of the most pervasive themes throughout this volume is that more must be done to provide quality education to incarcerated people everywhere. To do this, more partnerships can be forged among correctional systems, educational institutions, and government officials. These chapters exhibit a constellation of arrangements, from the import model outlined in the chapter on Norway, to the cultivation of "deep relationships" described in the chapter on Mexico, to the political anarchy and entrepreneurial scramble described by Max Kenner in his history of college-in-prison in the United States.

Nevertheless, it is clear from the experiences of the authors in this volume that educational institutions need to make their cases more convincingly for the value of what they can offer. At the same time, correctional systems ought to openly support partnerships of mutual benefit, reducing barriers for educational institutions to bring their offerings behind the wall. Finally, lawmakers and government officials will need to commit to the work to encourage investment and the development of quality, ethically sound programs. Overall, these changes require deep commitment, trust-building across multisector landscapes, and resource provisioning that competes for time and energy with the direct service provision itself. Prioritizing how educational access in prison unfolds may be particular to each community, but there are general trends in the successes and challenges to this work that are visible when observed through the comparative gaze.

Though case studies from the United States, Mexico, and, to some extent, Italy and Poland show that higher education provided by colleges and universities can be highly successful interventions in the lives of incarcerated students, it is nevertheless clear that there is significant room to expand educational offerings. Opportunities for growth are abundant with increased investment by stakeholders, but ensuring that such growth is done with integrity, and not in a predatory way, is of utmost importance. To identify these opportunities and others, the chapters from Norway, Slovakia, and Mexico all speak of the utility of assessment when it comes to identifying exactly which educational interventions are the most effective. Moreover, as the chapter from Slovakia in particular points out, more must be done to determine the types of educational offerings that incarcerated students themselves even want. As the authors of that chapter argue, it is critical to ensure that education serves the needs of the incarcerated and not primarily the needs of prison or education systems. A stakeholder-centered model can best address this concern.

Increased effort must be given to face the challenges that stand as barriers to more effective and pervasive education in prison. For example, the chapters from Austria, Poland, the Netherlands, and Mexico all lament the lack of greater technological resources available for education in prison, especially when technology could be an exceptionally powerful tool in spaces where some cannot enter and many others cannot leave. Other resources, from writing materials (e.g., Slovakia) to quiet, ample study space (e.g., Poland) to materials in other languages (e.g., Italy) are common problems and could be addressed with more institutional commitment from stakeholders. In the United States, we face many of these same barriers, with layers of restrictive policies that college-in-prison programs face daily while working to expand college access to incarcerated people. Several authors highlight innovations that could very likely serve to mitigate some of these barriers, such as peer mentoring (e.g., Belgium), cultural mediation (e.g., Italy), expanded e-learning (e.g., Austria and the Netherlands), and testing for learning disabilities (e.g., Norway). There is much space for innovation in the realm of addressing the many challenges that abound.

In sum, the state of education in prison—in the countries surveyed here, at least—is strong and methodically improving, but more must be done. The goal of this volume is to help educators in prison work together across and within their countries to provide even better programs and interventions. This does not necessarily mean that all the authors think incarceration is the best way to solve the problems in their given case study, and many of us think that public safety is overdue for reframing. But as long as people remain behind bars, they deserve access to quality education that can play a transformative role in both their self-actualization and their ability to change their material circumstances.

As Max Kenner points out at the beginning of this volume, though there are many challenges facing education in prison around the world, there is also hope. To that end, we hope that this volume will be an impactful addition to the critically important conversation of the significance of education in prison. It is our firm belief that education brings hope and restores humanity, that people around the world are better off for having access to it, and that increased access can only be achieved by working together.

Works Cited

European Commission. 2000. "Charter of Fundamental Rights of the European Union." https://eur-lex.europa.eu/legal-content/EN/TXT/?uri=CELEX:12012P /TXT.

United Nations. 1948. "Universal Declaration of Human Rights." http://un.org/en /universal-declaration-human-rights/.

CONTRIBUTORS

Arve Asbjørnsen, PhD, is a professor of logopedics at the University of Bergen. He has published journal articles on language acquisition, cognitive impairments, and learning challenges, and on similar impairments associated with psychiatric disorders such as major depression, schizophrenia, and posttraumatic stress disorder. In addition, he has made major contributions to learning in a correctional context. Dr. Asbjørnsen is the leader of the Bergen Cognition and Learning Group, which has been responsible for major research projects on correctional education in Norway.

Natasha Bidault Mniszek is undersecretary of the Campeche State Penitentiary System, Prevention and Social Reinsertion Division, Mexico. She was coordinator of the Higher Education Program for Social Reintegration Centers of Mexico City (PESCER) of the Autonomous University of Mexico City (UACM). She previously served as the director of multiple reintegration sites in Mexico for incarcerated people and returning citizens. She has a master's degree in crime prevention and penal systems from the Legal and Penitentiary Investigation Institute in Mexico City.

Paal Breivik, a candidatus rerum politicarum in sociology, is a former associate professor at the University in Stavanger and currently holds the position of senior advisor at the County Governor of Vestland, Norway. He is the national coordinator for correctional education in Norway and has lectured and published articles about education for inmates and cross-professional collaboration.

Dorien Brosens is an assistant professor in the Department of Educational Sciences of the Vrije Universiteit Brussel and a senior postdoctoral researcher at the Flemish Research Foundation (Belgium). She is one of the coordinating members of the research group PArticipation and Learning in Detention (PALD). Her research mainly focuses on peer programs, active citizenship, and innovative types of learning in prison.

Michelangelo Capitano has served a long professional career within the Police Justice and Juvenile Prison in Palermo, Italy, including as the director of Italian Juvenile Services. Now retired, his publications on the subject of incarceration include "Devianza adolescenziale. Dalla norma sociale alla norma giuridica" (Adolescent deviance: From the social norm to the juridical norm, 2020; with M. Garro); and "I servizi a tutela del minore e della comunità. Il Sistema Giustizia Minorile" (Services for the protection of minors and the community: The Juvenile Justice System, 2021; with L. La Bua).

Jennifer Coreas is the coordinator and cofounder of the program Literacy for Reconciliation for ConTextos in El Salvador and Chicago. She holds degrees from El Salvador in English as a second language and applied linguistics, and she received a master's degree in English from Middlebury College in 2018. Her work extends from curriculum development and teaching to advocacy, training, and facilitation of dialogue. She has led the work and the vision for ConTextos's work in prisons and communities, accompanied authors in their journeys of self-discovery, and brought their stories to hundreds of teachers, psychologists, and social workers in professional development spaces. She has been recognized with numerous fellowships and scholarships including the Rocky Gooch Memorial Scholarship and the Esperanza Fellowship.

Liesbeth De Donder is a professor at the Vrije Universiteit Brussel (Belgium) and head of the research group PArticipation and Learning in Detention (PALD). Her research focuses on social inclusion, community development, and change, with a particular interest in participatory methodologies. She is chairwoman of Klasbak vzw, the Flemish branch of the European Prison Education Association.

Maria Garro is a psychologist, senior researcher in dynamic psychology, and instructor of social psychology and forensic psychology in the Department of Psychology, Educational Science, and Human Movement at the University of Palermo (Italy). She is the author or coauthor of numerous books and articles on forensic psychology and prison, including "Immigrant Prisoners in Italy: Cultural Mediation to Reduce Social Isolation and Increase Migrant Prisoner Well-Being?"(2022, with M. Schirinzi, C. Novara, and E. Ayllon Alonso) in *International Journal of Prisoner Health*; "Reversing the Trend: A Psychosocial Intervention on Young Immigrants in Sicily" (2018, with M. Schirinzi) in *Journal of International Migration and Integration*; and "The ECHR Condemns Prison Overcrowding in Italy: The Total Reorganization of the Institution and the Social Reintegration of the Prisoner" (2017, with F. Cirami) in *Journal of Prison Education and Reentry*.

Mneesha Gellman is an associate professor of political science in the Marlboro Institute for Liberal Arts and Interdisciplinary Studies at Emerson College, where she teaches on themes of human rights and international comparative politics. She is the founder and director of the Emerson Prison Initiative, which brings a bachelor of arts pathway to incarcerated students at state prisons in Massachusetts. Gellman is the editor of *Education Behind the Wall: Why and How We Teach College in Prison* (2022), and the author of *Indigenous Language Politics in the Schoolroom: Cultural Survival in Mexico and the United States* (2023) and *Democratization and Memories of Violence: Ethnic Minority Social Movements in Mexico, Turkey, and El Salvador* (2017). She has published widely on democracy, education, and human rights in both academic journals and popular outlets. Gellman serves as an expert witness in asylum cases in US immigration courts for people from Mexico and El Salvador.

Walter Hammerschick is a vice head and senior researcher at the Department of Applied Sociology of Law and Criminology (IRKS) of the University of Innsbruck, located in Vienna, Austria. He earned his doctorate in law from the University of Salzburg followed by postgraduate studies in Sociology at Bowling Green State University in Ohio, United States. Before fully dedicating his professional career to scientific work, he worked for the Austrian Association for Probation Assistance and Social Work. He joined the Institute for the Sociology of Law and Criminology in 1991 as a researcher and was its executive director from 2008 to 2021. Prison research is and has been one of his major fields of interest, including the labor market situation and reintegration of formerly incarcerated people. He has headed and participated in numerous national and European studies in this field, regularly speaking at conferences, giving lectures, and publishing.

Max Kenner is the executive director and Tow Chair for Education and Democracy at the Bard Prison Initiative (BPI), which he founded as an undergraduate in 1999. A pioneer among college-in-prison programs, BPI enrolls over three hundred incarcerated students full-time in academic programs culminating in degrees from Bard College; Bard is also home to the Consortium for the Liberal Arts in Prison, which cultivates leaders and institutions in its field, nationally and internationally.

Torfinn Langelid, a candidatus philosophiae in history, is a former senior advisor at the County Governor of Vestland. He was the national coordinator for correctional education in Norway, a member of the Nordic Network for Prison Education for many years, and a member of the steering committee of the European Prison Education Association (EPEA) from 1997 to 2007. He has published articles, reports, and books on prison education and historical perspectives of correctional education.

Gioacchino Lavanco is a professor of Psychology of Community and director of the Department of Psychology, Educational Science, and Human Movement at the University of Palermo (Italy). He is a trainer for the Prison Service and a lifelong educator. He is also the author of several articles and books about social services and well-being in the community, including "Adolescenti e giovani detenuti fra legalità e cultura criminale: la gestione degli eventi critici" (Adolescents and young prisoners between legality and criminal culture: The management of critical events, 2018), and "Comunità chiuse, comunità aperte: rimanere chiusi "fuori" dal carcere" (Closed communities, open communities: Staying closed "out" of prison, 2017; with C. Novara).

Chester Lee is the director for Faculty and Academic Support Services on Emerson College's Kasteel Well campus in the Netherlands. He holds a bachelor's degree in history and journalism from the Chinese University of Hong Kong, and he received his master's degree in media communication technology and policy from Macquarie University in Australia. He went on to complete his PhD in 1997 at Macquarie University, specializing in cross-cultural communications. His academic concentration is now on areas such as human rights and migration, the European criminal justice systems in a global context, and sex work in Europe (decriminalizing vs. legalizing prostitution), with a focus on promotion of cultural awareness, cross-cultural understanding, and intercultural dialogue.

Marek Lukáč is an associate professor at the Institute of Romani Studies at the University of Prešov (Slovakia). His research focuses on social exclusion, the education of marginalized adult Romani, and the education of incarcerated persons. He has published books and articles related to the education of Romani adults, second-chance education, social exclusion, and education in prison. He is a member of the executive committee of the Association of Adult Education Institutions (AIVD) in Slovakia.

Silvia Lukáčová is an assistant professor at the Institute of Pedagogy, Andragogy, and Psychology at the University of Prešov (Slovakia). In her research, she focuses on education of the incarcerated, second-chance education, and the education of adults from socially excluded communities. She has published several books and scientific articles and is one of the leading experts on second-chance education in Slovakia.

Terje Manger holds a doctoral degree from the University of Bergen, Norway, and is a professor emeritus of educational psychology at that university. He has published books and journal articles on topics such as general educational psychology, behavioral psychology, and gender differences in mathematical achievement in school. Dr. Manger and his colleagues in the Bergen Cognition and Learning Group at the University of Bergen have a long record of contributions to research on prison education, and have in recent years conducted several large-scale studies in Norwegian and Nordic prisons, resulting in national and international publications.

Silke Marynissen is a PhD fellow conducting fundamental research for the Flemish Research Foundation at the Vrije Universiteit Brussel (Belgium). Her research focuses on informal learning and music participation in prison, viewed from the perspective of realist science. She is a member of the research group PArticipation and Learning in Detention (PALD).

Justin McDevitt is director of the Women's College Partnership at Indiana Women's Prison in Indianapolis, a college-in-prison collaboration between the University of Notre Dame, Marian University, and the Bard Prison Initiative. He previously served as assistant regional director for alumni and reentry services with the Notre Dame Programs for Education in Prison (NDPEP) in the Center for Social Concerns at the University of Notre Dame. He has taught courses in American politics, urban politics, race and politics, global migration, and interfaith dialogue, and also an interdisciplinary course entitled "The World in Pandemic." Justin holds a JD from Loyola University Chicago, where his work included field research on labor migration in Chile, farmworkers' rights in central Illinois, and gender-based violence in Tanzania. He is currently completing a PhD in American politics at the University of Notre Dame, where his dissertation research focuses on the political development of collateral consequences with felony convictions. He is also cofounder and executive director of Life Outside, a nonprofit reentry organization based in South Bend, Indiana.

Maria K. McKenna is a professor of the practice, with a joint appointment in the Department of Africana Studies and the Education, Schooling, and Society program at the University of Notre Dame in Indiana. She is the director of the AnBryce Scholars and Transformational Leaders Program Initiatives, serving first-generation and historically under-resourced undergraduate students. She received her PhD in Educational Foundations from Saint Louis University after completing undergraduate and graduate work at the University of Notre Dame and Northwestern University. Her teaching and research span the disciplines of education and ethnic studies while focusing on the social, cultural, and philosophical contexts of American education. She and her husband Mark have four children and reside in South Bend, Indiana.

Lise Øen Jones, PhD, is a professor at the Institute of Psychosocial Science at the University of Bergen, Norway. She has published books, chapters, and journal articles on topics such as reading and writing difficulties and efficacy beliefs among people in prison, special education in schools, and use of educational technology. Over the last few years, Dr. Jones and her colleagues in the Bergen Cognition and Learning Group have conducted several large-scale studies in Norwegian and Nordic prisons.

Massimiliano Schirinzi is an English lecturer in the Department of Psychology, Educational Science, and Human Movement at the University of Palermo (Italy). He is a teacher of Italian L2/LS, a linguistic and cultural mediator, and an oral examiner at the University for Foreigners of Perugia (Italy). He is also the coauthor of the book *In Partenza: An Introduction to Italian* (2013, with R. Guarino) and coauthor of the articles "Immigrant Prisoners in Italy: Cultural Mediation to Reduce Social Isolation and Increase Migrant Prisoner Well-Being?" (2022, with M. Schirinzi, C. Novara, and E. Ayllon Alonso) in *International Journal of Prisoner Health*, and "Reversing the Trend: A Psychosocial Intervention on Young Immigrants in Sicily" (2018, with M. Garro) in *Journal of International Migration and Integration*.

Grzegorz A. Skrobotowicz, PhD, MBA, is an assistant professor in the Department of Criminal Executive Law, Faculty of Law, Canon Law, and Administration at the John Paul II Catholic University of Lublin (KUL) in Poland. He received his PhD in 2012 from KUL, with a dissertation entitled "Mediation in Criminal Proceedings: Enforcement of Mediation Settlements in Research." His latest research is on why mediation, an extremely important tool for restorative justice, is rarely used in Poland. In 2019, he served as a visiting faculty fellow with the Nanovic Institute for European Studies at the University of Notre Dame, where he was able to observe an example of American higher education in prison, and he presented to several classes through the Moreau College Initiative, an academic collaboration between Holy Cross College and the University of Notre Dame in partnership with the Indiana Department of Correction.

Dominika Temiaková is an assistant professor in the Department of Pedagogy, Faculty of Education, at the University of Constantine the Philosopher in Nitra (Slovakia). Her research focuses primarily on the theory and practice of adult education, specifically penitentiary education and staff training. She is the author of the publication *Penitentiary and Post-Penitentiary Education* (2015, writing as D. Kadlubeková), and *Education of Women in Penitentiary Conditions*, which examines the education of convicted women in Slovakia (2021).

Justin George Watson, PhD, is the Brother John Driscoll Distinguished Professor of the Liberal Arts at Holy Cross College in Notre Dame, Indiana. Watson earned his doctorate in English at the University of Notre Dame, and he has served as the book review editor of *Religion and Literature*. He also served as chief academic officer of Holy Cross College from 2014 to 2021, where he worked closely with the Moreau College Initiative, an academic collaboration between Holy Cross College and the University of Notre Dame, in partnership with the Indiana Department of Correction.

INDEX

310 INDEX

Brandeis Series in Law and Society

ROSALIND KABRHEL, J.D. AND DANIEL BREEN, J.D., EDITORS

Justice Louis D. Brandeis once said that "if we desire respect for the law, we must first make the law respectable." For Justice Brandeis, making the law "respectable" meant making it work in the interests of humankind, as a help rather than a hindrance in the manifold struggles of persons of all backgrounds to achieve justice. In that spirit, the Law and Society Series publishes works that take interdisciplinary approaches to law, drawing richly from the social sciences and humanities, with a view towards shedding critical light upon the variety of ways in which legal rules, and the institutions that enforce them, affect our lives. Intended for practitioners, academics, students, and the interested general public, this series will feature titles that contribute robustly to contemporary debates about law and legal reform, all with a view towards adding to efforts of all sorts to make the law "respectable."

For a complete list of books that are available in the series,
visit https://brandeisuniversitypress.com/series/law

Unlocking Learning:
International Perspectives on Education in Prison
Justin McDevitt and Mneesha Gellman

We're Here to Help:
When Guardianship Goes Wrong
Diane Dimond

The Common Flaw:
Needless Complexity in the Courts and 50 Ways to Reduce It
Thomas Moukawsher

Education Behind the Wall:
Why and How We Teach College in Prison
Mneesha Gellman

When Freedom Speaks:
The Boundaries and the Boundlessness of Our First Amendment Right
Lynn Levine Greenky

Pain and Shock in America:
Politics, Advocacy, and the Controversial Treatment of People with Disabilities
Jan A. Nisbet